NONE OF
YOUR DAMN
BUSINESS

OF YOUR DAMN BUSINESS

Privacy in the United States from the
Gilded Age to the Digital Age

LAWRENCE CAPPELLO

The University of Chicago Press

Chicago and London

The University of Chicago Press, Chicago 60637
The University of Chicago Press, Ltd., London
© 2019 by Lawrence Cappello
Published 2019
Printed in the United States of America

28 27 26 25 24 23 22 21 20 19   1 2 3 4 5

ISBN-13: 978-0-226-55774-8 (cloth)
ISBN-13: 978-0-226-55788-5 (e-book)
DOI: https://doi.org/10.7208/chicago/9780226557885.001.0001

Library of Congress Cataloging-in-Publication Data

Names: Cappello, Lawrence, author.
Title: None of your damn business : privacy in the United States
    from the gilded age to the digital age / Lawrence Cappello.
Description: Chicago : The University of Chicago Press, 2019. |
    Includes bibliographical references and index.
Identifiers: LCCN 2019005346 | ISBN 9780226557748 (cloth :
    alk. paper) | ISBN 9780226557885 (e-book)
Subjects: LCSH: Privacy—United States—History. | National security—
    Social aspects—United States.
Classification: LCC BF637.P74 C36 2019 | DDC 323.44/8—dc23
LC record available at https://lccn.loc.gov/2019005346

♾ This paper meets the requirements of ANSI/NISO Z39.48-1992
(Permanence of Paper).

For Carol and Ethel Campbell – who taught
their children to respect other peoples'
privacy, and without whom, nothing.

CONTENTS

INTRODUCTION

Capitol Hill, early afternoon, Tuesday, April 10, 2018. Having set aside his signature dark grey T-shirt and jeans for a smartly fitted navy blue suit and tie, Mark Zuckerberg, the thirty-three year old chief executive of Facebook and bona fide American wunderkind, walked into the Senate Chamber to face the first of two marathon public hearings where he would endure ten hours of questioning from ninety-one lawmakers on the subject of privacy.

He looked confident, all things considered. Taking time for a few polite handshakes as he made his way toward the witness table where a large group of press photographers were patiently waiting for him. About thirty-five in total. Cameras at the ready—tightly packed in efficient rows and assembled in such a way that their positioning had essentially transformed them into a single wall of lenses. When Mr. Zuckerberg reached the table, the wall started shooting. And for two painfully awkward minutes the only sound in the room was the sustained rapid-fire clicking and shuttering of professional-grade digital cameras. When Zuckerberg finally sat down the wall closed in around him, abandoning any previous regard it had for his personal space as it fired from all angles. Later, during a routine break, one photographer from the Associated Press considered it fair play to take photos of, and then post on the internet, two pages from Zuckerberg's private notes that had been accidentally left on the witness table. The irony was not lost on the millions of Americans watching from home.

The chamber is called to order. "Mr. Zuckerberg, in many ways you and the company that you created, the story that you've created represents the American Dream," opened Senator John Thune, chairman of the Commerce Committee. "Many are incredibly inspired by what you've done. At the same time, you have an obligation, and it's up to you, to ensure that that dream does not become a privacy nightmare for the scores of people who use Facebook."[1]

The purpose of the inquiry was widely known. A month prior, a whistle-blower named Christopher Wylie announced to the press that a British political consulting firm called Cambridge Analytica had improperly accessed social media data on more than fifty million Americans with the intention of influencing the 2016 presidential election. A few weeks later Facebook admitted that the actual number was probably closer to eighty-seven million. The recent hacking of the Equifax credit bureau, which had affected about half of the nation's adult population, was still fresh in people's minds, as was the knowledge that the European Union was scheduled to implement a drastic and sweeping new privacy law the following month. But the hearings were about more than just the inability of an American company to protect sensitive information. Facebook's lax privacy standards, it seemed, may well have bled into the fabric of our democratic system.

This is not a book about the Cambridge Analytica scandal. But watching Congress try to make sense of it over those two days it soon became abundantly clear that in these early decades of the internet age the protection of personal privacy has become one of the foremost concerns facing the United States. That our current social and political struggles over privacy have both the urgency and resonance capable of defining an era.

It was also clear that as a social and political issue, privacy is incredibly difficult to understand. Almost every lawmaker present agreed that Americans had a "reasonable expectation of privacy" that was worth protecting. But when it came time to engage the precise privacy problems at play, few of them were able to articulate exactly what privacy means or why it's important. Nor did the conversation ever move toward a meaningful discussion of how we as a civilization arrived at this particular conundrum in the first place—all we heard is that technology was somehow to blame. It seemed as though the problem had grown too big to understand. As the noticeably frustrated Senator Bill Nelson put it to Zuckerberg: "Let me just cut to the chase. If you and other social media companies do not get your act in order, none of us are going to have any privacy anymore. That's what we're facing . . . it's the advent of technology."[2]

So how did we get here? That's what this book is about. If we want a sense of what privacy is and why it matters, there is a lot to be gained by looking at it historically.

This book examines five key privacy debates in US history from the Gilded Age to the internet age with the aim of providing some much-needed clarity about that very complicated word—*privacy*. Each chapter focuses on the interplay between privacy and one particular force that pushed against it in the name of the "public interest"—on a specific context in which privacy first became threatened, then defended, then ultimately circumscribed in the face of that threat. And because historians have the privilege of hindsight, every chapter offers a more comprehensive analysis of the privacy problems at play in each historical moment than privacy advocates themselves were able to at the time.

At first glance the popular narrative shared by most Americans is very much in line with what Senator Nelson was trying to say. This narrative holds that technology is to blame—that after computers burst onto the scene in the 1950s technology kept evolving, which made our lives easier and more efficient, and so Americans willingly traded a little privacy for a little convenience and more national security until we all woke up one morning and realized things had perhaps gone too far. By then it was far too difficult to roll things back. We had become too dependent. Worse, we had become too complacent. And now privacy is circling the drain. QED.

But the real story of American privacy is considerably more nuanced. The origins of our modern debates about privacy date back to the late nineteenth century—inspired in part, yes, by new technologies that many found unsettling, but also very much by changing standards of public decency and the reality that information was being democratized. From there—from the Gilded Age—the American conversation about privacy branched out in a variety of directions across an array of contexts throughout the twentieth century. Because privacy is such a multifaceted concept, this was not one conversation but many, occurring simultaneously on multiple overlapping fronts and grappling with such important questions as the proper role of the media, government intrusions on civil liberties, the rise of the welfare state, the wars on poverty and crime, new understandings of gender and the body, and, as was the case with Facebook, commercialized data collection.

While these topics are largely distinct from one another, it is important to understand that the key privacy debates of the twentieth century tended to follow a particular pattern. First, privacy would become threatened by some legitimate countervailing force. That force was almost always framed by its proponents as serving the "public interest"—and those arguments were not entirely wrong. Privacy advocates, feeling intruded upon, would then typically raise the general alarm that privacy, that timeless and cherished value, was under siege and perhaps dying, and they would also voice more focused and specifically tailored arguments outlining exactly how privacy was being endangered in the moment and, of course, why it was worth defending. And so with each new threat to privacy came new articulations about its value and the consequences of it being imperiled. As a result, American understandings of privacy grew increasingly complicated over the twentieth century, and much harder to keep track of, because they were continuously being refashioned to meet new threats. But whatever the threat, the thing to remember is that American claims to privacy were conspicuously *reactive*.

We must also understand that those Americans who took up the cause of privacy tended to make the same kinds of mistakes while defending it. First, the key privacy debates of the twentieth century often assumed an "all-or-nothing" character—and thus were framed incorrectly as questions of *whether* legitimate public interests were more important than privacy, instead of as examinations of *how* privacy could be protected while simultaneously embracing those public interests. Second, these privacy advocates tended to position privacy as an *individual* right while ignoring its larger *societal* value. This crucial error often allowed those forces that pushed against privacy to argue for the "greater good," while those defending it frequently spoke of individual harms—a somewhat weaker position as the needs of the many generally outweigh the needs of the few. And finally, because privacy is such a difficult concept to define succinctly, the rhetoric used to support privacy claims was usually either too narrow, or too broad, or relied on flawed metaphors that fell flat as instruments of social and political change.[3]

As the twentieth century marched on, more and more ominous predictions were made that in the not-too-distant future privacy would be little more than a memory. And this, in turn, made the prospect of such a future more digestible to the public. As Americans increasingly lost more control over their personal information and decisional freedom, the expression "privacy is dead" crept further into the popular lexicon. So too did the altogether frustrating question "if you're not doing anything wrong, then what do you have to hide?"[4]

So what is privacy, exactly? What is it we fear we're losing? Here's where things get difficult. Privacy is just a word. An umbrella term. One that continually evades any tight compact definition and reminds us that language is an imperfect medium. Much like any analysis of the words *liberty* or *freedom* or *love*, the closer we look at *privacy* the more we realize that it fails to fit easily into a single category. This ambiguity is one of the reasons privacy has been so hard to protect. It is also why, when pressed for personal information they don't want to reveal, Americans often just avoid lengthy justifications altogether and take refuge in the delightfully simple phrase: "None of your damn business."

The book begins in the Gilded Age—where the changing landscape of the newspaper business gave rise to the first modern debates about privacy and the proper limits of a free press. From the popular tabloids and civil trials we can see that in the 1870s, on the heels of one of America's most sensational sex scandals, the lines of privacy in journalism were being largely redrawn in the face of growing demand for a new genre: "human interest" reportage. Distinctions between those considered deserving of the press's attention and those who were its victims were growing much more fluid, and while many railed against these new invasions, calling them an "assault on privacy," others aggressively sought them out in the pursuit of notoriety. By the 1890s these problems grew more severe as newspapers began replacing wood-cut illustrations with "instant photographs."

The marriage of photography to mass-market journalism prompted one of the most famous legal essays ever written about privacy, penned by one of the most famous jurists to ever sit on the Supreme Court. It brilliantly repositioned our understanding of privacy away from older legal notions of property rights toward something much more modern—the right to safeguard one's personality and psychological well-being. In response, those media moguls who saw their bottom lines balloon from the new "human interest" genre devised an ingenious defense of their practices. Instead of leaning on predictable First Amendment arguments, they acknowledged their role in harming privacy, even going so far as to lament its decline, while simultaneously positioning themselves as mere humble servants of public curiosity serving up "thin-skinned" Americans to the court of public opinion. If their crimes against privacy were so egregious, they argued, people would stop buying their papers. But until that day, they had a duty to provide information the people deemed newsworthy. This defense against privacy claims was firmly in place by the 1920s, and it is still used by the media today.

From newspapers it moves to a very different pressure on privacy: national security during the many military conflicts of the twentieth century, both hot and cold. The nation's first federal domestic surveillance apparatus was born out of the First World War, where in the pursuit of enemy agents, purported radicals, defeatists, and labor organizers who might impede the war effort, the Justice Department's fledgling Bureau of Investigation (the germ of the Federal Bureau of Investigation) debuted an array of novel techniques to acquire information. The result was a fundamental alteration of the capabilities, and the will, of the federal government to invade the privacy of its citizens and the flowering of the "good citizens have nothing to hide" ideology. Years later, opponents of Franklin D. Roosevelt's New Deal used national security rhetoric and the fear of subversion to further their political aims with a new rhetorical flourish in this vein: "un-Americanism." Ambitious members of the legislative branch used their investigative powers to paint New Deal liberalism as a dangerous tool akin to the ideology of the Soviet Union; before you knew it, liberals and Reds were practically the same thing. Such attacks depended greatly on privacy infringements— not for any specific legislative purpose, but to directly and indirectly assassinate the characters of political enemies.

The "privacy versus security" debate, which crystalized in the McCarthy era, is part of a well-established American tradition of subordinating the societal value of privacy to self-styled crusaders against dangerous domestic subversives. Of course, these enemies were not entirely imagined. But the terms surrounding the tradeoff between privacy and security were often framed incorrectly, lacked proper safeguards, and exploited to serve ends that had little to do with national security. The persistent and flawed argument increasingly heard in interrogation rooms, job interviews, and committee hearings at midcentury was inelegant but efficient: "the republic comes first; if you're not doing anything wrong, then you should have nothing to hide." At the same time, the executive branch, when faced with the same threat of congressional investigation, came to articulate its own right to privacy: "executive privilege."

From national security we move to pressures of physical surveillance technology. Almost every society in human history has used some form of physical surveillance to enforce social norms, punish taboos, and protect its citizens. In the United States, the balance of power between privacy and disclosure after the Second World War shifted unmistakably in favor of those individuals and organizations who engaged in physical surveillance. This imbalance was the result of four important overlapping developments: scientific breakthroughs in miniaturization technology in the 1940s, the rapid growth and professionalization of the private detective field in the 1950s, the aggressive commercialization and marketing of surveillance technology to law enforcement *and* the public at large in the 1960s, and the legitimization of surveillance through tropes in American pop culture for the rest of the century.

The surveillance phenomenon of the postwar period—simultaneously economic, political, and cultural—quickly outstripped the original social and legal controls intended to constrain eavesdropping. Wiretaps, microphones, and miniaturized video cameras were enticing, relatively easy to install, and in most states not illegal to own. The response from the American public was loud, constant, and uneven. Many spoke of Orwellian doomsday scenarios. Others of a golden age of crime prevention. Naturally, positions varied depending on who was doing the surveilling, what was being surveilled, and the justifications given for that surveillance. Yet in the grand scheme, both sides were proven wrong. Big Brother did not rise in postwar America, nor did Jeremy Bentham's panopticon come to dominate the social and political landscapes. Instead, the power generated by surveillance flowed through a variety of channels; was harnessed by a host of actors, both public and private, for a variety of reasons; and was both condemned and applauded by the public—often at the same time.

From physical surveillance we move to the pressures of large-scale data collection, commonly known today as Big Data. Two developments—the rise of the New Deal welfare state and the advent of mainframe computers in the 1950s (known affectionately as "Big Iron")—are most responsible for elevating the privacy problems associated with data collection. Governments must acquire information about their citizens before they can effectively extend them social and legal benefits. As the federal bureaucracy expanded throughout the twentieth century in the interest of public welfare, the amount of information it collected grew exponentially. Big Iron made it possible to manage and understand this data. It provided a means through which information could be stored, accessed, and shared with both the public and private sectors. By the 1970s the practice of sharing government-collected data with private entities like insurance companies, advertisers, and lending institutions had become commonplace. Big data's potential seemed limitless.

But the public soon recognized the many problems inherent in the rise of big data. Unauthorized data sharing, informational errors, and denying citizens access to their own data were somewhat abated by the terms of the Privacy Act of 1974, but that law didn't do all that it might have. In the legislative process it had been eviscerated by corporations and their lobbyists, who argued that privacy controls on their consumer databases would cripple their businesses. In the end, private companies were excluded from the provisions of the law entirely.

By the 1980s those companies that profited from big data found a powerful ally in President Ronald Reagan, who from his earliest days in office called for a marked increase in data mining. Not to enhance the distribution of social welfare benefits, but as a powerful tool through which the waste and inefficiency of "big government" could be eliminated. The regulation of computer matching—the cross-referencing of information held in one database with that held by another in either the public or private sector—effectively legitimized it and eventually confirmed the establishment of a de facto national database despite public opposition. Ironically, the history of American data mining reveals that while New Deal liberalism played the greatest role in the expansion of data collection, it was fiscal conservatives in the 1970s and 1980s who brought a marked increase in the aggregation, processing, and sharing of that data, in the name of efficiency, free enterprise, and "small government." Powerful corporations and commercial interests supported these efforts vigorously, while privacy advocates struggled—and often failed—to enact adequate or comprehensive protections against the improper circulation and misuse of personal information. These advocates were forced to settle for "sectoral" or patchwork policy remedies that regulated different industries such as banking or libraries or insurance companies in different ways, often on a state-by-state basis, instead of for the more effective "omnibus" remedies adopted by other advanced democracies that established a uniform set of rules about particular kinds of information that apply to every industry. Privacy and profits did not mix, and as a result Americans lost a considerable amount of control over the storage and use of their personal information. At the dawn of the Internet Age, the country was woefully ill-equipped to handle the tidal wave of new data privacy problems soon to arrive.

From Big Data we move, finally, to reproductive rights and the role of privacy in the feminist movement. For all the various ways privacy has captured the attention of the public since the Gilded Age—whether from problems inherent to photojournalism, or public interrogation, or surveillance, or data collection—it was the fight over access to contraception, strangely enough, that prompted the Supreme Court to definitively recognize a constitutional "right to privacy" in the mid-1960s. Despite the word *privacy* not appearing once in that document, the Court cited it when overturning an arcane nineteenth-century statute prohibiting the distribution of contraceptive devices—even if the recipients were married or could demonstrate a clear medical need. That the law would seek to regulate the behavior of married couples in their private bedrooms was an idea so repellant to the Court that it determined that "specific guarantees in the Bill of Rights [contained] penumbras, formed by emanations from those guarantees that help give them life and substance," and that those guarantees "create zones of privacy." Any attempt to penetrate the privacy of the marital bed conflicted "with a right of privacy older than the Bill of Rights—older than our political parties, older than our school system." The ruling would be instrumental in the Court's *Roe v Wade* decision eight years later.

That landmark case, *Griswold v. Connecticut*, was a key victory for privacy, but the campaign behind it was not waged by privacy advocates but by feminists and medical professionals. It was the result of a carefully orchestrated legal campaign that spanned decades, aiming to facilitate broad social change and gender equality. And so to understand this crucial moment for privacy, we have to look at *Griswold* as part of a larger social and political discourse about two overlapping developments: the women's rights movement and sexual morality laws. Gender-specific notions of privacy arose in the early industrial period with the maturation of distinct public and private "spheres," rooted in understandings of feminine norms, restricted access, peaceful seclusion in the private home (or "woman's place"), and what Barbara Welter once called the "cult of true womanhood." A century later that same discussion centered largely on reproductive rights, with a "woman's privacy" evoking a freedom to choose contraception or have an abortion. It is no coincidence this transition occurred against the backdrop of American rights consciousness and the sexual revolution, a period where the idea of the home as a haven for privacy and femininity was increasingly rejected. In the social and cultural realms, the decisional privacy rights affirmed in *Griswold* and *Roe* moved well beyond reproductive issues. Access to birth control helped to create new powers, new norms, and new expectations of self-determination among women—and indirectly among all Americans.[5]

In their own way, every one of these pressures—modern journalism, national security, surveillance, big data, morality law—forced Americans to think more deeply about privacy. They instilled a sense of national ambivalence that convinced many of us, either from excitement or exhaustion, to relinquish at least some privacy in some circumstances in exchange for genuinely positive benefits.

The rise of human interest journalism helped awaken Americans to the problems of modern information *dissemination*—when true information about a person is revealed to others without that person's consent. This is not so much the elimination of secrecy as it is the spreading of information beyond expected boundaries. Such unchecked disclosure can damage reputations, inhibit people from authoring their own self-narratives, and make them prisoners of their recorded past. And yet people found the new human interest genre also has many positive aspects, so Americans met this threat to privacy with a sense of ambivalence. Gossip is entertaining. Always has been. In the eyes of many, the Gilded Age newspapers were merely amplifying gossip beyond the confines of small towns, where it had lived for centuries, onto a national stage. These papers also frequently reported on the indiscretions of the elite, much to the delight of the masses, who welcomed it as a positive act of egalitarian class leveling.[6]

The "privacy versus security" debates helped awaken Americans to the ways in which the high-stakes atmosphere of wartime can be exploited by opportunists to justify drastic infringements on privacy rights. The assault on privacy in wartime used many tools: loyalty boards, deliberate or ham-fisted disclosure of suspects' private information, public interrogations laden with ad hominem attacks, and the coercion of private information through threats of economic ruin. And yet because national security is inherently positive, Americans met this threat to privacy with a sense of ambivalence. Domestic terrorism, industrial warfare, atomic espionage, nuclear holocaust—these things all rightly arouse the public's fear and respect. It is understandable that many might take a "better safe than sorry" position, especially if those whose privacy was being compromised were strangers.

Great leaps in surveillance technology helped awaken Americans to the ways in which the threat of constant observation can facilitate self-censorship and new definitions of what constitutes an "unreasonable search." Unconstrained surveillance carries the potential for starkly antidemocratic tendencies and prevents private social and political groups from enlivening and undergirding a pluralistic society. And yet, once again, considering the many positive attributes of surveillance, Americans met this threat to privacy with a sense of ambivalence. Wiretaps and bugs help cops catch dangerous criminals. CCTV cameras help protect businesses. Productivity soars when bosses can better monitor their employees. And private detectives help individuals and organizations eliminate uncertainty and reduce risk.

The pressures of big data helped awaken Americans to problems of information *aggregation*—or the gathering of information about a person through snippets that combine to form a new but not always accurate digital portrait. Aggregation moves information out of its original context. It can also reveal *new* facts, beyond those originally collected. And yet because large-scale data collection also has many positive attributes, Americans met this threat to privacy with a sense of ambivalence. The extension of social welfare benefits, the ability of social scientists to better understand the power structures in society, advances in business and governmental efficiency, the modern credit and insurance industries, and the ability of individuals to tell a good investment or employee from a bad one—all made possible by the wonders of data collection and interpretation.[7]

The pressures of morality law and gender inequality helped awaken Americans to possibilities of using privacy as an intellectual weapon through which to demand a larger swath of rights. While on the path to *Griswold* and *Roe*, feminists aligned the benefits of "decisional privacy" in contraception and abortion with the rights of women to reject the traditional private sphere and code of morality imposed on them by a patriarchal society. By choosing to delay childbirth or to not have children at all, women were partially freed from gendered roles of nurturer and caregiver and "subjugation through confinement." When combined with employment and pay equality, decisional privacy could transform the home into a place where women could find the same comforts as men—a place that enabled not the exercise of dominion over others but reliable opportunities for solitude, self-reflection, and selected intercourse with others.[8]

I am hardly the first writer to take up the question of privacy. Over the years, a number of scholars and legal theorists have produced an extensive body of work on the subject, and two, in particular, have made intellectual contributions that are essential to the bones of this book. The first, legal scholar Daniel Solove, made a key breakthrough on the problem of definition when he introduced his "taxonomy of privacy" in 2006. Solove encourages us to reject the idea that any single perfect common denominator exists when attempting to define privacy. In its place, he offers an elegant series of categories and subcategories that explain the power behind specific privacy problems and why they're objectionable. Readers will become intimately acquainted with many of these categories as they work their way through the pages that follow. The second, philosopher and technology expert Helen Nissenbaum, convincingly argues that threats to privacy can never be understood without first understanding their distinct social contexts—what she calls "contextual integrity." This book agrees wholeheartedly and uses a dialectical approach to better illuminate the contexts in which privacy has been threatened and defended throughout our history.[9]

Before we begin, a word about the structure. Historians have been rather late to the game when it comes to writing about privacy. An unfortunate oversight to be sure, but one that we are starting to make amends for. The growing scholarship of recent years, much of it very good, often places different kinds of privacy problems side by side in a chronological fashion to show, as the excellent historian Sarah Igo puts it, how "the proper threshold for 'knowing' a citizen in a democratic, capitalist nation would become in the twentieth century one of Americans' most enduring debates."[10] This chronological approach has proven very useful to the field and has helped legitimize privacy as a subject of historical inquiry.

This book, on the other hand, takes an aggressively thematic approach—one privacy debate at a time. The aim is to help readers clearly identify the key differences inherent to the various privacy debates that have come up in American history in a highly digestible way and to offer some perspective on how recent discussions about privacy have tended to turn on these different issues. These debates were sometimes informed by one another, and where they were is certainly noted. But at the end of the day this book is designed to call attention to how privacy generally means different things to different people and why those distinctions are important. This book is about the differences.

That said, it is my hope that readers will not stray too far from its overarching theme. Every one of these debates is ultimately about the competition between privacy and a legitimate public interest. Understanding this point—that claims to privacy almost always push against a legitimate counterweight that other people care about—is a crucial framework for understanding the persistent ambivalence Americans have demonstrated about the erosion of their privacy over the twentieth century. The right to privacy is by no means a uniquely American concept. Yet if there is something particularly distinct about American understandings of privacy, it is our tendency to frame privacy in all-or-nothing terms and to package it too frequently as an individual right while those pressures that push against it argue for the greater good.

These stories about American privacy have an interesting cast of characters—few of whom were entirely heroes or villains. They were titans of the Supreme Court who pushed the Constitution to its limits. They were titans of business preaching the gospel of corporate efficiency. They were the disciples of FDR's New Deal sowing the seeds of social welfare. They were two-bit bookies and bootleggers objecting to evidence collected via wiretaps and secret microphones. They were journalists and cameramen looking for a scoop. They were civil rights activists crusading for social justice. They were women's rights activists crusading for reproductive choice. Some fought with vigor as champions of increased privacy protections. Some fought against such protections to further their own financial and political agendas. Many, all the while, simply shrugged their shoulders and remarked knowingly (and quite incorrectly) that privacy was "dead."

Lastly, it is my sincere hope that if someone should ask you what you're currently reading, you'll be as accurate as possible when it comes to the title.

1

WHAT WE TALK ABOUT WHEN
WE TALK ABOUT PRIVACY

I

Philadelphia, midmorning, Tuesday, May 29, 1787. The twenty-nine gentlemen sat, somewhat uneasily, in the East Room of Independence Hall exchanging rumors, theories, and conjecture. They didn't know each other particularly well, but then they certainly had a lot in common. They were all men of status and means. Men of comfort and learning in a land made up of mostly poor uneducated farmers. They were men of reputation. Patriots. A few of them were bona fide celebrities. Thomas Jefferson, sadly, was abroad in France, and John Adams was tending to the nation's affairs in England, but George Washington was there. The retired general had ridden into the city two weeks earlier like a conquering hero to the sound of cheers, ringing bells, and celebratory cannon fire. Benjamin Franklin had come as well. At eighty-one Pennsylvania's favorite son looked more like its great-grandfather—his insides torn apart by kidney stones and his joints aching from gout. Nevertheless, the legitimacy added by his presence was no small matter. As they waited for the day's proceedings to begin, the twenty-nine gentlemen all knew, quite frankly, that their purpose for being there was dangerously unclear and that their authority was murky at best.[1]

It is James Madison we should keep our eye on. While most of the delegates to the Constitutional Convention were late to arrive in Philadelphia, thirty-six-year-old Madison had shown up eleven days early, with a plan. The present government, as it stood, was wholly unsuited to meet the needs of the people it meant to serve. Each state was essentially a sovereign nation, the economy was in shambles, conducting foreign relations was a nightmare, and a small rebellion had just recently been put down by force in the Massachusetts countryside. In their zeal to prevent the tyranny of a king the founding fathers had fallen victim to the tyranny of the mob. The Confederation, as Madison saw things, didn't need to be fixed. It needed to be dismantled and replaced with something stronger. Madison was resolved to say as much and he was resolved to say it early. While his more patient colleagues waited to see which way the wind blew, he would seize the initiative and propose the creation of a new government at the first opportunity. If successful, the scheme would be nothing short of a second revolution.[2]

But before Madison could propose what we now call the Virginia Plan and take his rightful place in our historical memory as the "architect of the Constitution," there was a crucial matter of procedure that required the Convention's attention. As soon as General Washington called the day's meeting to order, George Wythe, known to his contemporaries as "Wythe the Just," rose to address the delegates. He had three proposals. First, everyone must agree that no notes or transcripts of their conversations would ever be reproduced without Washington's express permission. Second, no outsiders, under any circumstances, would be allowed access to the notes or transcripts kept by the Convention's secretary. And finally, nothing said behind the closed doors of Independence Hall that summer could ever be published or otherwise communicated to others "without leave." In other words, Wythe was suggesting the delegates all take a vow of secrecy. If they were to properly deal with the difficult task at hand, they would need to be frank with one another. And to do that they would need the confidence that comes with absolute privacy. Wythe's proposals were put to a vote. The framers agreed.[3]

The next person to speak was Governor Edmund Randolph, Madison's companion from Virginia, who immediately gave voice to Madison's ideas and set the republic on a path toward its new beginning. He was free to make such a radical proposal because he understood—they all understood—that any backlash would be contained in the room and not published in the nation's newspapers. After a summer of candid conversation it was decided the Confederation would come to an end. A new national government under a new Constitution would emerge. And while that document would be published widely and debated rigorously in the name of transparency, the notes and transcripts of the Convention would not be released for another fifty years. Were it not for Wythe the Just and his demand for privacy, it is unlikely that the gentlemen would have fared so well.

II

So what is privacy? Arguably the most influential privacy scholar of the twentieth century was a Columbia law professor named Alan Westin. He said, in the 1960s, that privacy is "the claim of individuals, groups, or institutions to determine for themselves when, how, and to what extent information about them is communicated to others." Perhaps the most influential privacy scholar of the nineteenth century was a Supreme Court justice named Louis Brandeis. His definition of privacy, coined around 1890, had a bit more punch: "the right to be let alone." To be fair, neither of these definitions would survive wholly unscathed under a philosopher's lens. Not all privacy concerns have to do with information, and being "let alone" is a rather broad way to describe something so nuanced. But again, privacy is a slippery concept, and when speaking generally about the wide range of intrusions that constitute "privacy problems," these two sentiments expressed by these two giants are as good a place to start as any.[4]

Let's work backwards. Let's say that you already have some basic intuitive sense of what is meant by the word *privacy*. Let's say that if a stranger approached you on the street and asked politely for unfettered access to your wallet and your electronic devices that you would feel a powerful urge to refuse: that even if you could ensure your banks accounts would not be drained and credit would not be ruined, you would still regard such a thing as a violation. This is about more than just money. "But if you aren't doing anything wrong, then you should have nothing to hide," says the stranger. Maybe, but the answer is still no.

So why refuse? There's more than one reason. Most people have at least one or two emails sitting in their inbox that, while neither immoral nor illegal, are incredibly personal. Other communications might not be so intimate but, if taken out of context and broadcast to others, could certainly be misunderstood and potentially damage personal or professional relationships. Perhaps you have a medical condition you'd prefer did not become common knowledge. Perhaps you have sensitive material that was given to you in confidence by a friend or employer that he or she wouldn't want shared. Perhaps your purchase history includes lice shampoo or bed-bug bombs, and you don't want others to think of you as that person who maybe has lice or bed bugs (first impressions tend to stick).

The important thing here is that privacy is not one single thing but a complicated assemblage of all the reasons you would instinctively refuse such a request. Some of your objections are easy to explain. Others not so much, but the feelings behind them are no less genuine just because they're difficult to articulate. Privacy is an umbrella term. Much like the word *freedom,* it speaks to a multitude of different yet related things. Some of these things are distinct, but in most cases they overlap in very interesting ways. And so a useful strategy when trying to make sense of privacy is to identify why it has value in the first place.[5]

III

One reason privacy has value is that it can create space for the kinds of radical discussions that push against the status quo and established political norms. The authors of the Constitution didn't travel to Philadelphia to design a new system of government. They had, in fact, been ordered by Congress and their home states to repair the old one. When we talk today about the Articles of Confederation, America's original constitution, it is usually to speak of their deficiencies. But there was a lot contained within that document that the founding fathers were understandably committed to preserving.

The Articles of Confederation represented, for the first time, a process of nation building that had been solemnly ratified by thirteen very different state governments. It was the product of hard-struck compromises that took years to negotiate. It established a national Congress, delegated powers to make war and peace, and outlined a basic economic framework. Nobody who had a hand in writing it ever claimed it was perfect, which is why the founding fathers built in an amendment process. With a few well-placed tweaks the Articles might have served the new republic for generations.[6]

Still, many Americans felt strongly that the negatives outweighed the positives. The Confederation Congress lacked the powers it needed to govern. It could request money but not levy taxes. It could negotiate foreign treaties but not enforce them. And because any change to the Articles could come only from the unanimous consent of all thirteen states, any one state could hold the nation hostage for any petty political reason (Rhode Island was particularly troublesome in this respect).

Then, in the winter of 1787, crisis. Amid a severe economic downturn armed gangs started springing up throughout the western counties of Massachusetts. Led by Daniel Shays, a former officer in the Revolution, a small army of debt-ridden soldiers marched on the federal arsenal at Springfield hoping to seize its guns, cannons, and powder. They were met there by General Benjamin Lincoln and quickly put down, but the larger implications of Shays' Rebellion could not be ignored. Armed insurrection spoke to growing conservative fears over the viability of the Confederation government. Henry Lee had seen the writing on the wall months earlier and warned George Washington that restlessness over the economy was "not confined to one state or to part of one state" but to "the whole." Smaller revolts had already sprung up in New Hampshire. Writing to a colleague, Washington later said the uprising left him "mortified beyond expression" and effectively rendered the republic "ridiculous and contemptible in the eyes of all Europe."[7]

So, in response, the Confederation Congress called for a "grand convention" with delegates from each state. Many, like Madison, saw the gathering as an opportunity to begin anew. But it is one thing to think such things and another to discuss them openly. Madison might speak his peace and at any moment some Confederation loyalist, or perhaps just some plainly opportunistic delegate, might start throwing around words like *treason*. Wythe the Just's call for privacy freed them to speak their minds.

The noted constitutional historian Carol Berkin once asked who, without the guarantee of privacy, "wished to be on record supporting measures their local governments opposed? Who would dare to exceed or ignore his instructions if such independent actions were made public? Who would vote 'yea' on overthrowing the government?" Alan Westin agreed, noting that "if the Convention's work had been made public contemporaneously, it is unlikely that the compromises forged in private sessions could have been achieved."[8]

Privacy is incredibly valuable to the democratic process, and not only because it gave us our Constitution. Consider how Americans choose their leaders. The United States has strict laws protecting the privacy of the ballot box—laws that were enacted in the 1890s to break up the power of parasitic political bosses. Back when such things were still a matter of public record, those who mustered enough courage to vote against their district's political machine could expect, if things didn't go their way, a loss of employment, a lack of municipal services, or even violent reprisals from hired thugs. The secret ballot helped fix that.[9]

Consider how, without privacy, independent political groups would be unable to effectively fight for popular causes and bring about much needed social change as they have throughout our history. Before a social movement can be effective, activists and organizations must first conduct private meetings and strategy sessions to plot out a course of action and hone an intellectual platform. It is unlikely that civil rights groups like the NAACP or Martin Luther King's SCLC would have been so successful if every strategy session they conducted was recorded and every sympathetic financial donor, especially southern whites, had their identity made public. The same can be said for labor unions. And for religious groups. And for women's rights organizations. And for the LGBT movement.

Americans have a legally recognized right to privacy in their political associations, and almost every western democracy has erected laws that limit access to the membership rosters and donor lists held by organizations that actively agitate the political system. Privacy carves out a space for such groups to hone and develop their platforms and strategies before taking them public. That, in turn, makes these groups more capable of effecting positive change.[10]

Even a casual glance at the Bill of Rights reveals how integral *privacy* was to the framers' understanding of liberty. The Third Amendment prohibits soldiers from being quartered inside peoples' houses. The Fourth Amendment prohibits unreasonable searches and seizures and protects the privacy of our homes and our personal effects. The Fifth Amendment gives citizens the right to remain silent about their personal affairs when being interrogated. And none who signed the Constitution, most especially James Madison, author of the Bill of Rights, would have forgotten that a vow of secrecy was needed to give it life in the first place.

These things—voter privacy, organizational privacy, the origins of the Constitution and the Bill of Rights—are important to remember when thinking about what it takes to keep the American system afloat. We sometimes lose sight of the fact that the right to privacy isn't just about individuals. Privacy has *societal* value. It advances the cause of liberty.[11]

Of course, one shouldn't be naïve. History also teaches us that too much privacy in our institutions can be disastrous for democracy and blind citizens to very real threats to their liberty. Democracies, as the saying goes, die in darkness. Over the centuries privacy has helped to mask corruption of all stripes: from elected officials embezzling public funds, to the solicitation of payoffs and bribes, to voter suppression, to limitations on marketplace competition, illegal surveillance operations, illegal military actions, and even illegal political assassinations. To be sure, transparency in government is an essential aspect of any free society. But so is privacy. The goal, then, is to find a workable interplay between these two competing and equally necessary values. The goal is balance. Only tyrants, fools, and zealots speak of such things in all-or-nothing terms.

IV

The desire for privacy is not a uniquely human trait. Complex political organs, shifting social and cultural hierarchies, superstructures and spheres—those powerful forces certainly influence how privacy is shaped and perceived over time, but a need for privacy is one of the most basic aspects of what it means to be alive. Naturalists and ecologists have discovered that most animals, especially mammals, seek periods of seclusion or small-group intimacy throughout their lives. This is often described as a tendency toward territoriality, where an animal will lay a private claim to a specific space and defend it against intruders. What Robert Ardrey called "the territorial imperative" has a variety of benefits, like providing a space for organisms to learn survival skills, to mate, and to safely raise young. Mammals in particular maintain complex norms of "social distance" through sensory perceptions like smells and sounds.[12]

While not unique to humans, privacy is most definitely part of the human condition. Anthropologists, as Westin reminds us, have found that individuals in almost every society seek some measure of privacy for themselves and practice "avoidance rules" rooted in personal space to minimize socially undesirable events or situations. These rules help people protect themselves from the stresses and strains of constant social interaction.

Virtually every civilization has employed rules governing privacy, at least with regard to the concealment of sexual activity, urination and defecation, and female genitalia. Margaret Mead, the famous anthropologist, once observed that most societies consider their spiritual rituals to be private, particularly rites of passage where an individual spends a period of time in isolation. Many religious societies throughout history believed that they were constantly being watched by a god or gods, and that communication with these entities required either physical or psychological privacy to be most effective. In the words of the New England colony's spiritual leader Cotton Mather: "a Godly man will sometimes Retire, that he may carry on the Exercises of Godliness."[13]

Privacy is good for the mind. Individuals, from time to time, need to carve out tiny pockets of isolation for emotional release, self-reflection, and a sort of mental recharging. We all know what it is to carry the weight of a day. We each have our own burdens, and we each juggle multiple versions of ourselves as our interactions shift among coworkers, strangers, acquaintances, friends, and loved ones. Social interaction, even in the best of circumstances, is mentally taxing, and the true significance of those interactions often only come to light after we set aside our social masks, in solitude, and reflect upon them.

Privacy creates space for intimacy. Think about how strong relationships are forged. People share confidences and complex emotional experiences with each other as a kind of currency—as a way to nurture trust and communicate the desire to establish a deeper connection. A first date in America is usually an exchange of information between two people who are sizing each other up for romantic potential. On a bad first date, the conversation stays superficial. But on a great first date, the kind of information exchanged gradually becomes more private and personal, which in turn fosters an atmosphere of intimacy.

The sharing of private information is a major component of constructing intimate relationships and keeping them healthy. "True knowledge of another person, in all of his or her complexity, can only be achieved with a handful of friends, lovers, or family members," notes the famous writer Jeffrey Rosen, and "in order to flourish, the intimate relationships on which true knowledge of another person depends need space as well as time: sanctuaries from the gaze of the crowd in which slow mutual self-disclosure is possible."[14]

Privacy also fosters creativity. Speak to any accomplished author, or musician, or actor, or speech writer, or painter, and most will tell you that the process behind wondrous artistic expression is, in truth, a grind. Creative work in its early stages is often quite fragile. It frequently must be nurtured through careful criticism between the creator and a small group of confidants. What the creator calls "finished work" is most often the product of numerous drafts and revisions— of great purges and frustration and of new directions forged. Privacy allows works-in-progress to develop in ways that would be impossible if the creative process was open for all to see. Constant observation has a tendency to blunt even the sharpest of edges.

Perhaps most important is that privacy protects individuals from being misinterpreted and judged out of context by their peers. Throughout the twentieth century, this is the privacy problem Americans encountered more often than any other. We know from social psychologists that first impressions are formed quite quickly, are usually based on only a few pieces of information, and are very hard to dislodge. Our opinions of others often have little regard for the depths of their lives and the capacity of all individuals to grow and change. While we all, as Walt Whitman put it, "contain multitudes," to live in modern society is to make snap judgments and place other individuals into neat little packages. The full spectrum of human emotion and experience is too often reduced to a small group of facts.[15]

And so, because all of us know how reductive human beings can be, privacy allows individuals to shape and protect their reputations and their public persona. Privacy helps us assert a measure of control over how we're perceived by others. It limits this kind of misrepresentation and allows us to shape our own self-narratives.[16]

The human condition. Mental health. Intimacy. Creativity. Protection from misrepresentation. These are only a few reasons why privacy has value on both an individual and a societal level. But while privacy is correctly categorized as a fundamental human right by nations on every continent, that doesn't mean it has a consistent moral or ethical *value*. As the prolific political scholar Alan Wolfe puts it, "Privacy in itself is morally ambiguous. Individuals can use private spaces to develop their character, demean others, plan rebellions, collect stamps, masturbate, read Tolstoy, watch television, or do nothing."[17]

V

Ancient civilizations took pains to embed privacy protections into their laws and social norms, but something about privacy changed around the mid-1800s with the onset of the industrial revolution.[18] The consequences of the industrial era—the rise of factories and mass production—in no uncertain terms gave privacy its modern character. With rapid technological innovation came the development of the nuclear family, the weakening of religious authority in day-to-day life, increased mobility, and the anonymity that accompanied the rise of modern cities whose populations swelled from the tens of thousands to the millions. When combined, these developments transformed privacy into something entirely unlike what preindustrial societies had enjoyed.[19]

So our story begins there, in the late nineteenth century, where the powerful new pressures brought by the modern age presented Americans with affronts to their privacy that preindustrial societies never had to grapple with. It was there, in the Gilded Age, where discussions about privacy became a permanent and uninterrupted fixture of American social and political discourse. And what made privacy in the modern age so confusing was that in some regards Gilded Age Americans also experienced *more* privacy. This push and pull, this dichotomy, this simultaneous expansion and contraction brings us to our most important lesson: there is always a counterweight. Modern privacy walks hand in hand with competing interests. Interestingly, these counterweights are rarely sinister. In fact, they are often as fundamental to society as privacy itself.

These interests include public curiosity—freedom of the press and the free exchange of ideas is a cornerstone of our national identity. National security—the need to detect criminals and subversives and to protect citizens from danger and bodily harm is among the most important functions of government. Technological innovation—the hallmarks of the computer age provide a level of interpersonal connection, economic growth, and personal convenience that dwarf everything that came before it and are as important, if not more so, to modern American capitalism. In every case these countervailing interests also push against the many positive benefits privacy has to offer; therefore lines must be drawn and proper balances struck.

To explore the history of privacy in the United States is to explore the interplay between privacy and these equally legitimate interests. Where Americans stumble when talking about privacy, and we stumble quite often, is by framing privacy and the forces that push against it as mutually exclusive. When we do that we abandon the search for a workable harmony. This is the source of our national ambivalence and confusion — this is the great defect in our reasoning.

2

SHOUTING FROM THE HOUSETOPS

The Right to Privacy and the Rise of Photojournalism, 1890–1928

I

There is a certain irony in the realization that Justice Louis Brandeis was photogenic. One of the earliest and most influential architects of American privacy law, the associate justice of the Supreme Court was fortunate enough to be blessed not only with the kind of keen legal mind that earned him a large degree of immortality in the history of that institution but also with the kind of physical features that hold up well for posterity. His deep-set blue eyes, when paired with his graying hair, gave the effect of complimentary shading. His healthy weight and clean shaven face accentuated the lines of his nose, jaw, and cheekbones, adding facial symmetry. And in most of the photos that remain of him, he seems genuinely comfortable in front of the lens. The irony here lay in the fact that the camera's affection for the man was noticeably unrequited.

"Instantaneous photographs and newspaper enterprise have invaded the sacred precincts of private and domestic life," charged Brandeis in his seminal 1890 law review on the right to privacy, and "numerous mechanical devices threaten to make good the prediction that 'what is whispered in the closet shall be proclaimed from the house-tops.'"[1]

Any proper history of privacy in the United States must set aside considerable space for the contributions of Justice Brandeis. His oft-cited *Harvard Law Review* article, "The Right to Privacy," written well before his ascension to the Supreme Court and coauthored with former law partner Samuel Warren, was among the first articles to examine the concept in depth, and remains a touchtone for generations of legal scholars trying to flesh out the relationship between privacy and the law. From the bench, Brandeis later railed against the dangers of technology and electronic surveillance in his famous dissent in the *Olmstead* wiretapping case of 1928—an impassioned and sophisticated examination of the problems associated with police surveillance that would be cited again and again as the justices slowly honed the intellectual framework required to recognize a constitutional right to privacy nearly half a century later.[2]

"The Right to Privacy" begins, as seminal articles often do, by identifying a problem: cameras and newspapermen. American privacy, wrote Brandeis and Warren, was under siege by the new social and technological developments of the Gilded Age, particularly in photography and journalism, and the law was not keeping pace. "It is our purpose to consider whether the existing law affords a principle which can be properly invoked to protect the privacy of the individual," they explain, "and, if it does, what the nature and extent of such protection is." Mixing first-rate legal acumen with innovative thinking, Warren and Brandeis begin by noting the fundamental principle that individuals have "full protection in person and property."

But what makes the article so impactful is how they expanded those age-old privacy protections beyond mere property ownership to include the "legal value of sensations." Brilliantly weaving in and out of established common law precedents concerning slander, libel, and intellectual property, Warren and Brandeis demonstrated for the first time in American legal history that existing law could be adapted to protect what they called "inviolate personality"—or simply, the "right to be let alone." Motivated by the countervailing pressures of new technologies and changing standards of public discourse in a rapidly growing media landscape, the authors warned that if privacy was to endure in the modern world it would need to be intellectually repackaged as something that included one's personality and psychological well-being. In doing so, they established themselves as among the first American intellectuals to articulate a distinctly modern understanding of privacy as something that required protection both from governmental intrusion *and* from commercial entities whose pursuit of gossip might have a deleterious effect on American lives and reputations.

Things were certainly changing, and changing rapidly. Between 1850 and 1890 American newspaper circulation had increased from approximately 100 papers read by 800,000 readers to 900 papers read by almost 8 million. With this added competition came a powerful drive for the "scoop"—and so standard journalistic practices became *much* more invasive.

By 1890 the "respectable" political newspapers and the "lowbrow" tabloid press outlets had both honed the rhetoric needed to fight off the kinds of objections voiced by the likes of Warren and Brandeis about the erosion of privacy, and they continued honing it well into the Progressive Era.

Amid these changes, in 1888 George Eastman introduced his single-button Kodak "instant camera" and revolutionized the already exploding field of amateur photography. For the first time people could walk around taking photographs without having to fumble with large contraptions that needed to be held steady for minutes at a time in front of a willing and frozen participant. Which means that for the first time individuals could suddenly have their likenesses captured in public by strangers in a candid and vulnerable fashion *without* their consent. Then, on the heels of this wondrous technological development came Stephen Henry Horgan's "halftone" process that made possible the widespread reproduction of photographs in newspapers. The age of photojournalism was born.

For all of its dry technical language and sharp legal reasoning, what stands out most about "The Right to Privacy" is the article's distinctly contemptuous tone. Warren and Brandeis's denouncement of the Gilded Age press is indignant and unrestrained. They not only attack—they *scold*. "The press is overstepping in every direction the obvious bounds of propriety and of decency," reads an early passage. "Gossip is no longer the resource of the idle and of the vicious, but has become a trade, which is pursued with industry as well as effrontery. To satisfy a prurient taste the details of sexual relations are spread broadcast in the columns of the daily papers." Warren and Brandeis's assault on the media was wide and relentless, charging that privacy invasions from "modern enterprise and invention" subject people "to mental pain and distress, far greater than could be inflicted by mere bodily injury." And worse, the quest for profits had steered newspapers and Americans toward an obscene obsession with sex.[3]

One could call them snobs and not be entirely off the mark. Never shying from melodrama (some bodily injuries are worse than others), the young lawyers fashioned themselves not just as legal experts but also as noble defenders of morality and intellectualism, offering a larger warning about the dangers of a technologically savvy, privacy-invading tabloid press that would stop at nothing in its pursuit of gossip while corrupting all that was decent and pure in American life.

Warren and Brandeis had reason to be confident that their high-minded attacks on the new press would be well received. Their learned peers in Boston's upper crust certainly agreed with their characterization. Upon the article's publication most of the faculty at Harvard Law and many senior scholars showered the authors with praise almost immediately, commending their legal prowess and innovative use of existing "common law" precedents to address privacy law in a broader sense than had been done before.

The few mainstream magazines and newspapers that took notice of "The Right to Privacy" were quick to dismiss its arguments as pompous and trite. *Life* magazine grouped Warren and Brandeis with a particular class of "ladies and gentlemen, criminals, and people of sensitive respectability" who were entirely out of touch with what real Americans expected from the media. "The feelings of these *thin-skinned* Americans," it concluded, "are doubtless at the bottom of an article in the December number of the *Harvard Law Review*." Whether snobbish, brilliant, or both, in 1975 the Supreme Court identified the piece as "the root article" of American privacy law.[4]

Privacy experts have also been quick to point out its short-comings. Perhaps the most glaring error is how Brandeis chose to define privacy as "the right to be let alone," a turn of phrase he borrowed from Judge Thomas Cooley. It's punchy, but defining privacy as the right to be let alone is inadequate on a number of levels. The definition is simply too broad. By such a standard, any physical assault would constitute an invasion of privacy. So would any offensive remark from a stranger on the street. The authors also try to wedge privacy into a loosely articulated philosophical concept they call "inviolate personality," or the right to determine to what extent one's thoughts, sentiments, and emotions shall be communicated to others, but again they do so without much clarification. Nor does the article mention what specific rights, if any, are essential to maintaining the right to be let alone. They leave us with a definition of privacy that is too broad to be of much practical use.[5]

When Brandeis put "instantaneous photographs" and "newspaper enterprise" side by side in his article, he was not necessarily concerned that people were being *observed*—they were also being *identified*. Distinctions between those considered deserving of the press's attention and those who were its victims were growing more fluid. Some railed against these new invasions and invoked, as Warren and Brandeis did, widespread intellectual "leveling." Others actively sought such invasions in the pursuit of notoriety. As the press came to embrace photographs, new privacy concerns arose over whether photographs were really objective in the first place and the extent to which the subjects of those photographs were more readily identifiable, more easily misrepresented, and more exposed. New norms of privacy in journalism were taking root. Gossip was no longer constrained by the limitations of word of mouth. It could be aired widely.

"The Right to Privacy" may well have arisen, as one scholar argued, from hypersensitive "spokesmen for patrician values" looking down on the "cultural values of mass society." But to accept this simple characterization is to ignore the larger point about the powerful transformation occurring in Gilded Age media. Motivated by significant changes in technology, visual culture, and perceptions of the public sphere, "The Right to Privacy" helps us examine the privacy problems of the Gilded Age and Progressive Era and the extent to which individuals required a new understanding of privacy to properly defend it.[6]

When discussing Brandeis, historians tend to draw a straight line from "The Right to Privacy" to his 1928 *Olmstead* dissent. But *Olmstead* concerns privacy problems raised by law enforcement, wiretapping, and the ability of the Constitution to address these specific concerns. Before we get to *Olmstead* there is an entire chapter of American privacy rooted in the history of journalism and photography. The associate justice was right: "time works changes, brings into existence new conditions and purposes," and so certain concepts must be revisited and their definitions expanded. The competing interest of public curiosity proved to be a powerful foe.[7]

II

In the summer of 1870 in Brooklyn, a tense Theodore Tilton listened carefully as his wife confessed to having an affair with his longtime friend and mentor, the celebrated Congregationalist minister Henry Ward Beecher. It began four years earlier, she told him, when he and the preacher worked together writing and editing the popular religious journal the *Independent*. As a poet, religious scholar, and prominent abolitionist, Tilton often left his wife alone for months at a time to travel the lecture circuit. The good reverend knew that the Tilton marriage was somewhat strained, and he began calling on Elizabeth at least once a week while Theodore was away. What started as a pleasant series of religious discussions between friends eventually grew into something physical. But the burden of sin had taken its toll. That July she returned home from her usual summer sojourn in the country and confessed all.[8]

It wasn't entirely her fault, she argued. And it wasn't entirely wicked. She had surrendered to Beecher, her husband's father figure, only after her "moral resistance" was chipped away by what she later called "repeated assaults upon her mind" by the great man's "overmastering arguments." Further, the recent loss of her infant child had placed her in a "tender state." And anyway, because their sexual exploits came from a place of "pure affection and a high religious love" she still remained, despite her adultery, "spotless and chaste." After securing a promise from her husband that he would neither cause Beecher harm nor speak a word of her confession, she returned to the country and awaited his next course of action.[9]

Tilton forgave her, but wrote a letter to Beecher demanding the minister resign his pulpit. A few weeks later, their mutual friend Frank Moulton was able to broker a truce between the two men. A few months after that, Beecher and Moulton bankrolled Tilton's new journal *The Golden Age*. The story might have ended there had the Tiltons not spoken of the affair to others. Accounts differ on exactly how the information got out, but it is clear that Theodore's sometimes chess partner Elizabeth Cady Stanton was at least partly culpable. The details of Beecher's infidelity soon found their way to Stanton's colleague Victoria Woodhull, the infamous suffragist and "free love" advocate, who was a long-standing target of the Beecher family. In 1872 Woodhull, then presidential nominee of the Equal Rights Party, used the rumor to accuse Reverend Beecher of a series of sexual indiscretions, not the least of which was "terrible orgies" with Mrs. Tilton carried on in the presence of her children. A church investigation eventually exonerated Beecher, essentially branding Tilton a liar, though not before details were leaked to the papers. In 1875 a humiliated and excommunicated Theodore filed a civil suit against the minister for adultery and alienation of affection. The public trial, what the *New York Times* later called "one of the most pitiful episodes in human experience," was replete with backstabbing, false testimony, and wild accusations.[10]

The Beecher-Tilton affair by no means marks the beginning of tabloid journalism, but it was undoubtedly one of the biggest stories of its time—the first modern sex scandal to receive long-term media attention absent a murder victim. For more than a year the press followed every minuscule development in the case. Even today numerous books and articles explore what the scandal reveals about prevailing perceptions of sexuality, religion, and gender in nineteenth-century America. But Beecher-Tilton also marked a watershed moment in the history of American privacy and the proper role of the media.[11]

The origins of the modern American newspaper, covering public life outside the arenas of politics and business, are generally attributed to the "penny press" of the 1830s and the "flash papers" of the 1840s—both of which provoked a measure of outrage from the moral reformers of their day for "licentious" and "revolting" content. These early newspapers were skillfully adapted from their forerunners in the United Kingdom to fit popular American modes of lewd banter, lowbrow witticisms, and wisecracking. The flash press enjoyed tremendously high circulation and, for the most part, was left to its own devices.[12]

The exponential growth of nineteenth-century newspapers was nothing short of a cultural and economic marvel. Over a few short decades, readership ballooned from the tens of thousands to almost ten million. Papers courted everyday Americans as readers and were rewarded with handsome profits. The steady increase in the circulation of these less-than-highbrow periodicals led to the sensationalist "yellow press" of giants like William Randolph Hearst and Joseph Pulitzer. What we now call "human interest journalism" addressed an ever-growing range of topics from crime to society gossip to the off-stage antics of popular theater actors and professional musicians.[13] And it wasn't just the words on the page. The success of human interest journalism in this period owed as much to pictures as it did to sensational writing. Much like today, a masterful use of imagery helped immerse readers in narratives by lending visual cues and a sense of legitimacy.

As demand for human interest reportage grew in the second half of the nineteenth century, these newspapers were increasingly legitimized in civic life. Not only in the political realm, but also in the day-to-day happenings of urban neighborhoods and rural towns. The illustrated press was able to gradually position itself as a legitimate representative of the public voice—the interpreter of what information, regardless of how private, could be disclosed to serve the "court of public opinion." With this legitimization, the press began its steady encroachment into aspects of life that had been considered out of bounds.[14]

This relatively abrupt change in the standards of privacy went neither unnoticed nor unopposed. In fact, what makes the Beecher-Tilton scandal so significant is that it shined a spotlight on exactly how drastically the lines of privacy were being redrawn.

Newspapers didn't only write about the scandal, newspapers wrote about newspapers writing about the scandal and about how much the scandal had changed the way newspapers themselves were functioning. Knee deep into the metaphysical and often bordering on the absurd, coverage of the Beecher-Tilton trial ushered in an extensive discourse over the social role of the media and the boundaries of individual privacy in cases when the public had a keen interest in a topic that clearly had no impact on their daily lives or on the state of the republic.

For the first time reporters covering Beecher-Tilton didn't speak only to the principal actors. They knocked on the doors of their neighbors and asked whether they'd had any idea of the improprieties down the street. They asked local grocers, butchers, and bakers if they ever detected the whiff of libidinous behavior or connubial strife between the Tiltons. Distant relatives were tracked down and asked about the character of their kin. Was there something in their childhood, perhaps, that might have foreshadowed some moral deficiency? Members of the congregation were asked whether they knew of any other adulterous occurrences among their flock.[15]

Until Beecher-Tilton, most mainstream newspapers refused to address the private lives of people not deemed public figures (mostly politicians, performers, titans of business, and heinous criminals) for fear that such invasions were either anathema to the public good or would make the papers look amateur and unreliable. Mrs. Tilton's infidelity helped undo this reluctance. The public's demand for every scrap of information on the Beecher trial granted the press new authority, so that even the most cautious and highly esteemed papers joined a consensus that established the press, in the words of scholar Glenn Wallach, "as the remorseless prosecution, defense, and judge in a court of public opinion." Investigative tactics once considered too brazen were suddenly permissible. The collateral damage to American privacy was deemed acceptable. Just give the people what they want.[16]

III

The mainstream press faced a conundrum. Editors wanted to fill as much space as possible with the scandal to sell more papers, but they also understood that by doing so they left themselves exposed to charges of impropriety and delegitimization from elite moral authorities—influential people like Warren and Brandeis—who still very much subscribed to old-school Victorian standards of decency and impropriety. To solve this problem, the mainstream media employed a brilliant brand of double-think rhetoric that allowed them to continue their constant coverage *and* absolve themselves of any wrongdoing. The solution was simple: blame the readers. It was genius.

The *New York Times*, though it did not yet command the status it enjoys today, had for years been positioning itself as one of the more "respectable" news outlets in the Northeast. While covering Beecher-Tilton, the editorial board published numerous statements calling the story a distraction from truly important news and lamented the "sudden and rapid growth of this nuisance." The paper took particular issue with the widening net of persons suddenly enduring the inherent prying of the journalist's interview. "For the last four weeks" it chided, "everyone who has, or is supposed to have, any possible information concerning the parties to the scandal, or concerning their relations and intimate friends, or their immediate ancestry, has been subjected to a searching examination by a crowd of so-called 'representatives of the press.'"[17] But in almost the same breath, the editors also declared the *Times* would continue to report on the scandal at length because of the public's insatiable appetite for gossip. The paper was but a humble servant to the court of public opinion, and so it was the people, not the press, that "should be heartily ashamed" because "the most disreputable of newspapers would not publish interviews [of people loosely connected to the scandal] if they were not eagerly read."[18]

This masterful self-absolution of any wrongdoing in their attacks on established norms of American privacy was mirrored by almost every press outlet that had been hesitant to cross that line. The *Times*, its defense now honed, opined that "when people get ready to respect themselves, they will have no difficulty making the newspapers respect them." Until then, as keeper of the public voice, "while the public demand a report of the trial now going on" it was the paper's "duty to supply it—a duty which we perform with very great disgust."[19] They held their noses all the way to the bank.

IV

The Gilded Age media's strange sense of self-awareness also spilled over into its treatment of images. Photographs would not grace the pages of American newspapers for another twenty years, but visual representations of the Beecher-Tilton sex scandal were a crucial aspect of its coverage. The masterfully detailed engravings in publications such as *Frank Leslie's Illustrated Newspaper* depicted not only the trial's key players but also persistent journalists at work. Again, news coverage about news coverage.

One *Leslie's* engraving from 1874 speaks to the lack of privacy afforded to Beecher-Tilton peripherals. The image depicts nine reporters crowding the steps outside a meeting of the Beecher trial's investigation committee. An official blocks the door, while two journalists brazenly lean over a banister in an attempt to peer into a nearby window. Another from that year shows more than twenty journalists crowding a Brooklyn parlor, hastily copying a statement by Beecher before handing off their transcriptions to waiting errand boys. An early report in the *Chicago Tribune* drove home how important the visual component was to the larger story, noting that "the greatest effort has been made to get a likeness of Mrs. Tilton. One house offered $1,000 for a photograph . . . nothing has appeared to

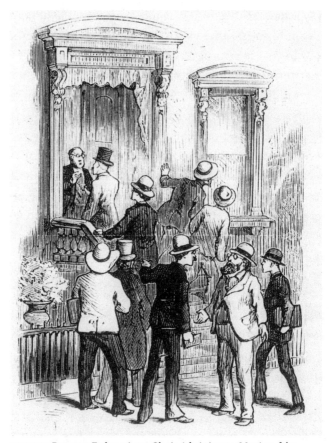

FIGURE 1. Reporters Endeavoring to Obtain Admission to a Meeting of the Investigation Committee at Mr. Storrs's House.

give the slightest idea of this now famous woman." The article then published Mrs. Tilton's daily routine, her "accustomed spheres," and made sure to mention that she was "greatly annoyed by the curious who crowded her privacy."[20]

By choosing to report (with pictures!) the changing nature of journalistic privacy standards, these papers effectively gave credence to arguments that such intrusions satisfied a legitimate public demand. And so the sexual indiscretions of a renowned minister gave occasion for human interest journalism to penetrate the private sphere in a very public way. It's exactly the kind of thing Justice Brandeis was to castigate. "The Right to Privacy" took pains to address the moral implications of these privacy problems and the distractions it posed to "brains capable of other things," but it was not, as some have said, the beginning of this discussion, but a reflection of a dialogue that had been going on for almost two decades. Indeed, the aristocratic Warren himself had had personal experience of this new dynamic. In 1883 he married Mabel Bayard, daughter of Senator Thomas F. Bayard, who was to become secretary of state. Throughout the 1880s the private affairs of both the Warrens and the Bayards appeared in the national press—a likely motivation for Warren's contributions to "The Right to Privacy."[21]

E. L. Godkin, founder of the *Nation* and one of the most important journalistic minds of his generation, was among the more prominent figures to attack these changing standards of privacy in journalism in the 1870s. In a series of scathing editorials Godkin credited "cheap periodicals" with ushering in the despicable rise of a new "Chromo-Civilization"—a people that shunned true intellectualism in favor of "a more simple-minded unconsciousness of truth." America, according to Godkin, was getting dumber, and it was the media's fault.[22]

We know Brandeis and Warren sympathized with Godkin's ideas. He makes a brief appearance in "The Right to Privacy" as an "able writer" who had "recently" discussed the evil of privacy invasions by newspapers. The particular piece Brandeis and Warren were referring to appeared in *Scribner's* and is filled with much of the same foreboding seen in Godkin's earlier work. As Brandeis and Warren would, he paints a picture of civilization's rise from savagery to an enlightened and genteel state, positioning the sanctity of a man's reputation as a linchpin of society. Public curiosity, Godkin said, was as old as time itself, but was effectively kept at bay because gossip was primarily oral and could never spread far. "In all this," he wrote, the advent of the newspaper had "converted curiosity into what economists call an effectual demand and gossip into a marketable commodity."[23]

Brandeis, Warren, and Godkin were hardly alone in their opinions. Their moral and intellectual objections fit squarely with the prevailing social and cultural ideas among New England gentility.

From this perspective, what scholar Rochelle Gurstein called "the reticent sensibility," for-profit journalism gave prominence to matters undeserving of a large audience, trivialized the quality of public conversation, corrupted good taste and judgment, and "made for an increasingly polarized society, where distinction would reside with the cultivated few who were capable of recognizing excellence."[24]

It is tempting, especially nowadays, to write off these Victorian sensibilities as prudish elitism. But it is important to understand that these ideas were part of a powerful and long-standing philosophy that recognized privacy, the sacred, and shame as core elements of the very deepest levels of individual consciousness. The reticent sensibility recognized limits to knowledge and approached the unknowable with a certain degree of wonder. Under this philosophy one made a *choice* to embrace civility, to have the strength of character to live by a code of ethics that held individual privacy in very high esteem. It was something to take pride in, something that separated Americans from the savages. What mortified Brandeis and his contemporaries most about the rise of the tabloid press was not simply that it was eroding good taste, but that it was attacking a larger social conception of intimacy and privacy.[25]

The Reverend Beecher defended himself rather well given the circumstances. In July 1874 a church investigating committee (stacked with some of his closest friends) was convened to settle the matter. When Elizabeth Tilton, who had by then decided to leave her husband, was called to testify, she vehemently denied the adultery had ever occurred. Despite a mountain of seemingly irrefutable letters and documentation submitted by Theodore, Beecher was exonerated. The legal trial that followed resulted in a hung jury. And Tilton, along with many of those who spoke on his behalf, were excommunicated from the congregation. Elizabeth was too, years later, when in a bout of guilt she issued a public confession admitting that the adultery *did* in fact occur. Her ex-husband—ostracized, cuckolded, and broke—fled to Paris where he lived in poverty, devoting much of his life to studying chess until his death in 1907. So which was more destructive—the act that wrecked the Tiltons' marriage or the exposure of three private lives?

V

Twenty years later, near the turn of the century when "The Right to Privacy" went to press, the tabloid media had achieved an unprecedented level of sophistication. Among the most notorious and widely circulated tabloid of the period was the *National Police Gazette*, a highly sensational and beautifully illustrated weekly run by the dubious Richard K. Fox.

The *Gazette* had been around since 1845 and began running scandalous crime stories after coming into the hands of former New York City Police Chief George Matsell shortly after the Civil War. But it wasn't until Fox took charge in the 1870s that it achieved national prominence, reaching an estimated circulation of 150,000 copies per week (the paper was a popular mainstay of barber shops, hotels, and saloons, and so actual readership was likely much higher). By the late 1870s the tabloid was successful enough to purchase a skyscraper at the Manhattan foot of the (then under-construction) Brooklyn Bridge.[26]

Its pages were large and bright pink and packed with first-rate woodcuts. The *Gazette*'s lifeblood was sports—bareknuckle boxing mostly—but as much space (and often more) was dedicated to sensational, graphic accounts of murder, robbery, vice, and gossip. Those stories overwhelmingly referenced sexuality, usually coupled with violence or some other illicit activity.[27] It was, in all respects, the very picture of the damaging modern periodical to which Warren, Brandeis, and Godkin allude.

Some of the subjects of these stories were prominent figures whose indiscretions would certainly have made national news at any time, like when congressman Thompson shot businessman Walter Davis on a train for plying his wife with drink, "debauching her," and making her "the victim, in her unfortunate condition, of his degraded lust." But most of those who found themselves in the *Gazette*'s crosshairs were not public figures at all.

A glance at just one pink page from an 1892 edition brings us first to a "ruined" Isabella Mariano cutting out the tongue of her former lover whom she caught in bed with a new paramour (the headline reads "A Jilted Woman's Revenge"), then to one Jacob Miller who fatally stabbed a Mr. James Bosworth after he saw him kissing his wife in a dimly lit kitchen ("Killed By Her Husband"), and finally the arrests of a man and his "pretty fifteen year old" lover who had spent two weeks in Chicago's Central Hotel ("Her Young Life Ruined, Romance of Christie Jackson, of Sharon Springs, N.Y., Eloped With a Rascal"). Of course, the paper fails to mention that its publication of Jackson's name, origins, and sexual history may itself have something to do with her "ruin."[28]

The vast majority of the *Gazette*'s stories exposed the private affairs of individuals in a manner that in no way could be justified as serving the public interest. For example, Miss Sabina Goudette suffered a gruesome disfigurement when her hair got caught in a cotton mill factory shafting. Her scalp, "with one ear and part of another, was torn off, one arm broken in two places and a shoulder dislocated." She lived but was not expected to recover. The paper made sure to mention her full name, town of residence, and upcoming marriage the following week. A similar tale involved Miss Annie McManus, of Reading, Pennsylvania, who was "disfigured for life" after the family pit bull "fastened its teeth in her face" in her father's library. Her full name, that of her parents, and her town of residence were published.[29]

Let's pause for a moment and take stock of what's going on here. The specific privacy problem concerns information dissemination—more precisely, a problem Daniel Solove's taxonomy terms *disclosure*. *Disclosure* occurs when certain true information about a person is revealed to others without the person's consent. It differs from regular breaches of confidentiality because the harm involves embarrassment or damage to the person's reputation. As Solove puts it: the "harm of disclosure is not so much the elimination of secrecy as it is the spreading of information beyond expected boundaries."[30]

Unchecked disclosure is damaging to individuals on a number of levels. As social animals, we use personal information about ourselves to shape the perceptions others have about us. What we choose to reveal and *not* to reveal allows us a measure of power when it comes to constructing our own reputations and the terms upon which we will interact with others. To broadcast personal information about someone else without his or her permission is to take that power away. The disfiguring of Goudette and McManus hardly seems relevant to the larger doings of society, but we can assume their anguish and embarrassment were amplified upon being broadcast to hundreds of thousands of strangers.[31]

If *disclosure* occurs in a media setting (like a newspaper), it makes one a prisoner of their recorded past. People grow and change—an existential reality reflected in our legal system by the presence of statutes of limitations. Part of the reason punishments for crimes have expiration dates is because we as a society recognize that people change over time. By making someone a prisoner of his or her recorded past, unchecked *disclosure* can also inhibit the ability to reform. While old newspapers were not as easily available as they are today, librarians and hobbyists did preserve them, so disclosures never truly disappeared. A fact made more troublesome when in 1893 members of the American Library Association called for the creation of a national newspaper index.[32]

Any arrest could make someone fair game for the *Gazette*, especially if there was a sexual component in the backstory. Let's return to that May 1892 issue. Rush Buck was lucky enough to grace Fox's pages after being knocked out and arrested for attempting to kiss and hug a female passerby accompanied by her husband. Miss Jessie Pierce and Miss Robbies Brown made the front page after being arrested for starting a factory room brawl. The reported cause of the brawl was "a spirited rivalry . . . supposed to have sprung from their claims on a common beau."[33]

Richard K. Fox had a preternatural sense for the newspaper business, and for all the crime and scandal he covered, what he was really selling his readers was sex, as the illustrations he commissioned demonstrated. The magnificently detailed woodcuts of the *Police Gazette* were not just mere accompaniments to its stories, they were the paper's backbone. By the mid-1880s the total space devoted to visual imagery spanned more than half the paper, covering eight full pages on top of the numerous smaller images that peppered the columns. Sexuality was a distinct feature in almost all of them. The depiction of the mangling of Sabina Goudette, for example, took up a quarter page and was aggressively provocative. As the overpowering gears lift her off the floor her back is arched in a blatantly erotic pose, her breasts are thrust forward (the attentive viewer can make out the contours of her right nipple), a helpless look on her face. The moment immediately precedes her disfigurement. The timing keeps her beautiful.

The paper's reliance on delivering sexual imagery under the guise of crime reportage undoubtedly informed the stories it chose to run. In this sense the words were more a guide to the images and not the other way around. A story like the mauling of Annie McManus was likely chosen less for its grotesque nature than for the sexual imagery it could yield. Like Miss Goudette her back is arched in an erotic pose as she lay on the floor. The beast is on top of her, his teeth sunk into her neck. Her face shows no pain, only a combination of shock and complete submission.

The image of Rush Buck is also noticeably salacious as he overpowers his victim from behind. She bends forward as she covers her face, her buttocks align with his hips in a posture that accentuates the curves of her body. Rush overpowers her, wearing a lustful gaze and slimy grin as her husband rushes forward with a fist cocked.[34]

The Pierce-Brown factory fight was among the *Gazette*'s more blatantly sexual front pages: the scene is filled with young women as one prepares to stomp another laying on the floor in the signature submissive and full-bodied pose found in other images. The aggressor's shirt has been ripped, promising to reveal her left breast.[35]

These pictures were the mechanism through which Fox sold sex and violence, and the profits gained from them were the driving force behind the disclosure of private affairs of many everyday Americans. Brandeis and Warren were plainly correct in claiming privacy invasions were entwined with a desire from newspapers to satisfy the "prurient tastes" of the public.

There can be no doubt the *Gazette* was aware of the privacy problems it was creating. The proof is in its noticeably defensive posture on the issue, printed on the bottom left corner of every first page

CAUGHT IN THE SHAFTING.

MISS SABINA GOUDETTE WHIRLED AROUND AND HORRIBLY MANGLED IN THE
NORTH GROSVENOR COTTON MILLS, NEAR PUTNAM, CONN.

FIGURE 2. Caught in the Shafting.

A GIRL'S FIGHT FOR LIFE.

MISS ANNIE M'MANUS' DESPERATE STRUGGLE WITH HER FATHER'S MADDENED
BULLDOG IN HER HOME IN READING, PA.

FIGURE 3. A Girl's Fight for Life.

RUSH BUCK KNOCKED OUT

BY AN INDIGNANT NIAGARA FALLS, N. Y., MAN, WHOSE WIFE HE HAD INSULTED IN PUBLIC
BY ATTEMPTING TO HUG AND KISS HER.

FIGURE 4. Rush Buck Knocked Out.

in the 1890s: "*The Police Gazette* is a newspaper in the real sense of the word. It prints the news of the week, but eliminates the filth. It selects the events with due regard to their importance from a news standpoint, and presents them to its readers in entertaining and readable shape."

Much like the *New York Times* during the Beecher scandal, the *Gazette* presents itself as a periodical of the highest character, but without the self-deprecation. While the *Times* denounced its own invasions outright and shifted blame to its readers, the *Gazette* embraced its privacy invasions while positioning itself as a noble crusader for the public good. The paper "never published anything that could give offense to the most punctilious person. Of a necessity it prints the offenses committed against the laws of society and State by men and women [because] it is needful for the public morals that the violators of the laws of man should be condemned and held up to public scorn and ridicule."

Hilariously, for all of Justice Brandeis's contempt of papers like

FREE FIGHT IN A COTTON MILL.
ANNISTON, ALA., FACTORY GIRLS JOIN SIDES IN A RIOT IN WHICH MISS BROWN IS FATALLY INJURED.

FIGURE 5. Free Fight in a Cotton Mill.

the *Gazette*, he adopted a notably similar posture in his Progressive Era attacks on the money trusts. Consider the *Gazette*'s statement of purpose in 1891:

> Were [criminal] offenses overlooked crime would become rampant, society rotten, and virtue would be at a premium. It is the fear of public condemnation that keeps many in the straight and narrow path. The electric light of the press holds them in check. If they sin in the dark and their offense is known only to themselves, they continue to pose before society as models of virtue. But on the other hand, if their crime is made

known they are punished and society is benefited. It is not the function of the newspaper to excite the appetite for scandal, but to expose all the frauds and shams with a view of correcting them. Such is the mission of the Police Gazette.[36]

And now Brandeis in 1913:

Publicity is justly commended as a remedy for social and industrial diseases. Sunlight is said to be the best of disinfectants; electric light the most efficient policeman. And publicity has already played an important part in the struggle against the Money Trust. The Pujo Committee has, in the disclosure of the facts concerning financial concentration, made a most important contribution toward attainment of the New Freedom. The battlefield has been surveyed and charted. The hostile forces have been located, counted and appraised. That was a necessary first step—and a long one—towards relief . . . there should be a further call upon publicity for service. That potent force must, in the impending struggle, be utilized in many ways as a continuous remedial measure.[37]

Yet only a fool would take the *Gazette*'s argument seriously. Even a casual glance makes clear its true motives, which were hardly "moral" by any standard. The important distinction between the paper and the justice is that Brandeis and his progressive comrades were talking about institutions whereas the *Gazette*'s subjects were individuals. But its ability to link privacy invasions of ordinary citizens with the public good is significant because it allows the paper to defend itself against the likes of Brandeis and Warren and their charges of immorality.

The paper frequently took measures to paint those who would call it immoral as hypocrites. A mainstay of the *Gazette* was its column on "Religious News," a space reserved exclusively for tales of deviant ministers who extolled purity by day while practicing debauchery by night. The heading of one column noted that "clergymen have much to say about the sins of the wicked world," but "when one of their own number strays from the path of virtue . . . their mouths are closed."[38] Brilliantly, the *Gazette* constructed a shield against its critics by claiming that all its invasions served the public good. All of them. Any charges of appealing to "prurient tastes" were made by men who would likely be exposed as reprehensible if their own private spheres had been invaded. The ministers *are* Warren and Brandeis.

As Fox's weekly expanded its circulation through the century's final decade, it also alluded to what was waiting for journalism in the next one. "The CAMERA FIEND is making life miserable for many people at seaside resorts," an 1891 article reads. "He is up early and late, and haunts the bathing grounds where handsome matrons and pretty maidens sport. It is no use trying to dodge him. He is loaded with enthusiasm and his camera is loaded with plates, and he is bound to have you whether you like it or not." Next to the piece, a woodcut features the object of its undoing: a camera. At the bottom of the page, a minuscule advertisement: Glen Cameras promises a full set-up for the aspiring amateur photographer, complete with instructions.[39]

VI

A "halftone" is a kind of optical illusion. A series of microscopic dots of different sizes and shapes are imprinted on a page to simulate the smooth tones of a photographic image. These thousands of specks can coalesce to create an image that is not actually a photograph — just a convincing reproduction of one. Students of impressionist painting might liken this technique to that of the great pointillist masters like Georges Seurat and Paul Signac: thousands of dots coming together to form a lifelike picture.

To make a traditional halftone, a cameraman shoots an image through a screen that breaks up the continuous tones of standard film into tiny droplets. Those droplets are then photoengraved onto a metal plate, allowing anyone to reproduce the original image as often as he or she likes through the use of a special letterpress or offset printing. The end result is the ability to replicate photographs on a massive scale, on regular paper. Just as a single woodcut can be dipped repeatedly in ink to stamp thousands of broadsheets, with the invention of the halftone the same could suddenly be done for photographs.

The introduction of the halftone process was nothing less than a revolution for news reportage. It quickly became a cornerstone of photojournalism, ushering in an iconographical revolution whose impact we still feel today. Credit for pioneering the process is generally attributed to Stephen Henry Horgan, who in the late 1870s while head of the New York *Daily Graphic*'s process department began punching a series of holes into cardboard sheets and then carefully rolling the sheets over controlled quantities of black ink to create images. They weren't exactly the best quality. Eventually, Horgan switched to meshed metal, and after some tinkering published the first newspaper photograph on March 4, 1880.[40]

Thanks to enthusiasts like Louis and Max Levy and Frederic Ives, Horgan's halftone process was slowly perfected, and by the early 1900s almost every newspaper in the country was inserting screens into their high-speed rotary presses, replacing the contrived images of the woodcut artist with the much more lifelike renderings yielded by the halftone process.[41]

As the capacity for reproducing photographs matured so too did the technology for capturing them. Photographs had long been familiar to Americans; Louis-Jacques-Mandé Daguerre introduced the first commercially successful photographic process (his "Daguerreotype") as far back as 1837. But the process was cumbersome and expensive. In the late 1880s the engineer and entrepreneur George Eastman made a key breakthrough with the single button Kodak "instant" camera. Unlike earlier cameras that used glass plate negatives, the Kodak model #540 used Eastman's new "flexible film" rolls and rotating barrel shutters. No longer did subjects have to sit still for agonizing minutes. The instant camera sold for $25 and came preloaded with a 100-shot roll of film. When the film was spent, customers could mail the whole camera to Kodak for developing and printing.

As the technology spread and continued to improve, more and

more individuals found themselves in front of the lens—whether they wanted to or not. The candid shot was born. Life could be captured as it truly was (kind of). And as the camera and the halftone process matured in tandem, the entire system of packaging visual information was irrevocably transformed. Once photographs could be printed alongside words, newspapers and magazines achieved a new level of influence and authority still recognized today. And as Justice Brandeis began his slow ascent to the Supreme Court, his predictions concerning privacy problems brought on by these technologies started to ring true in the legal realm.[42]

The camera is to blame for one of America's earliest privacy cases. In 1902 the very young and by all accounts very attractive Abigail Roberson filed suit against a New York business after a photograph of her was used without permission in an advertising campaign. A friend of Roberson's had seen her photograph a year earlier and asked permission to sketch it. The sketch eventually ended up in the hands of an executive at the Franklin Mills Flour Company. The businessman was so taken by Roberson's beauty that he ordered her likeness to be printed on approximately 25,000 lithographic prints and posters, which, according to court records, were "conspicuously posted and displayed in stores, warehouses, saloons, and other public places." The posters were essentially one big shot of Roberson's face, with the words "Flour of the Family" written above and "Franklin Mills Flour" written below.[43]

Roberson sued the company on grounds that the unauthorized use of her likeness was a violation of her privacy. The posters, she said, caused her to be "greatly humiliated by the scoffs and jeers" of people who recognized her face from the advertisement, and "her good name" had been attacked, causing her "great distress and suffering both in body and mind." She also alleged that the constant harassment had made her so sick that she "suffered a severe nervous shock, was confined to her bed and compelled to employ a physician." She asked for $15,000 in damages and demanded that Franklin Mills and the Rochester Folding Box Co. (which had produced the posters) be "enjoined from making, printing, publishing, circulating, or using in any manner any likenesses of her in any form what-ever."[44]

She lost. There was, at the time, no common law right to privacy in the state. But the court was not entirely unsympathetic. In the majority opinion, the justices noted that complaints grounded in privacy were largely new and that their existence did not seem to have been asserted prior to 1890, "when [the issue of privacy] was presented with attractiveness and no inconsiderable ability in the *Harvard Law Review* in an article entitled, 'The Right of Privacy.'"[45]

Eventually widespread popular criticism of the court's decision prompted the state legislature to adopt a bill to prevent "the unauthorized use of the name or picture of any person for the purposes of trade." Roberson still did not receive damages, but her case had a significant impact on New York privacy law. Seven years later, an almost identical ruling came down from the Rhode Island Supreme Court, which found against James N. Henry, who had sued the Cherry & Webb Company for publishing an unauthorized photo of him in an advertisement for waterproof coats. The judges in the case agreed that Henry was wronged but noted unanimously that up to that point no state law was on the books to prevent such practices.[46]

So what's the real danger here? There are at least two specific privacy problems at play in these cases: *appropriation* and *secondary use*. *Appropriation* is the use of one's identity (or likeness) to further the goals of someone else. Every advanced democracy has laws (along with social barriers) against unauthorized appropriation. The heart of the problem, as with other privacy issues, is that our likeness is an essential component of how we present ourselves to society. We have a right, as freeborn individuals, to play a large role in shaping how we are perceived by others. Unauthorized appropriation takes away that freedom and potentially destroys or distorts our reputations in ways we find objectionable: not because of our own actions, but because of *someone else's* priorities.[47]

Secondary use, while generally more applicable to informational privacy, is the sharing of material for purposes that are different from the original reasons the material was provided. Both plaintiffs,

Roberson and Henry, concede they willingly allowed themselves to be photographed. But that doesn't necessarily mean that anyone can use those photographs for any purpose. It's not that a person should have complete control over how his or her likeness or information is presented—one can hardly prevent someone from hanging a photo in his own living room by citing secondary use. But when a person allows him- or herself to be photographed, a secondary use of the image, such as in an advertising campaign, is rarely anticipated. In this sense, Roberson and Henry were absolutely victimized.[48]

Another privacy case in this period that came down in favor of its plaintiff arose in 1905, when Paolo Pavesich sued the New England Life Insurance Company for using his image in an advertisement in a Georgia newspaper. The difference here was in the rather insulting way Pavesich's likeness was distorted.[49] The ad was one of those before-and-after items. Pavesich, fully recognizable, was the "before" image, placed next to an embellished image that showed him poorly dressed and very sickly looking, seemingly on the verge of death. Pitching life insurance, the advertisement positioned the words "Do It Now—The Man Who Did" under the image of the healthy Pavesich and "Do It While You Can—The Man Who Didn't" under the sickly one. The ad concluded: "These Two Pictures Tell Their Own Story."[50]

Pavesich testified that the photo brought him into "ridicule before the world" because it falsely portrayed him as having been sick and weak and claimed he had made statements pertaining to life insurance that he had never made. Massachusetts Judge Andrew Cobb wrote in the unanimous decision "that the publication of one's picture without his consent by another as an advertisement, for the mere purposes of increasing the profits and gains of an advertiser," was an invasion of "common-law privacy." Pavesich, an artist by trade, was awarded the princely sum of $25,000.[51]

The cases of Abigail Roberson and Paolo Pavesich both support Brandeis's idea that a "common law" right to privacy should extend beyond property rights to protect what he called "inviolate personality"—the realm of private thoughts, sentiments, and emotions that are present in all of us. Both used privacy as a mechanism to articulate their legal right against the embarrassment and psychological trauma they experienced due to their diminished ability to control their own self-narratives. But whatever success these plaintiffs had should not be confused with any widespread acceptance in this period that inviolate personality, on its own, was solid legal footing from which to seek a redress of grievances.

For the most part, claims of mental anguish caused by privacy invasions generally succeeded only when coupled with accusations of libel, slander, or fraud. That's why Pavesich won, but Roberson didn't. The courts, it seems, were much more comfortable with privacy claims rooted in some sort of defamation or profit motive (a person's likeness being a form of personal "property"). But then again, it can't be denied that with the rise of the camera legal questions about the relationship between a person's likeness and the right to privacy were popping up more and more. Brandeis's predictions were ringing true—traditional understandings of privacy were becoming less rigid and more complicated.[52]

VII

Brandeis was also right about the implications of the blossoming marriage of the instant camera to the mainstream press. By the 1920s, around the time he was laying the groundwork for a constitutional right to privacy in his famous *Olmstead* dissent, sensationalist journalism had reached magnificent new heights—or depths. The turn-of-the-century yellow press of Hearst, Pulitzer, and others shattered the boundaries of excess in news reportage. In 1927 three New York tabloids—Hearst's *Daily Mirror*, Bernarr Mac Fadden's *Daily Graphic* (affectionately known as the "porno-graphic"), and Captain Joseph Patterson's *New York Daily News*—were chasing each other, as historian Robert Rutland writes, "through a series of alternative horrors and heroism until the reading public was limp." In the process each paper used faked photographs and sent out reporters who acknowledged no rules of privacy. One study that year found the three tabloids devoted one-quarter to one-third of their space to "anti-social news."[53]

Patterson's paper, founded in 1919, was built on a steady diet of crime reportage, sex scandals, and human interest stories that bolstered its circulation to over one million by 1926. Most of the *Daily's* coverage was similar to that of its predecessors like the *National Police Gazette,* but its innovative use of aggressive tactics and halftones greatly amplified its ability to invade privacy through unauthorized disclosure. From its inception the paper enlisted the public's help on this front by advertising that it would pay for tips on stories or photos. Every tipster who disclosed a sensational story about his neighbor or colleague got fifty cents, no matter how many had called before him. The average tip received $2 to $5, and by 1927 the *Daily* was paying upwards of $1,000 a week to an assorted army of whistleblowers, gossips, tattlers, and rats.[54]

"Think in terms of pictures," Patterson repeatedly told his editors. Sensational tabloids were first and foremost a photographic experience, designed for glancing more than reading. Philip Payne, who was privileged to have edited both the *Daily* and Hearst's *Mirror* in the 1920s, later claimed that the chief goal was to illustrate every story in the paper. Payne called photos "the very essence of tabloidism." Atop every issue the *Daily* made its intentions clear: it was "New York's Picture Newspaper"—with an image of a camera permanently fixed to its masthead.[55]

By 1928 photography was so integral to the news media that the Associated Press established its first wire photo service.[56] The true power of newspaper photographs, like the earlier illustrations of the Gilded Age, lay in their ability to instill a measure of vicarious experience to the narrative accounts they accompanied (or accompanied them). By extension, the rise of photographs in newspapers marked the end of the old illustrated weeklies and, sadly, the end of woodcuts. Photographs, by their very nature, convey a significantly larger degree of verisimilitude than even the most skilled illustrations. People see illustrations as *representations* of life; they see photographs as *actual* life—snippets of reality that have been captured. Even better, they transport viewers into other lives, exciting ones. And in this way vicarious experience, a product bought and sold since Antiquity, became that much more lifelike. It is here, in the early 1900s, that the marketplace made space for the great visual narratives that would later mature into movies and television.

This is why photographs, when embraced by journalists who cared little for the rights of others, were so perilous to privacy. People thought they were real.[57] Photographs, of course, aren't really that objective. The process of turning three dimensions into two is a tricky business, with both artistic and mechanical considerations. Decisions made by photographers concerning framing and timing are crucial. Photographers can influence lighting, setting, and perspective; and subjects often act quite unnaturally upon realizing their image is about to be captured, usually either playing to the camera or freezing up."[58] Let's illustrate this with an experiment. In 1896 the author Henry P. Robinson challenged readers to examine various photographs of several different people. All were photographed in a rural location, all were dressed similarly, and all conveyed a series of emotions. Half of the models were shot while experiencing true emotions. They were told a joke, and if they laughed their genuine laughter would be captured on film. They were told a sad story, and if their faces expressed genuine sadness the cameraman would shoot. By no means were they to play for the camera. The other half were told to act: hold poses and project feelings that they weren't really feeling. Readers were then asked which subjects were showing genuine feelings and which were faking it. The fakers were overwhelmingly thought to be genuine. Robinson's experiment highlights the blurred lines between verisimilitude (something that resembles truth) and verity (actual truth), and how difficult it can be to distinguish one from the other.[59]

And yet, the power of the photographic image is such that both in the 1920s and even today, most people believe in its objective truth. Susan Sontag, the famous essayist and filmmaker, noted that for many people "a photograph passes for incontrovertible proof that a given thing happened. The picture may distort; but there is always a presumption that something exists, or did exist, which is like what's in the picture. . . . [It] seems to have a more innocent, and therefore more accurate, relation to the visible reality than do other mimetic objects." Cultural scholar Miles Orvell agrees, noting "because the photograph was made by sunbeams it was understood to provide information of an unbiased kind." This isn't true, of course, but there is something to the idea that photographs have *some* kind of relationship to reality.[60]

This has real implications for privacy, since all individuals have a compelling interest in safeguarding the way they present themselves to society. When tabloids publish embarrassing photos of people, seen by literally millions of readers, those people become forever tied to them—no matter how artificial, manipulated, or out of context they may be. Perhaps worse, those people might also be more easily recognized by strangers (something much less likely in the days of woodcuts). Having your photo taken while leaving a precinct house after a night in jail, or while enjoying drinks in a bar with questionable company, or even while just walking down the street further inhibits the freedom you should have to write your own self-narrative. (If you are a public figure, the calculus is a bit different. We'll get to that.) This is not to say that people deserve complete autonomy in these matters—that would be unrealistic. But once the halftone was on the scene, Americans suddenly had significantly less autonomy in this realm than they used to.[61]

In 1926 the *Daily News* ran a front-page feature announcing the engagement of seventy-three-year-old Bernedetto Ferrara to Rosalia Glarraputo, "the loveliest of all the dark-eyed maiden's in Canarsie's Little Italy." Glarraputo was fifteen. The piece was packaged as a tale in which Ferrara (who had been imprisoned briefly for making advances to the girl four years earlier—"a horrid experience") was "righting his wrong" by marrying his victim. And while the paper refrained from any outright consternation, it provided a large and clear halftone of Glarraputo so that she could be quickly identified by those good citizens who would perhaps be interested in extending their opinion on the matter in person. The paper also offered up Ferrara's home addresses and that of his new fiancée's parents.[62]

VIII

Among all of the scandalous tabloid photos published while Justice Brandeis sat on the bench, one stands above all others.

Ruth Brown, a typist at *Cosmopolitan* magazine, married Albert Snyder, a rising art editor at *Motor Boating* magazine, after a brief courtship in 1915. Daughter Lorraine came three years later, prompting the couple to leave their small Brooklyn apartment for a larger one in the Bronx; eventually, as Albert advanced in his career, the couple moved to a modest home in Queens Village. The move to the suburbs was a mark of success. They owned a car and good furniture, and they had some money in the bank. Ruth quit her job and settled into a new life as a housewife and mother.[63]

But she and Albert were incompatible. Ruth liked to go out to restaurants and parties; Albert—twelve years older—preferred to stay in. Ruth loved animals and children; Albert forbade any animals in the house save one canary and often remarked that Ruth's pregnancy was an unwelcome accident. He also spoke frequently of an earlier fiancée, now deceased, as "the finest woman I have ever met" and insisted on hanging her picture in their home. Ruth's mother, Josephine Brown, suggested to her daughter more than once that she consider divorce. Instead, Ruth took a lover.[64]

Her affair with Judd Gray began in 1925. A corset salesman (the joke went that he knew his way around the female body) described as "a fit man of modest height," Gray spent two years wining and dining Mrs. Snyder at various Manhattan hotels. Tabloids eventually reported that the bellhops at the posh Waldorf-Astoria hotel saw them so frequently that they even knew their pet names for each other—hers was "Momsie," his was "Bud."[65]

It's unknown exactly when Ruth decided to murder her husband, but in early 1927 she purchased a $48,000 life insurance policy that would pay out double in the event of accidental or malicious death. On March 12, she let Gray into her home while her husband was out drinking and her daughter asleep on the second floor. Albert returned drunk and went straight to bed, whereupon Gray tried to bludgeon Albert's head with a four-pound window sash weight. When Albert fought back, Ruth burst in with a chloroform-soaked rag and eventually strangled the fellow with a length of stiff wire.[66]

The plan was to stage a robbery and secure the insurance payout. So as Albert lay dead in the bedroom, the lovers hid some valuables and left Ruth bound and gagged as Gray fled the scene. Ruth then started banging on the wall, waking her nine-year-old daughter, who ran to the neighbors to call the police. Ruth told the police who arrived she had heard noises in the night, went into the hall to investigate, and was attacked by two men who struck her unconscious. All she offered by way of description was that one was mustached and both "looked Italian."

Things quickly fell apart. Detectives found little evidence of a break-in, but they did find Ruth's "stolen" jewelry box. When another started flipping through Ruth's checkbook he noticed Gray's name among the balances. "What about Judd Gray?" asked the policeman casually. "Has he confessed?" she replied. It didn't take long for the police to connect the dots and arrest the pair of master criminals. Both lost their heads, quickly confessing and blaming the other for the deed. Commentator Damon Runyon nicknamed the case the "Dumbbell Murder."[67]

The Snyder trial was one of the largest tabloid stories of the 1920s, second only to the Lindbergh kidnapping, and served as the inspiration for the acclaimed 1944 film *Double Indemnity*. Celebrities in attendance included D. W. Griffith, Will Durant, and Nora Bayes—and the famous evangelist Sister Aimee Semple McPherson was hired by the *New York Evening Graphic* to write about the drama unfolding in the courtroom. The scandal soon provoked a scoop-versus-scoop battle between Hearst's *Daily Mirror* and the *New York Daily News*. The *Mirror* went so far as to hire Charlotte Mills to cover the trial—Mills's mother had been murdered a few years earlier in another high profile case.[68]

"At each step of the legal process," the *Daily News* later wrote, "the lovers found themselves in the viewfinders of a dozen Speed Graphic cameras. They were quickly tried, convicted and condemned to the lap of Old Sparky at Sing Sing." Aware of the story's magnitude and not without precedent, Sing Sing's Warden Lewis Lawes agreed to admit two dozen witnesses, some of them journalists, to view the execution under the condition that cameras were strictly prohibited. Tom Howard, a legman for one the *Daily*'s sister papers and operating under Patterson's instructions, smuggled in a "camera the size of a fat billfold" by attaching it to his ankle. After a crying Ruth uttered her final words, the newspaperman raised his pant leg slightly and "released the shutter with a cable snaked up his trouser leg."[69]

It's a great shot. A chilling image of Snyder bound to the chair, head covered by a leather mask and electrodes, graced the covers of a special extra edition of the *Daily News* and its regular press run the next day under the headline "DEAD!" The *Daily* scooped every paper in the country. Patterson had no problem gloating and went on to describe at length how the photo was obtained and printed a caption under the image the next day calling it "the most talked of feat in the history of journalism."[70]

But the photo was quickly met with a flood of outrage from the public and the press. A few weeks later it was cited by the New York State Assembly as the key impetus behind a bill to bar press at executions, under which "the owner or publisher of any newspaper publishing any other report of such execution other than that released by the Commissioner of Correction shall be guilty of a misdemeanor and subject to a fine not less than $1,000 or not more than $5,000." News coverage of the bill categorized it as "a sequel to the recent execution of Mrs. Ruth Snyder." The measure failed, but the Snyder image remains the only known photograph of a woman being executed in America.[71]

Ruth Snyder was hardly the first woman to be executed by the state of New York, nor was she the first to die in the electric chair. Numerous authors have noted the power of shifting standards of decency regarding public execution in this period. Most broadly, Michel Foucault described the slow turn from the spectacle of public execution—a historically necessary display of the state's "majestic, awesome power of sovereignty"—to modern forms of social control, under which spectacle was unnecessary and perhaps even counterproductive to liberal democracy.[72] Annulla Linders notes

FIGURE 6. Execution of Ruth Snyder.

the power of humanitarianism in this transition, as "the rowdiness of the crowd made it increasingly difficult to maintain a clear distinction between a solemn execution and a festive holiday celebration." Austin Sarat, as well, argues that "a newly sensitized middle-class" developed a powerful aversion to public execution and that the modern state was forced to "find ways of killing in a manner that does not allow the condemned to become an object of pity."[73]

Changing perceptions of the role of the state *and* new standards of public decency had moved Snyder's execution away from the open air gallows into the private, controlled, and intimate space of the execution chamber—which the *Daily News* promptly violated. The public spectacle of execution was hardly erased; it was merely transmitted through the media, which made it just another commodity.

Press coverage of events leading up to executions—arrests, trials, sentencing, and imprisonment of criminals—were fair game for both esteemed papers and the tabloid press. In fact, reporters were invited, by the state, to describe Snyder's passing. The day before her execution the *Daily* and other papers ran photographs of the execution chamber and the halls Snyder would travel to her end, replicating her line of sight in her final moments.[74]

Yet the photograph capturing Snyder in the throes of death was deemed over the line by the public and the state. Why?

The specific privacy problem posed by the Snyder image concerns the boundaries of *exposure*—the exposing to others of certain physical or bodily things that are deemed deeply primal and can lead to feelings of shame and humiliation. Exposure deals exclusively with the body. And it has almost nothing to do with secrecy.[75]

We all urinate and defecate. Nearly all adults engage in sexual behavior and/or masturbation. We all experience physical trauma. And all of us will die. Nudity, sex, urination, defecation, masturbation, gross disfigurement, and death all involve, as Solove's taxonomy puts it, "primal aspects of our lives—ones that are physical, instinctual, and necessary." Every civilization has social norms that encourage people to conceal some or all of these activities one way or another. For thousands of years we have been conditioned, albeit in different ways, to believe that bodily functions should be granted a measure of privacy. Few are ashamed about having to go to the bathroom, but most would be ashamed to have that process photographed and publicized. The same could be said for a serious bodily injury. *Exposure* is similar to *disclosure* in that they both deal with the dissemination of true information.[76]

In the West, dead bodies are generally afforded privacy protections against unwanted exposure. At the very least they are almost always covered, even in the event that they cannot be immediately moved. Public viewings of the dead usually occur only after a professional has taken considerable pains, often with plastics and chemicals, to make the body presentable.

Protections from exposure have a long judicial tradition dating to the nineteenth century. They have shielded both the living and the dead from the dissemination of deeply personal images. Numerous states prohibit access to images of the dead for publication—whether autopsies, crime scenes, or accident victims. In 2004 the Supreme Court rejected a Freedom of Information Act request for autopsy photos of Vincent Foster Jr., a White House aide who committed suicide, claiming they "could reasonably be expected to constitute an unwarranted invasion of personal privacy." This brings us back to "Ruthless" Ruth Snyder. The regard for privacy as an aspect of legally defined decency is why cameras were banned from Snyder's execution chamber but narrative descriptions and even photos of the empty death chamber were considered acceptable.[77] At Judd's funeral, police took pains to prevent another embarrassment by surrounding the hearse with uniformed men to block press access. The *Daily News* reported this in a snippet only a few inches from another reproduction of the Snyder photograph. The body, the article reads, was being protected "from the gaze of the curiously morbid," and officers "waved the machines of newspapermen aside."[78]

IX

In some respects, Warren and Brandeis got it wrong. The American legal system wasn't properly equipped to address the flood of new privacy problems brewing in 1890. That much was clear by the time Brandeis, in his *Olmstead* dissent, urged a push for constitutional remedies against privacy invasions by law enforcement. It's understandable why "The Right to Privacy," which addressed the very different subject of the press's role in public discourse, promoted common law remedies over criminal ones. Criminalizing the publication of truthful speech was anathema to the free speech ideals of the period, whereas the common law by nature brings with it a certain versatility that is perhaps better equipped to handle that particular issue. Or maybe, as one Brandeis biographer argues, they thought that approach would make the legal community more amenable to their ideas. Either way, the piece failed to apply a sophisticated definition of privacy beyond calling it "the right to be let alone." But whatever its shortcomings, by repackaging privacy as something that extends not just to property but also to thoughts, sentiments, and "inviolate personality," it remains a dazzlingly influential turn in a very important conversation.[79]

They also got a lot of things right. "The Right to Privacy" was penned during a crucial social and cultural transition that everyone could feel as it was happening. The Beecher-Tilton scandal had broken established boundaries of privacy in the media just a decade earlier. And, as Warren and Brandeis predicted, "instantaneous photographs and newspaper enterprise" along with other technological and "mechanical devices" did indeed give rise to a multitude of privacy concerns over information dissemination, disclosure, and exposure that still endure. But again, just because these developments pushed against privacy does not mean they were not altogether bad. A truly free press in a truly free society *should* be constantly testing the limits of its reach—that's healthy. And when a free press attempts to reach into the private aspects of individual lives for reasons that have nothing to do with the well-being of the community or the republic, a truly free society has a right to establish laws and norms that will protect its members from those invasions. Again, the goal is balance. What makes this historical period so interesting is that America's conversation about privacy was so young, and its people so unprepared, that the public met these new problems with a flurry of activity while grappling with privacy's new counterweight—public curiosity.

Seventy years after Brandeis and Warren published their article, the eminent legal scholar William L. Prosser drew heavily from it when he devised his four privacy torts (or wrongs) establishing the firm parameters of a common law of American privacy. These four principles remain the legal basis for most civil privacy law in the United States: the intrusion upon seclusion or solitude, or into private affairs; the public disclosure of embarrassing private facts; unwarranted publicity that places a person in a false light in the public eye; and, of course, the unwarranted appropriation of an individual's name or likeness.[80]

To place "The Right to Privacy" in its proper historical context is to highlight the broader developments of the Gilded Age. The triumph of technology and industrial capital. The rise of the modern city. The glaring social and economic inequality. The sense among most Americans that change was coming more rapidly. "As the network of relations affecting men's lives each year became more tangled and more distended," writes Robert Wiebe, the accompanying "dislocation and bewilderment" meant Americans "in a basic sense no longer knew who or what they were." In many ways, "The Right to Privacy" was part of a much larger historical dialogue about this troubling period—the Gilded Age is the only period in our history that has intentionally been given a derogatory name.[81]

But the article is also a window into the history of America's free press and its visual culture. In the early 1960s, Daniel J. Boorstin famously argued the United States had achieved what he called a "graphic revolution": that the spread of technology in printing, telegraphy, photography, and later the moving image increased public demand for information and images to a point where that demand exceeded the supply of legitimately newsworthy events. And this was decades before the twenty-four-hour news cycle. Boorstin wasn't talking about privacy—he was indicting celebrity culture and actually displayed little understanding of what constitutes a privacy invasion. But his observation does help put into perspective the public demand for the private information of others that allowed papers like the *Times*, the *Police Gazette*, and the *Daily News* to disclose and expose the private affairs of individuals for profit while shielding themselves from accusations of privacy invasions.[82]

Most important, Warren and Brandeis were pioneers in seeing that privacy problems were going to be intimately entwined with technological innovation and needed repackaging. As the press grew more sophisticated and sensational, the boundaries of privacy grew more fluid. The distinction between acceptable and unacceptable targets of a newspaper's attention (be it a politician, a celebrity, a criminal, a young bride, or the victim of physical disfigurement) has always been open to debate. But the link between technological advances in visual and printing culture and their capacity to invade privacy is the real insight of "The Right to Privacy."

In the Gilded Age and the Progressive Era the tales told by tabloids shattered boundaries of privacy that had existed since the Revolution. Of course, local gossip and back-fence chitchat in small towns had always been a part of American lives. But up until that point such banter was confined by geographical limits. Word-of-mouth, on its own, rarely travels far. Photography and the commercial innovations of mass-market media amplified the gossip of tight-knit communities beyond the back fence and onto the regional (and often national) stage.

And so the rise of human interest journalism helped awaken Americans to the problems of modern information *dissemination*—not so much the elimination of secrecy as it is the spreading of information beyond expected boundaries. Unchecked, this trend has the potential to damage reputations, inhibit people from authoring their own self-narratives, and make individuals prisoners of their recorded past. "Whether one can be known accurately and authentically—and on one's own terms, rather than the larger societies," notes historian Sarah Igo, was a striking new "question animating privacy's presence in American public life." And yet because the countervailing force of human interest journalism also has many positive aspects, Americans met this threat to privacy with a sense of ambivalence. Gossip is entertaining. Always has been. Especially when it's about someone else.[83]

When challenged, the media moguls who saw their bottom lines balloon from the new human interest genre generally defended their practices in one of two ways. Some cleverly acknowledged their role in harming privacy, even going so far as to lament its decline, while simultaneously positioning themselves as humble servants of public curiosity. These papers admitted culpability and simply continued going about their business—noting that in a democratic society where information was becoming more democratized the people, in the end, get the kind of newspapers they deserve. If their crimes against privacy were so egregious, they argued, people would stop buying their papers. The rest merely shrugged off the changing privacy standards as harmless and argued that they were simply doing what people had been doing for centuries—just on a grander scale and with greater profits.

As Americans read more and more human interest reportage in search of vicarious experience and good gossip, the disclosure and exposure of private affairs grew exponentially. All the while, as the methods of capturing and reproducing images grew more sophisticated, a large chunk of the control Americans had over the freedom to author their own identities, to write their own self-narratives, was lost in the aim of selling papers.

3

EXPOSING THE ENEMY WITHIN

Privacy and National Security, 1917–1961

I

Wars, as a rule, bring a great need for secrecy. The stakes for leaders of nations are highest in such times. The outcomes of battles are uncertain. And as students of military history well know, even the smallest tactical mistakes can lead to catastrophe. Effective leaders understand the value of deception in warfare and the importance of obscuring their strategies and capabilities to keep their enemies off balance. They also understand that their enemies will actively employ operatives to wrench away that information. The necessity of privacy to the functioning of the state is perhaps never more apparent than when examining the need for operational security in wartime. Loose lips sink ships.[1]

The trouble is that while governments throughout history have used the high-stakes atmosphere of wartime to rightly justify decreases in state transparency, they've also frequently used it to justify drastic infringements on the privacy rights of their citizens. War places considerable stress on civil liberties, especially personal privacy, and the United States in wartime is no exception. The military conflicts of the twentieth century, both hot and cold, served as a powerful, and often disastrous, counterweight to American privacy rights. This unfortunate reality illuminates our second countervailing interest to privacy: national security in wartime.

A lot of this has to do with rhetoric. The closer we look for the power behind wartime pressures on privacy the more obvious it becomes that they are very much tied to a dangerous and highly effective catchall proposition that a citizen's personal life becomes the government's business whenever it is framed against the larger interests of national security—even if those interests are poorly defined. This argument—heard in interrogation rooms, job interviews, and committee hearings—is inelegant but devastatingly efficient: the republic comes first, and if one is not doing anything wrong, then one has "nothing to hide."[2]

This is not the easiest contention to argue with, especially if one happens to be standing tall before the powers that be. If you're not doing anything wrong, and you care about the safety of your fellow citizens, what could you possibly have to hide when the government comes asking about your private affairs? At first glance there seems to be something not quite right about the logic, something dangerous even, but exactly what is hard to pin down. Throughout American history thousands of citizens have found themselves on the receiving end of this sentiment. Those who pushed back by invoking their right to privacy often discovered that doing so carried serious consequences, including job loss, imprisonment, deportation, and the social ostracization that came with being branded "un-American."

II

The American "privacy versus security" debate in wartime runs parallel to a very rich array of bold and brash crusaders who subordinated privacy in the face of threats said to be coming from dangerous subversives within America. Let's be clear: foreign spies, enemy sympathizers, and terrorists of various stripes have certainly conspired on American soil, and the dangers raised by their presence were unequivocally real. But they were also largely exaggerated. Throughout American history the debate over the tradeoff between privacy and security was often framed incorrectly, lacked proper safeguards, and was repeatedly exploited to serve ends that had little to do with national security. Striking a proper balance between privacy and security was rarely a goal for those who infringed on the privacy of thousands, at times quite severely. And these crusaders are now often seen as embarrassing figures in our history that we package in cautionary tales for future generations that we hope will somehow do better.[3]

We begin in the early twentieth century, where the stresses of the First World War laid the foundations of America's first national surveillance apparatus. In the pursuit of enemy agents, radicals, defeatists, and labor organizers who might impede the war effort, the Justice Department's Bureau of Investigation debuted an array of techniques to acquire information about suspected subversives. Illegal raids to secure membership lists, the use of deep cover operatives, and the warrantless opening of mail all took place in the context of new laws like the Espionage and Sedition Acts and a strong anti-German sentiment. The war prompted a fundamental shift in the capabilities of the federal government to invade the privacy of its citizens and allowed for the flowering of the "good citizens have nothing to hide" rhetoric.[4]

Then came the Red Scare. With the Great War won, the Justice Department quickly identified a new national security threat in the early 1920s—bolshevism. The first Red Scare and its spectacular bombings came amid a backdrop of economic and racial turmoil that gave many Americans the impression that the nation was being torn apart. This atmosphere allowed for an extension of wartime practices, including the creation and indexing of special subversive files and catalogs by the bureau along with extensive raids and interrogations that trampled on Fourth Amendment privacy protections.[5]

Then came the New Deal. The Red Scare fizzled out almost as quickly as it began, but after the stock market crash in 1929 and the arrival of the Great Depression, opponents of FDR's social welfare initiatives used the rhetoric of national security and foreign subversion to attack fiscal liberalism and its champions. Fascism was on the rise in Europe, communism was riding as high as it ever would in the United States, and with a new rhetorical flourish— "un-Americanism"—members of Congress used their investigative powers to further their own political careers and paint liberalism as a dangerous tool of the Soviet Union. These attacks didn't merely *involve* invasions of privacy, they were centered around them. The subpoenaing of rosters and mailing lists from various left-leaning organizations and the use of public interrogation in hearings often had no specific legislative purpose. Instead, they were meant to facilitate character assassinations of political enemies.[6]

Then came McCarthyism—the culmination of tendencies that had been maturing for decades. As the Cold War hardened in the late 1940s and the 1950s, the privacy invasions of the crusade against subversion took on a much more aggressive character. Congressional committees continued their public interrogations unimpeded, while presidents stimulated national anxieties about communism and created an atmosphere of near-permanent crisis in order to enlist public support for their foreign policy. The assault on privacy in the McCarthy era came on a number of fronts: loyalty boards, the ham-fisted treatment of evidence that often led to the disclosure of suspects' private information, public interrogations laden with ad hominem attacks, the coercion of private information through threats of economic ruin, and the Smith and McCarran Acts. All the while, the Fifth Amendment, whose protections against self-incrimination are rooted largely in a recognition of privacy as a fundamental right, was being pushed to its limits.

III

Before we get into the finer points of these historical moments, a few conceptual tools to help put the privacy versus security debate in its proper perspective.

These events are by no means new territory for historians. It's just that historians tend to focus on the infringement of *civil liberties*, not exclusively on privacy. The difference between these two concepts is that attacks on civil liberties refer to a large host of individual and societal rights that are protected by the Constitution and the common law. These protections speak to the American aspirations toward limited government and serve as cornerstones of liberal democratic jurisprudence. Freedom of speech, the right to due process, the protection of personal property—all of these things are essential aspects of our democratic framework, and all of them have been attacked (and defended) in some form or another throughout American history. But privacy carries its own distinct attributes and vulnerabilities worth exploring separately.

First and certainly foremost, the basic terms of the privacy versus security debate are inherently flawed. When Americans talk about the interplay between these two concepts, the conversation is almost always framed as a choice *between* one or the other—that either we can have privacy or we can have security, but we can't have both. Or to put it another way: the only way Americans can be kept safe from harm is to sacrifice privacy to abet law enforcement.[7]

But talking about the relationship between privacy and security in such zero-sum terms perpetuates the dangerous fallacy that they are irreconcilable. They aren't. Worse, this line of thinking isn't just logically unsound, it's degenerative. It prompts both leaders and citizens to fixate on *whether* privacy should be protected and not *how* it should be protected while adapting to new threats. In fact, there are numerous ways that national security can be strengthened while also preserving and protecting privacy. Increased oversight of surveillance and investigative tactics by privacy professionals, firmer checks and balances between the branches of government, and specific innovations have proven very effective for other advanced democracies in striking an appropriate balance between these two important ideals. We can, for the most part, have both at the same time.[8]

The second problem concerns salesmanship. One reason privacy advocates tend to lose out in the back and forth between privacy and security is because privacy isn't always the simplest thing to articulate in a few short sentences on a news broadcast or in a debate. Unfortunately, because privacy is such a nebulous concept, arguments about its importance can quickly resemble boring academic lectures. National security's branding is very much the opposite.

Bombs exploding, spies stealing atomic secrets, domestic terrorism, nuclear holocaust—all of these things are easy to visualize and comprehend. They rightly deserve the public's fear and respect. What's more, they seem rooted in common sense. Most privacy advocates, by contrast, have a hard time explaining the value of privacy to a free society, often due to a poor use of symbols and impactful rhetoric. What we don't understand we can make mean anything.

This brings us back to the "nothing-to-hide" argument—which also rests on a logical fallacy. Saying good people have nothing to hide is problematic because, as Daniel Solove points out, it carries an "underlying assumption that privacy is about hiding bad things" and that "by accepting this assumption we concede too much ground and invite an unproductive discussion of information people would likely want to hide." Not all secrets are bad. It's foolish to suggest otherwise. Secrets allow space for intimacy and enable people to shape their own identities. Presuming that all secrets are criminal ignores the many benefits of privacy for the individual and society at large, and stands opposed to sentiments clearly expressed in our founding documents as the antithesis of tyranny. So perhaps the best rejoinder is simply: "I'm not doing *anything* wrong and I've still got *plenty* to hide." Or as Edward Snowden put it: "arguing that you don't care about privacy because you have nothing to hide is no different than saying you don't care about free speech because you have nothing to say."[9]

Reflecting, in his declining years, on the height of the crusade against subversion, Cold War titan George Kennan offered a sobering picture of the damage done to the republic by anti-subversion hysteria. "What the phenomenon of McCarthyism did," wrote Kennan, "was to plant in my consciousness a lasting doubt as to the adequacy of our political system. . . . A political system and a public opinion, it seemed to me, that could be so easily disoriented by this sort of challenge in one epoch would be no less vulnerable to similar ones in another."[10]

The challenge facing Kennan's next epoch lay in striking a workable balance between privacy and security. Thus far, the history of these two concepts has essentially been a story of imbalance.

IV

Sunday, July 30, 1916, 2:08 a.m. Manhattan residents are awakened by a series of explosions lasting several hours on Black Tom Island, a mile-long pier in New York Harbor near the Statue of Liberty and home to a major munitions depot used to transport arms and supplies to the Allies during the Great War. The explosions were so powerful that pieces of shrapnel wedged themselves into the clock tower of the *Jersey Journal* building, freezing the dial at 2:12. Shock waves shattered plate-glass windows as far east as Brooklyn and caused over $100,000 worth of damage to the Statue of Liberty. Initial reports claimed more than fifty people had died in the incident, though the final number was closer to ten. Over time, a growing body of evidence indicated the bombing was the work of pro-German saboteurs looking to stymie the flow of aid to their British enemies.

While it might not command much attention in our popular memory, an FBI did in fact exist before J. Edgar Hoover, and the Black Tom incident was a turning point in its development. The bureau dates to 1908, when President Theodore Roosevelt ordered Attorney General Charles A. Bonaparte to create a staff of twenty-three agents within the Justice Department.[11] The bureau's first major operation came with the passage of the 1910 Mann Act, an attempt to stem interstate trafficking of women "for the purpose of prostitution or debauchery, or for any other immoral purpose." It was nicknamed the "White Slave Traffic Act." The bureau spent most of its energies arresting immigrants and minorities, making national headlines with the dubious arrest of heavyweight boxing champion Jack Johnson. These investigations raised the bureau's national profile.[12]

The Black Tom incident, one of the earliest major terrorist attacks on the nation by a foreign government, spurred President Woodrow Wilson to expand the bureau's authority to include investigation of acts of sabotage by foreign agents. The following year America was officially at war, and with the passage of the Espionage Act, the Trading with the Enemy Act, and later the amendment familiarly known as the Sedition Act, the bureau, now four hundred agents strong, was given sweeping powers to root out subversion and peer into the private lives of foreigners and citizens alike.[13]

But the task of keeping America safe from the machinations of its enemies was a large one and would require the participation of the post office, the Immigration Bureau, both naval and army intelligence, the Treasury Department, local law enforcement, and others. To be effective, domestic intelligence operations would need some kind of nerve center. The Justice Department, as Charles McCormick notes, "with its U.S. attorneys in place in every state and many large cities, was in a good position to organize the resources of the multitude of state, local, and private police forces that constituted a national tangle of often overlapping or ill-defined jurisdictions."[14]

Just like that, an unprecedented federal surveillance apparatus was born with almost no objections from the American public. One with a stunningly centralized capacity to infringe on privacy rights. And even if the public *had* wanted to check or roll back its powers, popular will to do so would have been greatly diminished by the strong current of anti-subversive sentiment that swept through the nation during the Great War.

Some think *hysteria* is the better term. In 1917 and 1918 thousands of German Americans, being suspected agents of the fatherland, faced extreme prejudices from the rest of the public. German books were burned, the German language was dropped from school curriculums (understanding the enemy's language being, apparently, a thing to discourage), sauerkraut was renamed "liberty cabbage," and Beethoven and Bach were removed from symphony offerings. In Washington a man who refused to stand during the playing of the national anthem was shot dead by a sailor, drawing cheers from the crowd. In Indiana a jury took less than an hour to acquit a man charged with killing another for yelling "to hell with the United States."[15]

For the most part, the public even cooperated with the new domestic intelligence apparatus and enthusiastically helped redraw the lines of American privacy. Many official investigations into subversion leaned on an exciting new group called the American Protective League (APL)—a pseudo-vigilante organization supervised by the bureau that swelled to 250,000 members by the end of the war. Armed with murky authority, these civilians engaged in unwarranted surveillance operations and conducted illegal raids on businesses, private homes, and meeting halls. Almost entirely without training the people of the APL were, in the words of Ann Hagedorn, "hidden in the folds of American society, watching, trailing, and taping their bosses, colleagues, employees, and neighbors." They also frequently went through people's trash.[16]

No limits were placed on the APL's gathering of evidence, and its members blatantly ignored the Fourth Amendment's probable cause and judicial oversight protections in ways that we would consider criminal. All the while the bureau could cleverly skirt any potential constitutional challenges in court because its agents had not actually seized the evidence themselves; they merely accepted it from good citizens doing their patriotic duty. During the whole of its existence the APL arrested hundreds of supposed draft dodgers, deported scores of ethnic Germans, and caught not one spy.[17]

In 1917 the bureau and the post office also began monitoring, opening, and banning correspondence of suspected subversives, at times illegally, in what Peter Conolly-Smith calls "the first domestic surveillance program in the United States," which "led to the persecution of hundreds of ordinary citizens and the forced suspensions of dozens of English and foreign-language publications."[18] Some of the legal footing for tampering with correspondence came from the Espionage and Trading with the Enemy Acts. The former declared: "every publication, matter, or thing, of any kind, containing any matter advocating or urging treason, insurrection, or forcible resistance to any law of the United States" as officially "nonmailable." The latter included a provision that foreign language papers could not use the mails without first filing English translations with local postmasters and obtaining a permit. Penalties reached as high as a $5,000 fine and five years in prison. The delays and costs required to meet these guidelines squeezed most foreign language periodicals out of the periodical business. Note that nowhere in these laws is it stated that agents of the government are allowed to open mails. In fact, post office officials specifically informed the bureau that they had no such authority.[19]

For those "anti-American" periodicals that persisted, the surveillance was quickly extended from publishers to readers, with thousands of individuals suddenly deemed targets. They had all their correspondence flagged, read, and assigned to a bureau agent for physical surveillance, which could range from tailing a suspect to going through his trash, or both. New York resident Enrique Gomez Franco, for example, caught the attention of bureau agents after a postal informant related that suspicious handwritten notes were penciled into the newspapers he received. The presence of seemingly cryptic messages ranging from "yesterday I received 2 'Judges' and 1 'Life'" (names of two popular periodicals, it turned out) to "beans are cooked everywhere" (strange, but true enough) were deemed sufficient probable cause to arrest the fellow. He was detained for a period and eventually released for lack of evidence.[20]

This dubiously legal surveillance strategy was only the beginning. The bureau and the APL took their investigations further by opening the private correspondence of suspected subversives—an illegal act both then and now. When the bureau did file an official request to open mail in 1917, that request was denied by Solicitor General Judge William Lamar. The judge ruled the infringement on privacy was too severe, noting that the long-established protections associated with sealed mail were not explicitly overruled by the Espionage and Trading with the Enemy Acts. But Lamar, patriotically, did alert government agents that mail could be legally opened and read if it reached the post office's "dead letters" department. That's the office that handles mail sent to illegible or unknown addresses or with insufficient postage and no return address. This blatant end-around allowed the APL and the bureau to open any letter they wanted through the end of the war. Agents could simply scratch off some postage or black out a return address and *voila!*[21]

This opening of private correspondence was an unprecedented violation of the privacy protections traditionally demanded of mail carriers—protections that date to the colonial era. Prior to the American Revolution correspondence sent by public mails fell under the auspices of Queen Anne's Post Office Act of 1710, which set severe penalties for "wittingly, or willingly, or knowingly, to open . . . or suffer to be opened . . . any letters, packet, or packets." Mail carriers were required to take an oath swearing to protect their parcels from unwarranted intrusion. Benjamin Franklin, while a colonial postal employee in the 1750s, went further by prohibiting local postmasters from sorting letters inside their homes (as they had been wont to do) out of fear that unauthorized persons might come into contact with private letters. Franklin also ordered that carriers seal the mail for each town in a bag and open it only when they had properly identified each intended recipient. After independence, these protections were extended through acts of Congress.[22]

To be fair, *prohibiting* the mailing of controversial materials was not without precedent. There was the Postal Act of 1872. But even that law explicitly forbade the opening of suspicious packages and limited the discretion of postal employees to reading only the outside of any letter. That Judge Lamar came up with such a clever way around these protections speaks to his recognition of the established legal precedents and the strong privacy implications at play. It also speaks to the power and reach of anti-subversive ideologies.

It was no secret that the mails were being tracked and sometimes opened during the war. Bureau chief A. Bruce Bielaski himself boasted of the leads generated from mail on numerous occasions. But with this kind of public acknowledgment comes a distinct set of privacy problems.

Overt surveillance, when the public is aware that it is being watched, generally leads to self-censorship and inhibition. It instills a subtle yet fundamental shift that, according to Julie Cohen, "threatens not only to chill the expression of eccentric individuality" but also to "dampen the force of our aspirations to it."[23]

Overt surveillance is a tool with which governments subdue public criticism—what some privacy scholars call a *chilling effect*. John Lord O'Brian, head of the War Emergency Division, admitted shortly after the war that the Justice Department had been under "immense pressure" from the executive branch to engage in "wholesale repression and restraint of public opinion." Harvard Law Professor Zechariah Chafee, who was sharply critical of the Espionage Act, noted that its effects would likely "discourage wise men from publishing valuable criticism of government policies." In 1917, the Yiddish *Daily Forward*, an influential socialist paper, announced that it would cease publishing all editorials relating to the war and not "criticize the allies, in order to avoid suspending of mailing privileges." The settlement house crusader Jane Addams, previously a sharp critic of the war, explained her refusal to sign a petition speaking against Espionage Act prosecutions three years later by claiming she was "obliged to speak very softly in regards to all things suspect."[24]

This chilling effect can also be found in the bureau's undercover wartime operations against labor unions. Often called the "first industrial war," World War I was decided as much by the industrial output of the nations involved as it was by soldiers and strategies. Thus, maintaining production quotas was of paramount concern to the federal government. To help streamline the economy and place it on a war footing, President Wilson established various War Industries Boards in 1917 and put them under the direction of Wall Street financier Bernard Baruch. It worked, with industrial output increasing by more than 20 percent.

Baruch was clever enough to offer labor unions recognition of collective bargaining rights, and he lent his support for an eight-hour workday—in exchange for a no-strike pledge. Many union workers saw improved safety standards and significant wage increases under these terms. And while there were some hiccups, most of organized labor supported the war and the efforts of the federal government to reorganize the economy. Between the war and these reforms, unions prospered. So much so, in fact, that US membership ballooned from 2.7 million in 1916 to approximately 5 million by 1920.[25]

Historically, though, the labor movement was also home to a large number of groups and individuals that viewed the war as a capitalist and/or imperialist venture disguised as the great cause of freedom. Rather quickly, they became targets, so that the popular crusade against German spies and sympathizers came to envelope far-left labor and political organizations—some of them quite radical, others just antiwar. This was abetted by the staunchly pro-business leanings of much of the wartime bureaucracy. Federal intelligence agencies therefore went after the labor unions by adapting the methods the industrial elite had used in strikebreaking. They gathered information on suspect individuals, most of them foreign, through the use of undercover agents skilled at developing assets (sometimes paid — sometimes coerced). This deprived labor groups of meaningful levels of organizational privacy.

When it came to recruiting undercover operatives during the Great War, the bureau was hampered by the fact that it was still rather small, lacked training facilities, and had little in the way of experienced staff. And so the ideal applicants for the undercover "radical squads" were mostly quick studies with some legal and investigative experience who could learn on the job. Jacob Spolansky, a thirty-year veteran, recalled that his early training consisted of little more than a quick "pep talk" on selfless nationalism. Aided by the APL and other civilian groups, bureau agents did little legwork, relying instead on well-placed informants. The best among these, said Spolansky, were "men at the top of the special employee hierarchy, who worked themselves into midlevel leadership in radical organizations and remained there for years." They would, at times, go to jail to maintain their cover and were "indispensable as information sources and manipulators of radicals."[26]

One such case involved the Pittsburgh chapter of the Industrial Workers of the World (IWW). A syndicalist organization with a rich history of radical rhetoric, the IWW (or Wobblies) had long been an important voice in American labor and very much a thorn in the side of the business elite and its allies in Washington. But it wasn't until the flowering of the wartime anti-subversion ideology that Washington deemed a powerful assault on the union's organizational privacy to be warranted. The bureau argued that the union would try to subvert the war effort and infect the minds of America's labor force. Pittsburgh, with its massive production capability, was of considerable importance both to the government and to organized labor.

Instrumental to the bureau's Pittsburgh operation was agent Louis Wendell — who worked undercover as L. M. Walsh. By 1917 he had so convincingly infiltrated the Pittsburgh branch of the IWW that he was promoted to recording and financial secretary *and* organization committee member. His duties included keeping the branch's charter and paperwork, along with a passkey to the IWW Radical Library, which he copied for the bureau.[27]

Wendell's mission was to gather information, sow discord within the ranks, and assist Washington's efforts to destroy the union. Wendell successfully manipulated the proceedings of the People's Council of America, a pacifist political organization established in 1917 that tried to mobilize workers and intellectuals against the war through literature and protests, to position the IWW (and himself) in a dominant position in that organization. He gave the bureau the secret locations of hundreds of mailing lists, charters, private correspondence, literature, and other records. Raids seizing this information "broke the back of the Hungarian branch of the IWW [in Pittsburgh]" and coerced its secretary into becoming an informant himself. Wendell also tracked down sources of IWW funding that had proved particularly elusive. The raids on records and membership lists and donor information went a long way toward weakening the union, a major player in the push for labor rights.[28]

Many Wobblies spoke of their arrests with pride. But the IWW had difficulty gaining financial support from moderates or recruiting ambivalent workers who supported labor rights but feared investigation. While the identities of the informers were concealed by the government, the fact of a wide network of them was loudly trumpeted. This "dualism in American infiltration practice," argues Regin Schmidt, also "creates an atmosphere of suspicion and even paranoia . . . thereby disrupting political activities."[29]

And yet, when the operation came to a close, Wendell admitted to finding "no significant pro-German activity: no violence or plans for violence involving Socialists, Wobblies, or their hangers-on." He did find a strong current of antiwar sentiment among many laborers and evidence of organized draft resistance. But ultimately his reports illustrate "a fissured Left" that posed no threat of revolution as long as it remained divided.[30]

In one sense the IWW isn't the most sympathetic of victims. It was an avowedly radical organization that advocated violent methods toward establishing a syndicalist worker's utopia that would overthrow the capitalist system. But there are words and then there are deeds, and while some minor IWW strike pamphlets included phrases like "the avenging sword is to be unsheathed, with all hearts resolved on victory or death," its history featured no Haymarket bombings, no platoons of riflemen, no storming of government offices, but instead a strict adherence to pragmatism and results-oriented nonviolent resistance.[31]

It was widely assumed that wartime legislation would be repealed once the armistice was signed, but postal censorship continued into the 1920s even though President Wilson did not "believe it would be wise to do any more suppressing." Bielaski left the bureau in 1919, forced out by the embarrassment and criticism brought on by the BI's involvement in a massive "slacker raid" targeting New York City draft dodgers the previous year in which 75,000 people were detained for three days without probable cause. Less than 1 percent of those arrested had actually committed the crime for which they were arrested.

V

Once the guns of August fell silent, domestic intelligence gathering shifted its focus from a wide array of dangerous radicals to one kind in particular—the Bolshevik. With this shift, the United States began its generations-long surge of anti-subversive rhetoric aimed at rooting out the communist menace. This trend, though it would wax and wane, affected both foreign and domestic policy and placed considerable stress on privacy rights.

The Red Scare of the early 1920s spawned from a number of overlapping sources. Its immediate causes were the success of the Bolshevik Revolution in Russia, along with the formation of two communist parties in the United States in 1919—that, and a subsequent series of terrorist bombings aimed at political and business leaders.[32] It would be a mistake to view the reaction to these events as a spontaneous expression of fear and hysteria. Leading historians of this period see the Red Scare as merely one aspect of a much larger so-cial and cultural drive for conformity and homogeneity. Other pressures in society were also to blame, particularly the economic ones brought on by demobilization.

Americans, as historian Nathan Miller puts it, were to "stumble leaderless into a turbulent conversion" from a war economy to a peacetime one. Approximately nine million workers found themselves out of jobs at about the same time four million servicemen were returning from war without any state program to ease the transition other than a one-time payout of $60 and a train ticket home. Almost overnight $4 billion in government contracts had been cancelled once the armistice was signed. Deregulation of the economy proceeded rapidly. Inflation was rampant. And this untenable economic climate quickly prompted labor unrest in the form of more than 3,600 strikes involving over four million workers.[33]

In Boston, the entire police force walked off the job. Those business owners with enough money to hire armed guards did so. The ones who couldn't grabbed what pistols, rifles, and shotguns they could find and posted up to defend their property and livelihoods over several nights of lawlessness. In Seattle a general strike brought the whole city to a screeching halt.

Observers drew parallels with the early days of the Russian Revolution and placed most of the blame on foreign antagonists. Anti-immigration sentiment too, rooted in the anti-German campaigns of the early war years, exacerbated the fear of foreign subversion at a time when millions of immigrants, mostly from eastern and southern Europe, were flooding American cities.[34]

Racial tensions also played a role. The Great Migration of the early twentieth century saw many northern whites living, for the first time, in close proximity to millions of blacks for whom they held little understanding and great animosity. It was little coincidence the revival of the Ku Klux Klan occurred in the midst of this demographic reconfiguration. Black leaders, for their part, saw opportunities for economic advancement, and W. E. B. DuBois declared that in the wake of the war blacks should "marshal every ounce of brain and brawn to fight a sterner, longer, more unbending battle" against racism. Sixty-six lynchings occurred in 1919, including ten black veterans, some in uniform. These tensions exploded into twenty-five race riots across the nation—the bloodiest in Chicago. Remembered as Red Summer, many white newspapers, including the *New York Times*, fueled speculation that the riots were the inspired machinations of Bolshevik agents.[35]

Then on the night of June 2, 1919—amid this backdrop of nativist, economic, and racial tensions—a bomb ripped apart the front section of the home of Attorney General A. Mitchell Palmer. The explosion had been premature, killing only the bomber, who was gracious enough to leave behind his head and legs for investigators. Among the rags that were his clothes an anarchist text was found. Entitled *Plain Words*, its writer proclaimed that the proletariat was "ready to do anything and everything to suppress the capitalist class."

Seven more explosions occurred that evening, all of them murder attempts on government officials and private citizens including federal judges, prominent business owners, and the mayor of Cleveland. A few weeks earlier, thirty-six incendiary devices were found in the mails addressed to a veritable who's-who of government and corporate elites. The packages were detained because of inadequate postage. The senders were never caught, but the nation had no trouble immediately placing the blame on those foreign subversives, faraway communists.[36]

Congress had to do something and quickly. So it allocated half a million dollars for the establishment of an antiradical division within the Bureau of Investigation. A twenty-four-year-old attorney from the Alien Enemy Registration Section was placed in charge of the new force. He never quite succeeded in catching the bombers, but the promotion nevertheless set the stage for a remarkable career. His name was John Edgar Hoover.[37]

Hoover, hardworking and fiercely intelligent, had a preternatural understanding of the ways in which information can be a gateway to power. His first action as head of the antiradical division was to set his staff to cataloging an extensive criminal indexing system to streamline the information collection and processing of files regarding suspected subversives. A massive undertaking, this centralization of information served as the genesis of America's first national criminal database.

Before Hoover the bureau's criminal files were "a chaos in the records and organization" according to Attorney General Palmer himself. This sophisticated upgrade, a brilliant act of organizational foresight by the standards of the day, stemmed largely from Hoover's previous work at the Library of Congress. As news of the database spread, local and state law enforcement agents across the country along with various federal bodies began sharing information about "persons of interest" at never-before-seen levels. The size of the average criminal file held by the bureau increased exponentially.

The moment is a benchmark in the history of law enforcement data collection and American privacy. It summons a number of privacy problems associated with what Solove's taxonomy calls *increased accessibility*—or an amplification of the accessibility of information. The perils of increased accessibility are often hard to pin down.

On one hand, this information was already available to law enforcement agencies, did not breach any new levels of confidentiality nor reveal any new secrets, and increased the ability of law enforcement to effectively investigate criminals. If there is no new breach in secrecy, what then is there to object to? Why not have all in the information in one place?[38]

Because centralization, if done haphazardly, can have serious consequences for individual and societal privacy. Historically, increased accessibility and the expansion of criminal databases have brought with them three key problems.

First, criminal records are frequently used for matters that have nothing to do with law enforcement. Sixty years after the creation of Hoover's file catalogs a government audit revealed that almost *half* of all record requests received by the FBI's Identification Division were from non-criminal-justice entities—most of them private employers and licensing agents. Whether these organizations have a right to such information—information that many would regard as deeply personal and that carries the potential to have a considerable impact on one's social mobility—has been the subject of much debate. Even in the twenty-first century there are large disparities in state standards of access.

Second, those records are substantively incomplete or wholly inaccurate. One 1982 government report noted that one-third to one-half of all records in the FBI system did not include dispositions (whether the accused was found innocent or not guilty) and that "roughly one-fifth of criminal history records contained erroneous information," despite numerous acts of Congress in the 1960s and 1970s that demanded protocols aimed at greater accuracy. These errors can lead to wrongful imprisonment, painful embarrassment, and a loss of social standing and economic well-being.[39]

And third, there is a dire lack of proper political oversight regarding how records are maintained and shared. Even though great potential exists for criminal history databases to be exploited for personal and political purposes, Hoover's catalogues, for generations, were never subjected to any measure of congressional or advisory board oversight.[40]

Information is power. It brings the potential for blackmail, personal and organizational exploitation, and a host of other nefarious activities. It is for all these reasons that governments pass laws regulating the flow and exchange of information considered sensitive. Yet the history of Hoover's tenure at the FBI is largely one of a man unencumbered by such regulations. A story of a man whose preternatural ability to acquire the private information of others allowed him to wield considerable political might and achieve a continuity of power that many have called a "fourth branch of government." And its privacy-eroding germ was the centralization of criminal records in 1919.[41]

It was easy in 1919—amid the labor unrest, the race riots, the demographic changes, the nativism, the global influenza pandemic—for the Justice Department to conflate left-wingers and labor unions with a subversive Bolshevik plot to overthrow the republic. "This association," argues historian Lynn Dumenil, "had long-term results, for the Red Scare hyperbole contributed not only to the crushing of the strikes of 1919 but toward crippling organized labor for over a decade." Sensing opportunity, America's corporate elite mobilized to roll back labor's wartime gains and spread fears of impending revolution.[42]

The assault on the labor movement's organizational privacy climaxed that November when Attorney General Palmer, who had pushed himself into the limelight as an anticommunist crusader (many say with presidential ambitions), orchestrated coordinated raids on the Union of Russian Workers that arrested more than six hundred people and paved the way for hundreds of deportations. Under the Alien Act of 1918, any noncitizen affiliated with an organization that "entertains or teaches disbelief in or opposition to all organized government" could be expelled from the country or imprisoned indefinitely without charges. The Justice Department now held that an alien did not need to engage in subversive activity or even hold radical views; he or she need only have some kind of connection with an organization deemed radical. The bureau maintained that a person's name on a membership list of a radical group was enough to warrant long-term imprisonment pending deportation, even if that person never attended meetings, paid dues, or was active. To be on such a list meant one might henceforth be regarded as a "usual suspect." The same chilling effect from these privacy infringements in wartime was apparent for all labor organizations in this period, though Palmer added the threats of deportation and imprisonment without trial.

The Palmer raids sought not merely to put Russians in handcuffs—they looked to capture information vital to the organizational privacy of Palmer's enemies: membership lists, minutes, donor rosters, all filled with names that would be fed into Hoover's criminal database, despite the fact that they were mostly acquired through illegal searches.

The following January, Palmer launched a second round of spectacular raids on two communist parties across twenty-three states and imprisoned thousands. But he had gone too far; the raids produced almost no quality evidence. After ominously predicting revolution to occur on May Day of 1920, Palmer was painted by many as the "boy who cried wolf," and his political descent thereafter was rapid. The lists and names he procured from those raids, however, still found their way to the Justice Department catalogs.[43]

However short lived, the first Red Scare had a far-reaching impact. It permanently damaged the American labor movement by conflating it with radicalism and was a significant factor in the anti-immigration legislation soon to come. It also, as Richard Powers observes, laid the framework for generations of national debate over communism by establishing the rhetoric that "the entire Left was somehow part of a communist plot to subvert the country." A decade later, the coarse tools of anticommunism would identify many fiscal liberals as among the most dangerous elements in the country. The victims of the APL and the Palmer raids, as historian Sarah Igo also notes, would soon find champions in the new American Civil Liberties Union (ACLU), "which mounted an organize response to the draconian wartime constraints on speech and dissent. But this did not amount to a defense of individual privacy or right to a personality—suggesting that privacy was not yet a plausible civil liberty equal to freedom of speech or association nor the most promising place to ground a claim for protection."[44]

The first Red Scare demonstrated how anti-subversive rhetoric could be fashioned to justify infringements on organizational privacy *and* how those infringements could then be used as weapons. It gave rise to J. Edgar Hoover, whose communist hunting had only just begun, and to the first centralized criminal database—a phenomenon whose privacy problems would be well documented by future generations. The tactic of targeting membership lists, mailing registers, and donor rosters, and then classifying the names on them as suspected radicals, became an intrinsic component of the anticommunist crusade. When a new Red Scare emerged in the 1930s, the privacy problems associated with this "mining for names" reached entirely new levels.

VI

While America's crusade against communist subversion came to its zenith with McCarthyism in the 1950s, popular history tends to forget that the buildup to the McCarthy era was a rather slow burn. It began with political attacks by fiscal conservatives during the 1930s and continued through World War II. Along the way, privacy rights came under incredible pressure on multiple fronts: public interrogations, government loyalty programs, the frequent subpoenaing of records and mailings lists held by private organizations, and new laws demanding the exposure of anyone affiliated with groups that had communist ties.

All the while, as these attacks grew more widespread, the political advantages of anticommunism's large umbrella became clearer to those who would exploit them for their own selfish motives. To be sure, these events constituted civil liberties violations that extended beyond issues of privacy. But privacy invasions were undeniably the linchpin of McCarthyism. On a tactical level, it was the point of departure on which most else was built.

McCarthyism wouldn't have been possible without mechanisms that legitimized widespread privacy infringements. Without the ability to invade privacy "the Red Baiters would have lost their power," reflects Marge Frantz, a longtime Alabama Communist Party member, because "their power was a power of exposure." Hoover confirmed as much to Congress in 1947 when he said "victory will be assured once Communists are identified and exposed, because the public will take the first step in quarantining them." As the power of exposure grew more apparent, the First and Fifth Amendments were eventually thrust center stage as the only legal privacy protections capable of shielding both the innocent and the guilty.[45]

There is an unfortunate tendency in American popular memory to refer to the excesses of the McCarthy era as "witch-hunts." While there are surely many aspects of this period that are rightly condemned, this widely used metaphor obscures how many, perhaps even most, of the people who encountered the political repression of the second Red Scare were either in or near the Communist Party.

Witchcraft isn't real. Communism is. The essence behind this metaphor speaks more to the way all communists were associated with treason and dangerous subversion. Such was the true evil of McCarthyism. This conflation ignored, among other things, the fact that some Americans, like Harlem's Howard Johnson, joined because of the party's stance on civil rights. Johnson later said that many "black intellectuals joined the party . . . because it was one organization that was really doing something, that was there. That was picketing . . . that was getting jobs for blacks." Others, like the schoolteacher David Friedman, did so because of his cultural heritage and positions on organized labor, remembering that his father, like many Jews from Russia, "brought with them the socialist tradition." Such associations did not make one a KGB agent.[46]

VII

After the first Red Scare, harassment of the American Communist Party subsided for a time. To most on the far-left in the 1920s, Russia was viewed as a veritable utopia of socialist thought. The party got both its funding and its cues directly from Moscow as a proud participant in the Comintern—an international movement derived from the Russian Revolution. By the 1930s, the Great Depression and the rise of European fascism transformed American communism into one of the most dynamic political expressions on the left.

Membership in the actual party would remain quite small. Most of the American intellectuals who would be later called communists were in fact part of a broader nonrevolutionary antifascist coalition called the Popular Front. The Front boasted over 50,000 members by the end of the 1930s, but by any reasonable measure communism never held much potential as a legitimate political threat to American democracy. Nor did it ever come close to possessing the numbers or organizational sophistication required to subvert the government in any meaningful way.[47]

The second Red Scare officially began in 1930, after Congress approved the creation of a special committee in the House meant to investigate and identify American communists for deportation. The committee was the brainchild of Representative Hamilton Fish, a New York aristocrat, who served as its chair. Fish justified the deportation of communists as a way to create jobs for "honest, loyal American citizens who are unemployed" on account of the Great Depression. These early hearings were, for the most part, hilarious testaments to the ignorance of America's leaders about Russian political culture. In one exchange, Chairman Fish asked witness Peter A. Bogdanoz why, if he truly had been a prisoner under the Czar, he didn't "know how many political prisoners there were in Siberia?" Bogdanoz laughed while his interpreter replied, "he says that the Czar didn't send him to Siberia to count the number of prisoners."[48]

The committee's hearings lasted six months and produced a report crediting the party with approximately 12,000 members and a proposal that membership in the party be made illegal. It also took pains to attack the ACLU as communist sympathizers.

The origins of the notorious House Un-American Activities Committee (HUAC) belong to a different New Yorker, Representative Samuel Dickstein, who in 1938 proposed its creation as a way to use the investigative arm of Congress to protect his beleaguered Jewish constituents from the rising tide of anti-Semitism brought on by Nazi sympathizers on Manhattan's East Side. However noble Dickstein's intentions, in the late 1930s Congress wasn't about to prioritize the protection of Jews. They were, however, more than willing to take advantage of the committee's broad mandate—investigating "un-Americanism"—to suit their own political ambitions and take cheap shots at their enemies.[49]

Nobody with any sense could claim to be surprised at what HUAC would eventually become. The writing was on the wall from the very beginning. Texas Representative Maury Maverick, who led the opposition to its creation, warned that such a committee would give "blanket powers to investigate, humiliate, meddle with anything and everything . . . from the German Saengerfest to B'nai

B'rith" and that "Un-American is simply something that somebody else does not agree to."[50]

Even before they began investigating communists, committee members demonstrated a particular disregard for the reputations of those they accused. Dickstein started putting into the congressional record the names of suspected fascist organizations and individuals from the sealed files of other congressional committees. The files had been sealed because the original committees that acquired them did not follow established rules of evidence gathering. When Dickstein was eventually confronted with affidavits signed by six people denying any ties to Nazism and demanding that their names be removed and their denials placed on record, Dickstein aggressively refused, arguing "if out of these hundreds of names that I have buttonholed as fascists and Nazis or whatever I have called them, only six filed a protest, I think I have done a pretty good job." This same line would be taken more than a decade later by Senator Joseph McCarthy.[51]

Dickstein created HUAC to fight Nazis. But he was quickly pushed out by colleagues with bigger plans—who tarred him with his own immigrant status. The congressman was a rabbi's son from Russia; as Representative Shannon of Missouri explained, many members of Congress felt "that an investigation of this kind should not be headed by a foreign-born citizen." The chairmanship was given to the Texas Democrat Martin Dies, a staunch opponent of Franklin Roosevelt and his grand (and who knows, possibly communist) New Deal.[52]

Anti-communism in the 1930s and 1940s was not a monolithic ideology. It is best categorized, as historian Ellen Schrecker notes, as "a coalition that gradually attracted groups and individuals. Each element in the network appealed to a different constituency and used its own tactics; the mixture of offensives became far more potent than any single campaign would have been."[53] At first, the movement was largely driven by anti-labor/anti-New Dealers like Dies, mostly Republicans and southern Democrats looking for a more effective way to fight FDR than by just opposing the economic merits of fiscal liberalism. But the party did itself no favor when in 1939 it tried, absent all intellectual consistency, to justify the Nazi-

Soviet nonaggression pact as some sort of masterfully conceived contribution to global peace and democracy. By the late 1940s the combined impact of "losing" China to Mao Zedong, the stealing of atomic secrets, and the later stalemate on the Korean peninsula created an excellent path through which the political right could hammer its enemies as "soft on communism."

It was clear even in these early years of the second Red Scare that *disclosure* would be a crucial weapon of the anticommunist arsenal. While the party's top leaders were well known to law enforcement, most rank and file members hid their affiliation. Communists rarely obstructed the core economic and political activities of the organizations they joined. In labor unions, for example, most who rose to senior positions saw themselves as labor leaders first and communists second. But even during the height of the Popular Front years, most civil servants and labor leaders knew that the majority of Americans distrusted communists and that they would lose a large amount of credibility, possibly their jobs, if their party membership was known. Ironically, most American communists operated in secret precisely because they knew communism was thought be a conspiracy.[54]

Thus, exposure became the anticommunist coalition's weapon of choice. Take the sage advice given by the American Legion's magazine on how citizens might best fight communists: "The salesman and peddlers" will be "skillfully disguised," a 1948 article instructed, "'liberals' at breakfast, 'defenders of the world' at lunch, and the 'voice of the people' at dinner . . . every art of human cunning is necessary to protect themselves and their subversive mission from exposure." Citizens should immediately contact the FBI "if some of your local or prominent people have sponsored or lent their names or contributed money to indubitable CP fronts" and "perform a friendly advisory service." Widespread exposure was the key because "mercilessly and tirelessly exposing and putting these fronts out of business is manifestly almost as vital as detecting and exposing actual Communists and spies."[55]

Hoover also stressed the importance of obliterating the privacy of communist sympathizers when he addressed HUAC in 1947, noting that he "always felt that the greatest contribution this committee could make is the public disclosure of forces that menace America," and that the committee "renders a distinct service when it publically reveals the diabolical machinations of sinister figures engaged in un-American activities." There was certainly much exposing to be done because, according to Hoover, the menace was everywhere. Amid "liberals and progressives" who had been "hoodwinked and duped." Amid "ministers of the gospel who promote their evil work and espouse a cause that is alien to the religion of Christ and Judaism." Amid "local school boards and parents" who "teach our youth." And, of course, amid "American labor groups" that had already been "infiltrated, dominated, or saturated with the virus of communism."[56]

Almost all of the anticommunist measures Congress considered were aimed at exposure and the obliteration of the organizational privacy of suspected sympathizers. The Smith Act of 1940, for example, allowed for the prosecution of anyone exposed as a member of the Communist Party. The justification behind the Internal Security Act of 1950 (the McCarran Act) — requiring all communist members, organizations, and affiliates to register with the government — grew out of the notion that all party members, regardless of their rank or length of tenure, were ideologues who actively pursued the violent overthrow of the American government because books written by Marx and Lenin instructed them to do so.[57]

When explaining why he chose to veto the McCarran Act, President Truman was quick to point out the larger dangers inherent in such a widespread disregard for organizational and individual privacy. He noted that it was "not because we have any sympathy for Communist opinions, but because any governmental stifling of the free expression of opinion is a long step toward totalitarianism." The potential for misuse was simply too severe for Truman, who argued that "the provision could easily be used to classify as a Communist-front organization any organization which is advocating a single policy or objective which is also being urged by the Communist Party . . . such as low cost housing."[58]

Truman's veto didn't hold up. That Congress was able to override it speaks to the power of anti-subversive sentiment in the early Cold

War. It also illustrates the eagerness with which the societal benefits of organizational privacy were deemed invalid. While many in the anticommunist coalition argued that they recognized the potential harm of such a law but were willing to make necessary sacrifices to keep the nation safe, those sacrifices were not borne equally by all.[59]

And so perhaps the most important lesson to be learned from the McCarran Act is that when individuals say they are willing to give up privacy rights in exchange for security, they're usually talking about sacrificing the rights of others—not their own.

VIII

There's an old saying: organizations do not bleed, but their members can. By far the most iconic aspect of the McCarthy era was the colorful public interrogations by members of Congress seeking to expose suspected communists. Powerful men posed questions to an assortment of witnesses, some defiant, some capitulatory, about past and present affiliations and the cards they carried. "Are you now or have you ever been . . ." and all that. But to understand why these public interrogations were particularly problematic from a privacy standpoint, it is important to first understand how congressional hearings work, as well as what it means to be a name on a list in a climate of fear and political opportunism.[60]

Lawmakers need some way to investigate issues of national concern before passing laws. This is a widely accepted principle, and rightly so. Democracies thrive on an informed consensus. But the reality of how it plays out of the floors of the legislature is far from simple. Congressional investigations are largely unrestricted, for practical purposes, and do not have to produce new legislation or justify the relevance of an inquiry's subject matter. Committee members have subpoena power but they are *not* bound by the same rules of evidence or conduct as a court of law. Most important: the presumption of innocence is not a prerequisite. Prosecutors are not restrained, defendants are not shielded, there is no right to cross-examination, and in practice the conduct of the committee's investigation generally flows from the personality and objectives of the chairperson.[61]

Historically, these conditions have proven to be a double-edged sword, bringing both positive and negative developments. Throughout the Progressive Era, congressional investigations helped rein in the power of money trusts, fraudulent bankers, and government corruption. After the Teapot Dome scandal, when Andrew Mellon complained that "government by investigation is not government," Felix Frankfurter (not yet on the Supreme Court) famously wrote that it was in the interest of good government that "the power of the investigation should be left untrammeled," and later that "the safeguards against abuse and folly are to be looked for in the forces of responsibility . . . within Congress."[62]

Yet many such investigations have been conducted in the absence of any clear legislative intent or public good. Instead, they were used to wage smear campaigns and further individual political goals. It's worth noting that Justice Frankfurter, decades later when the abuses of the McCarthy years were cresting, retreated from his earlier position and advocated reforming Congress's investigative rules and procedures.[63]

Public interrogation is a distinct category in the taxonomy of privacy. Interrogation is a form of searching. It is the pressuring of individuals to divulge information, and it harms others because a degree of coercion is almost always involved. An interrogator is almost never unbiased. Most often, he has a preconceived picture of the truth and is asking questions that seek to confirm that picture, however flawed. "People take offense when others ask an unduly probing question," argues Solove, "which is why there are social norms against asking excessively prying questions. Interrogation makes people concerned about how they will explain themselves or how their refusal to answer will appear to others." Interrogation has been used throughout history to impinge upon freedom of association and belief. The Spanish Inquisition and the English ex officio oaths of the Middle Ages are perhaps the two most widely known examples.[64]

Public interrogation—whether in a courtroom or before a congressional committee—also brings great potential for the distortion of information. Skilled interrogators can paint whatever picture they want of a subject. They possess extraordinary control over what information is teased out of a person and in what context that information should be interpreted. They are not interested in context or the whole story—only those snippets of information that suit their aims. For these reasons, most advanced democracies along with the United Nations have adopted into their laws some form of legal protection against self-incrimination. This prevents the government from forcing people to testify against themselves and has been categorized by judges and legal scholars as insulating citizens from "the essential and inherent cruelty of compelling a man to expose his own guilt," a "safeguard of conscience and human dignity," and a way for a society to reflect its "respect for personal integrity."[65] In the United States, our powerful protections against interrogation are embodied in the Fifth Amendment.

So how did the McCarthy-era Congress determine who should be interrogated? As we saw in the first Red Scare, they went "mining for names" on lists. Some were provided by uncover agents. Others by volunteer witnesses. And others by former party members who had seen the light. But none of these resources ever came close to the treasure trove Congress could acquire by seizing or subpoenaing membership rosters and mailing lists from organizations with known communist links.

Most committee interrogations were designed to expose someone. The witness, whose name was either given by an informant or was found on a list from a Popular Front organization, would invariably be asked under oath whether they he or she was currently or formerly a member of the Communist Party. If yes, he or she was ordered to provide more names. Often, a member of the committee would then read aloud a list of suspected communists and ask the witness to confirm their party membership. Since the committee usually already had these names, it was clear that the goal was not information but exposure.[66]

The leverage of the HUAC interrogators wasn't prison. People weren't being carted off and placed behind bars. Its leverage was the ability to deprive witnesses of their lives and livelihoods. Punishments for uncooperative witnesses and those with communist ties was generally economic. They would be fired from their jobs and suffer a loss in social standing. Subpoenas were frequently served at peoples' places of work or business, leading to some being fired before they even took the stand. With the aid of the private sector and federal employer guidelines, the scope of the economic sanctions was severe. No sector was immune, not the entertainment industry, not science labs, not Wall Street, and certainly not the academy.[67]

Thus, the committee hearings would likely not have had such coercive power were it not reinforced by the private sector. The collaboration of these employers with the government was necessary to legitimize the anticommunist network's activities. Ralph Brown, who conducted an exhaustive study of loyalty tests and the economic penalties of the second Red Scare, put the number of politically motivated dismissals as likely over 10,000. This significant level of coercion placed considerable pressure on witnesses to publicly reveal private information they otherwise would not have out of fear that silence would be seen as an admission of guilt. Even later, as congressional witnesses increasingly invoked the Fifth Amendment when faced with hostile lines of questioning, the popular perception that "silence equals guilt" was a powerful tool for prying interrogators.[68]

In 1938 Martin Dies had proclaimed that because "it is easy to smear someone's name or reputation by unsupported charges or an unjustified attack, but it is difficult to repair the damage that has been done," HUAC would "treat every witness with fairness and courtesy" and never have any "preconceived views of what the truth is respecting the subject matter of this inquiry." A laughable statement in hindsight. Whatever his original intentions (likely opportunistic), the committee's ham-fisted treatment of names found on Popular Front mailing lists under Dies and those who followed him showed tremendously little regard for "fairness and courtesy."[69]

In HUAC's first year Dies leaned heavily on mailing lists and magazine subscriptions provided by former-traveler-turned-anticommunist J. B. Matthews. Left-leaning magazines were of particular interest to Dies because they included so many individuals associated with the Roosevelt administration and the Works Progress Administration (WPA). A subscription list allowed Dies to fire a well-placed broadside against the WPA's Federal Theater Project, an organization where, in all honesty, ideological fidelity to capitalism was not in large supply. This attack contributed heavily to the defunding of the project. A New York theater critic suggested a tombstone be put up with the words KILLED BY THE COMMUNISTS OF NEW YORK. But for men like Dies, "who judged plays by their titles and were never accused of having actually witnessed any of the productions that outraged them, virtually all theater of the time was subversive."[70]

The following year the committee used the same list-based approach to attack the American League for Peace and Democracy (ALPD), one of the more important antifascist Popular Front organizations to receive financial support from the American Communist Party. Prominent New Dealers such as Harold Ickes, Robert Jackson, and Elmer Benson had all complimented the organization publicly in the mid-1930s, as did the *New Republic* and many other mainstream liberal periodicals. Early in the session committee agents seized a cache of records from the ALPD's Chicago and Washington offices, and found that the membership of the league's Washington, D.C., chapter was made up almost entirely of government employees, including a number of high-ranking New Dealers. That September, the committee's conservative members suggested publishing these names to "out" communist sympathizers in the Roosevelt administration. By October the committee had issued a press release linking the names of 563 federal employees culled from the ALPD mailing lists. It was a blatant political attack on FDR and the Democratic Party. These were merely names on a mailing list of an organization that opposed fascism, nothing more. Now Congress was saying they were "out-ed Reds."[71]

Like most membership and mailing lists, those of the ALPD contained the names both of devotees and of persons with only a remote connection to the organization. Some were communists; most were not. Because the ALPD was a Popular Front group it attracted an array of individuals, many with conflicting political ideologies, but all aligned in their abhorrence of fascism. To join the Popular Front in the 1930s meant only that one hated fascism, not that one embraced communism. By publishing the list Dies and the committee were trying to obliterate all such distinctions.

Backlash ensued. Dies and the committee faced widespread criticism for releasing the ALPD names. Its ulterior motivations were a little too clear for most, and the unvetted list was also filled with inaccuracies, like that of an award-winning D.C. schoolteacher who had no connection to the organization whatsoever. The ALPD called it a "twentieth-century inquisition." Roosevelt himself condemned this "sordid procedure."[72]

Committee member Noah Mason (R-IL) was unrepentant: "If there were mistakes of names being on the list that were not members it was not the mistake of the Dies Committee, it was the mistake of the local chapters of the League." Other committee supporters echoed the familiar anti-subversion argument that if one felt wronged and had nothing to hide, one should be able to come to Congress and speak for themselves.[73] Logical fallacies such as this reveal why privacy protections are so necessary. In a single stroke the committee demonstrated a flagrant disregard for the context of the information it publicized while simultaneously demanding more of it. That lawmakers would grandstand in such a way is precisely why many social and political organizations feel they have a right to keep their membership and mailing lists secret (and why many individuals demand the groups they join do so as well).

Unsurprisingly, the committee's lists were often obtained illegally. Former FBI Special Agent M. Wesley Swearingen, for example, admitted late in life to performing numerous illegal break-ins in the 1950s, "bag-jobs we call 'em," at the behest of the Domestic Intelligence Division. "We found things like membership lists," he later recalled, "or what could be construed as membership lists, and correspondence . . . but never any evidence of anything illegal. Well, of course, the Communist Party was considered subversive—but we never found evidence of any crimes, it was all political."[74]

The problem with HUAC's use of lists is really two problems—

what Solove's taxonomy calls *aggregation* and *secondary use.* Aggregation refers to the fact that information is most often collected in snippets and without much context. When information is aggregated carelessly it can heighten the potential for drawing incorrect inferences. Sometimes this happens accidentally. Sometimes this is intentional. Without proper context, these little snippets can be used to paint false pictures that might carry significant consequences. Secondary use, as we know, is the sharing of information for purposes that are different from the reasons for its original disclosure and without consent. When people joined a mailing list or sent a donation to a group, they may not have agreed to do so if they had been aware that their information would be shared with others.[75]

To understand the privacy problems of the McCarthy era one must first understand that its targets were, in many regards, fighting a battle over context. The troubling and often illegal methods used to acquire information about them are certainly important, but when that private information was made public it was the absence of context that made Americans fear their information would be misinterpreted by political opportunists and anticommunist zealots in ways that might bring negative consequences. This fear of misinterpretation was heightened in the McCarthy era because the potential consequences—loss of employment and social standing—were severe and growing increasingly more common as the phenomenon progressed.

Sure, individuals whose names were publicized by the committee could try to add that missing context by testifying. But doing so would be to assume a defensive posture, seeking a remedy for a privacy infringement in a public forum that had a reputation for grandstanding, frequently employed manipulative questions to ensnare those it disliked, and lacked the protections found in most courts of law. Both the committee and those it interrogated understood the power of accusation. As Mark Twain put it, "a lie can travel halfway around the world while the truth is putting on its shoes."

And so it is unsurprising that by the mid-1940s various organizations began resisting the committee's subpoenas of records. Among the more publicized of these refusals concerned the Anti-Fascist

Refugee Committee (AFRC). When HUAC Chairman John S. Wood (D-GA) in 1945 demanded membership records "in the interest of saving time," the AFRC put the distinguished gentlemen through three comical rounds of bureaucratic "buck-passing" before a young executive secretary, Helen R. Bryan, flatly refused on the grounds that the subpoena was "invalid." Incensed and embarrassed, Wood initiated contempt charges against all sixteen members of the AFRC board and Bryan. The board members, lacking in originality, called it "the beginning of fascism in America," and all received up to one year in jail and/or a $500 fine. All filed appeals, which were denied, and despite the clear First Amendment implications the Supreme Court refused to consider the case on grounds that the remedy for such abuses of power, if they were indeed abuses at all, rested either with Congress itself or with the people, not the courts.[76]

The Court would eventually take up the subject of membership lists and organizational privacy, just not in the context of anticommunism. In 1956, when the civil rights movement was gaining traction in the deep South, the NAACP found itself in a situation similar to HUAC's targets. The attorney general of Alabama, looking to check the organization's growing influence after the Montgomery bus boycott, pressed a state court judge to order that all NAACP membership lists and employee rosters (with names and addresses) be made public if the group wanted to continue operating in the state.

Anti-segregationists saw the ploy for what it was—an attempt to intimidate both current and potential supporters. Fearing widespread reprisals and a chilling effect that would inhibit new membership, the NAACP refused on the ground that it had a right to organizational privacy. After much back and forth between lower judicial bodies, the case came before the Warren Court in 1958.[77]

The decision was unanimous. "The Court has recognized the vital relationship between freedom to associate and privacy in one's associations," wrote Justice John Harlan II, who went on to discuss the practical effect of compelling an organization to disclose membership lists, especially when that organization can demonstrate that doing so exposed members to "economic reprisal, loss of employment, threat of physical coercion, and other manifestations of physical hostility." Simply put: information disclosure can inhibit association, association is speech, and speech is protected by the Bill of Rights.[78]

NAACP v. Alabama isn't just a benchmark in the history of First Amendment jurisprudence — it's a benchmark in the history of American privacy. Its core tenets were upheld again two years later when Arkansas tried the same exact membership list tactic (*Bates v. City of Little Rock*), and it was cited repeatedly in the mid-1960s when the Court officially recognized a constitutional right to privacy for the first time.

This reading of the First Amendment, however, was not enough in the eyes of the Court to constitute a blanket privacy protection over one's associations. The following year the Court ruled against the appeal of Lloyd Barenblatt, a professor of psychology whom HUAC held in contempt for refusing to answer questions about his religious and political beliefs on First Amendment grounds. Justice Harlan wrote there that the First Amendment did not protect witnesses from all lines of questioning, and that as long as congressional interest was pursued to "aid the legislative process" and protect government interests, then it was legitimate. Justices Black, Warren, and Douglas dissented in the 5–4 ruling, arguing that such interrogation impedes "the interest of the people as a whole in being able to join organizations, advocate causes, and make political 'mistakes' without later being subjected to governmental penalties for having dared to think for themselves."[79]

The First Amendment, despite its associational protections, was simply not enough to ensure the safety of individual and organizational privacy in the McCarthy era. To shield themselves against congressional interrogations, individuals would require the more explicit protections afforded by "taking the Fifth."

IX

When confronting HUAC some people were content to aggressively defend their privacy along religious lines, like theologian

Willard Uphuas, who waved his bible before the committee and reminded its members that "Jesus stood before Pilate and He didn't
answer a single question when asked" (to which special counsel
Richard Arens cleverly replied, "well, He wasn't asked whether He
was hooked up with Communist conspiracy"). But for most others,
the more secular remedy of the Fifth Amendment was the only safe
course of action to protect their privacy while under interrogation.[80]

The criminal justice system was always somewhat limited in
its ability to reinforce the contention that to be a communist was
to exist outside of the law. "There were few laws under which the
offenders could be tried," according to Ellen Schrecker, "because
being a communist was not a crime and the statute of limitations
precluded most espionage prosecutions." The usual charges faced
by Cold War defendants—perjury and contempt—therefore "bore
little relation to the presumed offense for which they were on trial."
There were indeed a few big criminal trials, like those of Alger Hiss
and the Rosenbergs, but for the most part anticommunists took on
their enemies with the weapons of exposure and penalties from the
private sector.[81]

HUAC's witnesses didn't start using the Fifth Amendment in any
meaningful way until 1948. Defendants refused to answer certain
questions lest they incriminate themselves prior to that year, but as
the public became more conscious of anticommunism and of the
fact that the committee sought exposure, not convictions, taking
the Fifth was increasingly viewed as a safe and pragmatic choice.
In a report in August 1948, the committee expressed its frustration
by calling for laws to cope with the "new communist tactic of evad-
ing detection and impeding the process of legislative investigation
through an unwarranted and unjustifiable means of the protections
[the Constitution] rightfully provides for those unjustly accused." As
anticommunism peaked in the early 1950s, so too did the use of the
Fifth Amendment by defendants.[82]

A congressional chamber is not a court of law—and a witness has
little with which to defend himself. There is no impartial judge present to balance opposing interests. The pace and tempo of the questioning is controlled by committee chairs. Evidence can be com-

pletely withheld from the accused, however baseless the accusations seem to be. And defense attorneys often have no right to cross-examine their own clients so that their positions could be articulated without interruption from committee members. If the committee wanted someone tainted, that person usually got tainted. As chair J. Parnell Thomas said in 1948 to one witness who took the Fifth: "the rights you have are the rights given to you by this Committee. We will determine what rights you have and what rights you have not got." Even if defendants felt no shame in their actions, nor committed any crime, nor would object to speaking about their associations with complete strangers, when standing before Congress their only hope for establishing any context was to invoke their constitutional right to privacy.[83]

This battle over context was fought by the innocent and the guilty alike. In February 1947, the German communist activist (and likely spy) Gerhart Eisler refused to take the stand at HUAC unless he was first permitted to deliver three minutes of remarks uninterrupted. His request was denied, so Eisler refused to be questioned and was cited with contempt. That same year Howard Lawson, after much back and forth about the premise of the committee's questioning, responded to the usual inquiry (was he or had he been a member of the party) with "I am framing my answer in the only way any American citizen can answer a question," adding that while he had no desire to keep his affiliations secret from the public, the clear bias of the committee forced him to refuse to answer questions in that particular room. "I will offer my beliefs and my associations to the American public and they will know where I stand," scolded Lawson — "as they already do from what I have written."[84]

Folk singer Pete Seeger's appearance in 1955 stands as one of the more enduring episodes in HUAC's history, marked by a mixture of privacy claims and appeals to the importance of context. When asked whether he had sung for a communist group at a particular venue in June 1949 to further its "propaganda," Seeger would not answer the question directly. Instead he replied that he had "sung for Americans of every political persuasion . . . sung in hobo jungles [and] sung for the Rockefellers," and that he "never refused to sing for someone because [he] disagreed with their political positions." Seeger refused to take the Fifth, saying only that he would not "answer any questions as to my association, my philosophical or religious beliefs or my political beliefs, or how I voted in any election, or any of these private affairs . . . under such compulsion as this. I would be very glad to tell you my life if you want to hear of it." Unsurprisingly, his remarks got him cited for contempt. Seeger didn't seem to mind.[85]

But then this wasn't altogether bad for the committee. That witnesses would take the Fifth Amendment brought certain advantages. Again, a key privacy problem concerning interrogation is the tendency for those who refuse to answer questions to be seen as guilty—at times of much more than their charged transgressions. The typical hearing opened with the reading of several dozen names of suspected communist subversives, the purpose of which was to place on the public record the names already known to official agencies. "It is pretty clear, I think," said Richard Nixon (R-CA) to a witness in 1948, "that you are not using the defense of the Fifth Amendment because you are innocent."[86]

Taking the Fifth brings with it a certain rigidity that both helped and hurt congressional defendants. The Supreme Court upheld the absolute nature of the Fifth Amendment in its landmark *Dennis v. United States* (1951) ruling, affirming that witnesses could use it to refuse answering even seemingly innocuous questions such as "where do you live?" and "what is your age?" because such questions had the potential to form "links in the chain" of evidence toward self-incrimination. But *Dennis* also ruled that a witness, in certain instances, did *not* have the right to pick and choose which questions warranted Fifth Amendment protections. One either took the Fifth down the line or left him- or herself open to potential contempt charges.

Interrogators, particularly grandstanders, were able to turn the all-or-nothing nature of the Fifth to their advantage. When faced with a witness taking the Fifth down the line, committee members frequently asked about baseless espionage activities and other farfetched and inconsequential matters meant to paint the witness as uncooperative or build up a "refusal to answer score" for the amusement of the press. Teachers could not deny actively brainwashing their students. Business owners could not deny laundering money to aid violent subversive plots. Professors could not deny attempting to incite revolution. Silence was as satisfactory as a confession, and inquisitors could claim victory and trust that the private sector and the public at large would mete out the proper punishment.[87] Accusations have a power all their own. These "Fifth Amendment communists," while able to safeguard their privacy, invited disaster upon themselves in the process. The protections provided by the court were but legal ones, and they did not shield against notoriety and loss of employment.

If an accused Red came before the committee and stood hat in hand, a bit slouched, the proper mix of shame and humility on his face, confessed to the evils of his past affiliations, and proceeded to name names of other Reds for the honorable gentlemen to subpoena, he would be commended for doing so and dubbed a reformed traveler. A good American once again. We all make mistakes, after all.

But for those who didn't, which was most, there would be extralegal penalties. Among the more blatant of these penalties was inclusion in a popular publication called *Red Channels*. It wasn't quite a book—more a really big list in book form. The brainchild of three former FBI agents who called themselves the American Business Consultants, *Red Channels* was first published in June 1950 as a 213-page compilation of names. To plead the Fifth down the line was to guarantee that one's name would appear in the next edition.[88]

Red Channels was little more than an ingeniously well-marketed blacklist. Most American corporations adhered to a policy of not hiring anyone found it its pages either out of patriotic zeal or, more often, self-defense. Good public relations demanded that any private sector corporation avoid any hint of controversy, and as television producer Marl Goodson (and amateur wordsmith) testified in 1962: "non-clearability meant unemployability."[89]

Some witnesses recognized the pitfalls involved in taking the Fifth and sought a kind of middle ground. In 1954 John T. Watkins, vice president of the Farm Equipment Workers Union, who had admitted years earlier to being associated with communists though never a party member, showed a remarkable understanding of the committee's tactics and motives when he delivered a statement to HUAC contrasting those of his peers:

> I would like to get one thing perfectly clear, Mr. Chairman. I am not going to plead the Fifth Amendment, but I refuse to answer certain questions that I believe are outside the proper scope of your Committee's activities. I will answer any questions which this Committee puts to me about myself. I will also answer questions about those persons whom I knew to be members of the Communist Party and whom I believe still are. I will not, however, answer any questions with respect to others with whom I associated in the past. I do not believe that any laws in this country requires me to testify about persons who may in the past have been Communist Party members or otherwise engaged in Communist Party activity, but who to my best knowledge and belief have long since removed themselves from the communist movement. I do not believe that such questions are relevant to the work of this Committee— nor do I believe that this Committee has the right to undertake the public exposure of persons because of their past activities. I may be wrong and the Committee may have this power, but until and unless a court of law so holds and directs me to answer, I must firmly refuse to discuss the political activities of my past associates.[90]

Watkins was cited for contempt, indicted, and found guilty. He received a twelve-month suspended sentence and a fine of $500. In 1957, the case went to the Supreme Court, which reversed the conviction. Chief Justice Earl Warren declared for the majority that "there is no Congressional power to expose for the sake of exposure," that "no inquiry is an end to itself; it must be related to, and in furtherance of, a legitimate task of the Congress." Ultimately the Watkins case was inconsequential because the decision was based on a narrow legality of procedure. Nevertheless the journalist David Lawrence devoted a three-page editorial to the decision in *U.S. News* the following week, announcing that "treason has won its biggest victory."[91]

HUAC's condemnation of the "hand-wringing" nature of Fifth Amendment in its 1948 report was not without irony. That same year, former chair J. Parnell Thomas was caught having billed the US government from 1940 to 1945 for salary payments to persons who did not work in his office; he had kept the money himself. He was charged by the Justice Department with payroll padding and indicted by a grand jury. In preliminary hearings, to the delight of many, he invoked his Fifth Amendment privilege and ruined his career.[92]

X

The McCarthy era was named for a member of Congress, but the executive branch was just as responsible (if not more so) for the anticommunist hysteria of the second Red Scare. After World War II, the Truman administration launched a large public relations campaign aimed at garnering popular support for his foreign policies. To sell the Truman Doctrine and the Marshall Plan to a nation emerging from fifteen years of depression and war, he actively stimulated concerns about national security and put in place a number of mechanisms that were later exploited by the anticommunist coalition. The executive branch is, after all, home to the Justice Department. By putting communists on trial and condoning large-scale surveillance operations like Director Hoover's COINTELPRO, a counterintelligence program that spanned fifteen years and often used extralegal means to stifle political dissent, Truman helped legitimize the image of party members as not merely political ideologues but as dangerous criminals.[93]

These policies may have been successful in the global arena, but they ended up hurting Truman politically. After his surprise election victory in 1948, Truman quickly found himself facing new tactics from political enemies who had no problem turning the Cold War fears he helped generate into ever more hysterical charges that the Democratic Party had been too soft on communism in the first place. In response, Truman had to spend much of his domestic political capital playing defense against a psychological current of anti-communism that he himself helped inject into the national conversation. Chickens coming home to roost and all that.[94]

Among the many initiatives taken by the executive branch in this period, it was the loyalty-security program and the consistent claims of "executive privilege" in the face of congressional pressure that were most significant for American privacy rights. To keep from being labeled soft-on-communism, in 1947 President Truman issued Executive Order 9835 announcing that "there shall be a loyalty investigation of every person entering the civilian employment of any department or agency of the executive branch of the Federal Government." On top of the usual security protocols, all current and future government employees would have their names cross-referenced against the files of the FBI, military intelligence, the HUAC files, and "any other appropriate source."[95]

The loyalty-security program was, at its core, a political test. Any person currently or formally connected to the Communist Party or any allegedly subversive organization listed by the attorney general, even in the most tenuous way, was eligible for disqualification or termination. The operative term was "sympathetic association," which like "un-American" was intentionally vague to allow considerable latitude for investigators, who could condemn a wide array of political activities and impose their own biases.

The move was a blow to the privacy rights of every American with a public sector job, even those unrelated to national security. It's not that people who worked for the federal government shouldn't have been examined. It's that the nature of these examinations became much more invasive and considerably more arbitrary. "Whenever derogatory information with respect to loyalty . . . is revealed" read the order, agents would conduct "a full field investigation" and refer suspects to a "Loyalty Review Board," who would then "disseminate such information to all departments and agencies."[96]

If a loyalty investigation turned up any suspicion of questionable political activity, the employee would receive a written "interrogatory" listing specific charges. The employee would then submit to a hearing before a loyalty board, which was under no obligation to disclose the names of informants or to share any details. Employees could contest the charges, but the process was often humiliating and expensive and had murky procedures that, like the congressional committee hearings, included no mechanism to balance opposing interests. About 12,000 employees who received interrogatories simply resigned instead of fighting for their positions. Some appealed to the Supreme Court to challenge the constitutionality of the loyalty-security program, but the judiciary, a conservative body at the time and sensing a political minefield, did little to curb the practice until the ascent of the more liberal Chief Justice Earl Warren in the mid-1950s, and even then only in cases that concerned the most blatantly illogical dismissals.[97]

So what exactly is the problem here? Doesn't the government have a right to protect itself from spies and subversives? Indeed it does, but the privacy problems at play in the loyalty-review process were very similar to those in the congressional hearings of the day: the improper aggregation of information, the secondary use of that information, the exclusion of the accused to pertinent information, and the glaring absence of context. All of these factors create a significant power imbalance against the accused, an imbalance that would be impermissible in almost any civil or criminal hearings today.

A closer look at a famous 1954 loyalty case offers a good illustration. In February a mailman received an interrogatory that he was under investigation by the regional office of the US Civil Service Commission. Among the list of charges:

"3. In January 1948 your name appeared on a general mailing list of the Joint Anti-Fascist Refugee Committee. . . .

5. Your wife . . . was a member of the Club of the Young Communist League.

6. In 1950, Communist literature was observed in the book-
shelves and Communist Art was seen on the walls of your residence. . . ."[98]

The mailman presented himself before a review committee and
said that he never had any affiliation with the AFRC, and that even
if he had, the organization was not listed by the attorney general as
suspect when he was hired (implying that a court of law would consider the accusation *ex post facto*). He also denied his wife's having
any affiliation with the YCL and in fact never even lived close to any-
where the league operated.[99]

To the particularly troubling claim that the committee's reach had
extended inside his own residence, the witness responded that he
"had no idea of what relationship there might be" between communism and the art he owned, and that he had been assigned *Das Kapi-
tal* in college but found the few chapters he read "dull and tedious."
The employee and his attorney then lobbied for any information
concerning the source of these accusations. The request was denied.
The employee terminated.[100]

Another 1948 case involving a federal meat inspector shows how
these cases often led to firings for reasons unrelated to national security or communism. Despite testimony from no less than ten character witnesses that the fellow had always been staunchly anticommunist and quite religious, the loyalty board discovered that he also
been a vocal supporter of desegregation. The agency's lawyer made
sure to ask every character witness whether the employee "had ever
discussed the Negro problem," and the chairman took up a series of
hypotheticals involving the dangers of a communist meat inspector
with an "evil design to contaminate a large amount of meat without necessarily being detected until it had got out and had done the
damage." The employee's attorney tenaciously placed on the record
a series of objections that the board had spent considerably more
time "on the racial situation" than his alleged associations with communism. The employee was terminated regardless. It took seven
years and a series of appeals for him to get his job back.[101]

By the early 1950s even state governments began establishing loyalty investigations for municipal employees. The political upsides of such programs had rippled out, and the privacy rights of governmental employees grew that much more constrained. A government job of any sort in the McCarthy era came with a significantly diminished level of personal privacy. FBI Special Agent Swearingen later recalled that if a fellow agent had a personal gripe with a person, or if "you got someone who was just a miserable personality . . . then you might pick on him and get him fired all the time. Every time he gets a new job you go in and tell them that this guy's really dangerous. That's all they have to hear and they'll figure out a way to get rid of him."[102]

Herbert Brownell Jr., attorney general to President Eisenhower, later admitted that the FBI often "went too far" in the investigation of federal employees, especially when "using anonymous information" to convict people. "On the government employee program," he recalled, "I think we could have confined it to people whose job was to handle security information instead of examining all government employees." Peter Szluk, a former State Department security operative, also revealed years later that false accusations from malicious coworkers or homophobes was rampant, and that the public would "be surprised how rotten people are to one another, simply because some guy wouldn't drop his pants for some woman or a man, I'm telling you! . . . the gay [sic] was a pretty large percentage of them . . . and if you did anything, regardless of how small or insignificant it might seem to somebody on the outside, to us it meant you've had it."[103]

These cases—the mailman, the meat inspector, and the thousands of others—are problematic not only because of the way private information was collected about the accused, but also because the accused were never allowed to access the information being used against them. The taxonomy of privacy calls this *exclusion*. The exclusion of individuals from understanding what personal information about them has been made available to others has been recognized by many governments today as anathema to liberal criminal procedures and fair information practices. No criminal court, for example, would ever allow a trial to go forward until a defendant's attorney properly reviewed all evidence being used by the prosecution. Despite the courtroom theatrics on television and in movies, surprise witnesses and last-minute evidence almost never occur in real life. It's simply too unfair to the accused in a society that prioritizes the presumption of innocence.

Exclusion reduces accountability on those who collect and process information about individuals. Because of this, exclusion reduces the accuracy of that information. Why worry about total accuracy if your target can never challenge your actions anyway? The real tragedy of exclusion is that it facilitates asymmetrical knowledge. They know more about you than you do about them. Or even worse—you don't even have a complete understanding of *what* they know. Exclusion instills in many a Kafkaesque sense of vulnerability and uncertainty. Information, after all, is power. And when individuals' information is used by others to make important decisions about them, people who are excluded from that information feel divested of control over their own lives in a way the law has deemed significant.[104]

Joseph Rauh, an anticommunist and anti-McCarthy "loyalty lawyer" who was regarded as one of the foremost defenders of civil liberties during the second Red Scare, noted that the exclusion of investigative findings was the toughest barrier most loyalty defendants faced. "You knew what was said, but you didn't know who the hell said it," he recalled, and "the people running the program didn't realize how outrageous not having confrontation was. You can't be fined for a traffic ticket without the policeman that gave it to you . . . but you could have your loyalty impugned and lose your job without ever knowing who said what about you. It was an absolute disgrace."[105]

"These interrogatories had no substance to them, they were statements that you're accused of this, this, and this," said United Public Workers attorney Al Bernstein. "These people were scared to death, livelihood at stake, their neighbors being quizzed about them, their position in the community—win, lose, or draw—never the same. I soon found out what the process was about; these were kangaroo courts. No cross-examination of witnesses—in fact, no witnesses. Not only was no witnesses, but no evidence . . . the prevailing rule guilt by association."[106]

The national security argument was bullshit. For the most part, at least. Simply too many Washington insiders admitted decades later that these privacy infringements were motivated not by a genuine concern for national security but by political opportunism. Clark Clifford, who as special advisor to the president met with Truman almost daily, later recalled that few in the executive branch were actually concerned with rooting out subversion. "We never had a serious discussion about a real loyalty problem," said Clifford, "the President didn't attach a fundamental importance to the so-called Communist scare. He thought it was a lot of baloney . . . it was a political problem and he had to recognize the political realities."[107]

Nothing better illustrates the executive branch's recognition of how privacy can be twisted to serve ulterior motives than its repeated invocation of "executive privilege" in the face of congressional inquiries. Executive privilege is an assertion of privacy. The Office of the President of the United States, in fact, has a long tradition of exercising a prerogative to keep its papers private from Congress and the American people. Among the more commonly known episodes are President Washington's refusal to hand over records relating to the controversial "Jay Treaty" with England, John Adams's decision to withhold letters concerning the inflammatory "XYZ Affair" with France, and the secrecy of Jefferson's negotiations for the Louisiana Purchase.[108]

Franklin Roosevelt gave Martin Dies a dressing down in 1940 after the congressman suggested Roosevelt consider coordinating activities and sharing files with the legislature. Offended, FDR replied that the committee's methods "defeat the ends of justice," and such a relationship would "be severely handicapped or completely destroyed by premature disclosure of facts or suppositions to the public, or by hasty seizure of evidence." FDR then invited Dies to the White House, only to make him wait in the anteroom while the president chatted away with Gardner Jackson—one of Dies's political enemies. Dies took the joke hard and complained of the "indignity" twice on the floor of the House.[109]

Truman, while hardly a warrior when facing the pressures of anticommunism, had his moment in 1948 when he refused to hand over the loyalty file of Dr. Edward Condon, a high-ranking government atomic science advisor who, because he was a vocal supporter of an internationalist foreign policy approach and New Deal liberalism in general, had become the target of a congressional smear campaign. Condon had also already been cleared by a Commerce Department loyalty board that February. When the House, by a vote of 300 to 29, ordered the secretary of commerce to hand over sections of Condon's FBI review, Truman reminded his press corps of Andrew Jackson's famous remarks to the Supreme Court a century earlier ("[he] has made his decision, now let him enforce it"). A month after the election, Nixon and other committee members gently admitted that their handling of the Condon affair had been "unfair" to the scientist and that the man was no security threat.[110]

To be sure, transparency in government is essential to any liberal society. But privacy is also a necessary component of state function, and not just the kind of privacy that deals with national security. For the same reasons that individual citizens need privacy so that they can better formulate ideas, assess their surroundings, and respond to problems intelligently, so too do government officials need privacy to reflect on the long-range effects of their policies and to engage in frank discussions aimed at finding intelligent solutions.

As we know, the Constitution of the United States was written behind closed doors, with its authors sworn to secrecy, and the notes of the debates were not released for fifty years. Alan Westin, perhaps the most influential privacy scholar of the twentieth century, once argued that "if the [constitutional] convention's work had been made public contemporaneously, it is unlikely that the compromises forged in private sessions could have been achieved, or even that their state governments would have allowed the delegates to write a new constitution." This understanding of privacy speaks to the importance of privacy for certain democratic processes *and* privacy about those processes afterwards (for a reasonable period).[111]

No president protected the privacy of his office more fiercely than Ike. Most famously in a 1954 memo he rejected a Senate subpoena from McCarthy himself for various documents concerning individuals with ties to his administration. "I will not allow people around me to be subpoenaed," he told Republican leaders, "and you might just as well know it now." Ike claimed it "essential to efficient and effective administration that employees of the executive branch be in a position to be completely candid in advising with each other." Arthur Schlesinger Jr. later called it "the most absolute assertion of presidential right to withhold information from Congress ever uttered to that day in American history." Even when the Supreme Court ordered the release of Nixon's secret recordings twenty years later, the justices made a point of noting that this precedent of executive privacy remained valid and that the Watergate situation was something altogether different.[112]

Eisenhower's invocation of executive privilege in 1954 amid the "Army-McCarthy" hearings was delivered on the cusp of McCarthy's (and McCarthyism's) downfall. Three weeks later, the senator publicly attacked the law firm of Joseph Welch, the army's special counsel, accusing it of harboring a communist lawyer named Fred Fisher. The prepared Welch responded by humiliating McCarthy with his now famous rejoinder, "You have done enough. Have you no sense of decency, sir, at long last? Have you left no sense of decency? . . . If there is a God in heaven, it will do neither you nor your cause any good. I will not discuss it further."[113] It was the final blow in a series of attacks on McCarthy that year, not the least of which was the senator's feud with CBS broadcaster Edward R. Murrow. McCarthy had finally destroyed himself on national television. The Senate appointed a committee to explore his activities over the previous years. The result was a unanimous condemnation of his brazen tactics and eventual censure by a vote of 67 to 22. Claiming betrayal, McCarthy remained in the Senate but was largely ignored by the press and his peers. A heavy drinker, he died three years later of a liver condition, at forty-eight.[114]

XI

If we're being honest, the damages inflicted by America's crusades against subversion are in many ways hard to quantify. The arrests, the blacklists, the congressional hearings, the mass deportations, the widespread loss of employment—what statistics we have on these developments are largely imprecise. It's also important to remember that when compared to other nations that encountered similar experiences, people were never rounded up and shot in the streets.[115]

Yet the developments brought on by the countervailing force of national security put considerable pressure on American privacy rights and, in the process, facilitated a widespread chilling effect on social and political expression. One of the better interpretations of McCarthy's legacy comes from historian Ellen Schrecker, who suggests that perhaps the damage is best appraised by examining "what *did not* happen" because of this hysteria. That by crippling the far-left, the nation lost a political network that created a space where serious alternatives to the capitalist model could be entertained. Also, any opposition to the Cold War was so quickly associated with communism that it was essentially impossible to challenge the foundations of America's foreign policy without inviting at least some accusations of disloyalty. On cultural matters, anti-subversive rhetoric contributed to the reluctance of publishers, television producers, and filmmakers to take on controversial social and political subjects.[116]

From a historical standpoint, the antidemocratic tendencies of anti-subversion campaigns continued well after McCarthyism was put to rest. Many scholars see the legacy of McCarthyism in COINTELPRO's harassment of political dissenters in the 1960s and 1970s, the Watergate illegalities and scandal of 1974, the Iran Contra scandal of the 1980s, and many documented Patriot Act abuses of the twenty-first century. That's because it was during these anti-subversion crusades that the rhetoric justifying blatant violations of privacy rights in the name of national security was honed and implemented.[117]

Of course these troubling episodes in our history also involve broader notions of civil liberties, but the aggressors involved also understood that widespread privacy infringements could serve as weapons. The circumvention of American privacy rights, whether by illegal searches or by politically motivated public interrogation, was the platform from which other civil liberties violations were able to flourish. Privacy is largely about self-defense. Take it away and one is vulnerable.

After the September 11 attacks, US appeals court judge Richard Posner noted "it stands to reason that such a revelation [as terrorism] would lead to our civil liberties being curtailed." Posner echoed the sentiments of former chief justice Robert Jackson in noting that the Constitution is not a "suicide pact." "Protections of privacy," according to Posner, should not be treated as "sacrosanct" to a point where "the battle against international terrorism must accommodate itself to them." Posner was confident in this logic because he noted that historically, once safety is restored the nation can roll back whatever security measures it put in place during the crisis. Solove refers to this popular notion as the "pendulum argument"—essentially, that during times of crisis the pendulum swings toward security and away from privacy, and at peacetime swings back toward liberty.[118]

But the pendulum argument doesn't hold up to historical scrutiny. If anything, the history of privacy shows us that it is precisely in times of crisis that we should be most aggressive in protecting civil liberties. In fact, such times are when both the state and the public have been far too willing to make unnecessary sacrifices that they often come to regret. Anti-German hysteria, the Palmer raids, Japanese interment, HUAC, McCarthy, the loyalty programs—these are not historical moments we remember as necessary sacrifices, but instead as warnings of what can happen when widespread fear meets political opportunism.[119]

History also shows us that among the biggest challenges to privacy rights throughout these crusades was the inability of many advocates to effectively position privacy as a larger societal good. Not as something anathema to security, but as a necessary component of any liberal society that must be balanced appropriately with opposing concerns. This was precisely the line taken by the NAACP when it faced down the state of Alabama in the early 1950s, and while it is hard to predict how such a position would have taken shape across the numerous fronts that comprised the crusades against wartime subversion, or whether it would have been successful, it did prove remarkably effective in that historical moment. But again, the absence of a broader societal movement is understandable when one considers that provocative threats of domestic terrorism are much more easily articulated than are philosophical theories about privacy's multifaceted nature. Perhaps Patrick Henry's "give me liberty, or give me death" would be a good place to start.

In 1952 Associate Justice William O. Douglas wrote an essay for the *New York Times Magazine* entitled "The Black Silence of Fear." In it he argued that an American returning from abroad would find "that thought is being standardized, that the permissible area for calm discussion is being narrowed, that the range of ideas is being limited, that many minds are closed. Fear is fanned to a fury. Good and honest men are pilloried. Character is assassinated. Fear runs rampant." Douglas believed the chilling effect of the time "will so narrow the range of permissible discussion and permissible thought that we will become victims of the orthodox school. If we do, we will lose flexibility. We will lose the capacity for expert management . . . and borrow the policeman's philosophy from the enemy we detest." Thirteen years later, Douglas would express similar ideas in his majority opinion declaring the Supreme Court's first official recognition of a constitutional right to privacy.[120]

4

WIRETAPS, BUGS, AND CCTV

Privacy and the Evolution of
Physical Surveillance, 1928–1998

I

Capitol Hill, late evening, Tuesday, January 10, 1967. Across the nation, radios and televisions broadcast President Lyndon B. Johnson's remarks on the state of the union into millions of American living rooms. "Most Americans are already living better than any people in history," he opened, quite correctly. But despite such prosperity America still faced "a time of testing." By Johnson's count the United States was engaged in at least three different wars. The first, in Vietnam, was "very costly" but should be continued with vigilance. The second, on domestic poverty, was also no "short or easy struggle," but the administration's efforts were in the process of relentlessly striking down "legal barriers to equality." Johnson's third war, however—a "war on crime" declared two years earlier—was in need of reappraisal. Crime was surely among the more pressing issues facing the nation, but the president believed that the surveillance techniques being used by law enforcement officials presented a larger danger:

> We should protect what Justice Brandeis called the "right most valued by civilized men"—the right to privacy. We should outlaw all wiretapping—public and private—wherever and whenever it occurs, except when the security of this Nation itself is at stake—and only then with the strictest governmental safe-

guards. And we should exercise the full reach of our constitutional powers to outlaw electronic "bugging" and "snooping."[1]

A month later, Johnson ordered Attorney General Ramsey Clark to send a proposal to Congress that would have banned wiretapping except in cases deemed by the president as essential to national security. But while members of Congress recognized the growing public concern over wiretapping, they were also receptive to the increasing "law and order" rhetoric rising from the political right—especially the "get tough" policies being floated by former Republican presidential candidate Richard Nixon whose star, once again, seemed on the rise.

Not wanting to be branded "soft on crime" Congress, after a series of hearings, let the provision to ban wiretaps die. Undeterred, Johnson declared that he would simply instruct the Justice Department to suspend the use of wiretapping. Unfortunately for the "right most valued by civilized man" Johnson's successor had different ideas about the appropriate use of government surveillance.[2]

II

The etymology of the word *surveillance* is binary in nature, derived from the French verb "to watch over." As in, watching over an individual or individuals to keep them safe, but also watching over them to ensure that they meet a certain standard of behavior. Conceptually, surveillance both enables and constrains. It is used both to protect and to control.[3]

Every society that has established norms has also established mechanisms to enforce those norms. Surveillance, in this regard, is a necessary tool—part of our common machinery that disregards the privacy of individuals and groups to protect the rights of other individuals and groups. Any conversation about surveillance must recognize this reality. Parents watch children. Police officers watch public spaces. Employers watch employees. Because there will never be a society in which every individual obeys every rule while also side-stepping every tension and taboo, authorities will always employ some kind of process to ensure a degree of social and cultural conformity. And that process will inevitably violate someone's—or everyone's—privacy. It's just part of the modern social contract.[4]

But surveillance can also be used to serve sinister ends. And precisely because surveillance is a powerful tool of social control, societies tend to impose limits on the ability of authorities to place individuals under surveillance against their will or without their knowledge. Among the cornerstones of liberal democratic practice is the necessary curtailment of surveillance claims made by monarchs and municipal authorities. The history of surveillance in any society is the story of the interplay between these two tendencies: a positive conception of surveillance as a necessary means of social control and a negative conception of it as a tool used to constrain liberty and privacy.[5]

The precise dangers of physical surveillance in the public and private spheres include more general privacy concerns: aggregation, secondary use, distorted narratives. But perhaps the most recognizable danger inherent to overt surveillance is that it causes individual inhibition and self-censorship. When people are aware that they are being watched, they tend to alter their behavior to fit what they believe to be general expectations of "normal behavior" so as not to draw attention to themselves.

This self-censorship often occurs even if a person is not doing anything wrong. Many people, for example, feel comfortable singing along to their radio while driving on a highway, but stop doing so at a red light or while in heavy traffic where other motorists are more likely to see them. "Pervasive monitoring," observes Julie Cohen, "incline choices toward the bland and the mainstream." Psychologists call this the Hawthorne effect, after behavioral studies Henry Landsberger conducted in the 1920s and 1930s at Western Electric's Hawthorne Works in Cicero, Illinois, which confirm the thesis.[6] Even worse, Alan Westin notes "a close correlation between the availability of privacy from hostile surveillance and the achievement of creativity, mental health, and ethical self-development."[7]

Physical surveillance gives watchers access to a subject's speech or acts, which technology allows them to reproduce. In this regard it differs from *data* surveillance. People take more care in their writing than they do with their impromptu speech and actions. Casual speech often includes offhand comments, partial observations, sarcasm, and false sentiments to either avoid argument or draw a subject out. To have such conversations made public is potentially catastrophic to an individual's reputation. A vivid example of this is in Milan Kundera's novel *The Unbearable Lightness of Being*, when describing how the police destroyed an important member of the Prague Spring resistance group by recording his conversations among friends and then broadcasting them over public radio: "Prochazka was discredited because in private, a person says all sorts of things, slurs friends, uses coarse language . . . makes a companion laugh by shocking him with outrageous talk, [and] floats heretical ideas he'd never admit in public."[8]

As Kundera's example hints, the problems of surveillance, detrimental on their own, become much more severe when performed irresponsibly by the state. Even if discrete and hidden surveillance abates the Hawthorne effect, surveillance retains incredible investigatory power. Surveillance doesn't just target specific information; it usually captures much more information than was originally sought. If watched long enough, any person may be caught in some form of illegal or immoral activity that can be used against him or her.[9]

Unconstrained surveillance by law enforcement also can abet starkly antidemocratic tendencies. It prevents private social and political groups from expressing themselves, to the detriment of a pluralistic society. The establishment of powerful surveillance apparatus is a hallmark of totalitarian regimes, which require complete fealty. In fascist and communist states organizational privacy is often condemned as "antisocial," "immoral," or "part of the cult of individualism"—especially in the early stages of totalitarian consolidation.[10]

In the United States, the architects of the Constitution strove for a degree of harmony between the competing values of privacy and surveillance. But we need to recall the technological realities of the late eighteenth century. When Madison wrote the Bill of Rights, sound could not yet be transmitted or recorded. The only means of penetrating private spaces were eavesdropping and physical trespass, and so *those* acts were constrained under the strict warrant controls of the Fourth Amendment. A considerable chunk of the framework of constitutional rights—especially those pertaining to free speech and press; prohibitions on the peacetime quartering of troops in private homes; the protections against unreasonable search and seizure; and protections against self-incrimination—were established with a mind toward limiting the historical surveillance powers of governments, which the founders deemed anathema to liberty.[11]

Although technology developed in the nineteenth century, of course, it wasn't until the twentieth century that the fragile balance that the framers had struck between privacy and surveillance was threatened. Major breakthroughs in the sophistication and miniaturization of surveillance technology, particularly after World War II, concomitant with political, social, and cultural trends, fostered an acceptance of widespread physical surveillance by not only the government but private citizens as well. Rather quickly, the old legal and social controls were outstripped. As historian Sara Igo notes, it was there, in the postwar period, where the threat to privacy "came not from one particular direction but from every corner of American society," including "the government and the military, corporations and workplaces, universities and hospitals, media and marketers."[12]

By the early 1950s new surveillance hardware could penetrate homes and offices without a physical trespass, and it could monitor unrestricted channels of communication like telegraphs, telephone lines, and radio frequencies. The technology was quickly commercialized and made cheaply available to the public. Futuristic devices like the bulky "button camera" and miniaturized tape recorders were relatively easy to install, and in most states they were not illegal to own. Soon they were being used by government agencies, private businesses, professional investigators, and individuals. At the same time, technologies like data-based phone connections and other early digital communications were increasingly coordinating personal, business, and governmental affairs.

The balance of power had shifted conspicuously in favor of those conducting physical surveillance. The response from the public was uneven and varied depended on who was doing the surveilling, what was being surveilled, and what justifications were given for it. Congress passed three major laws regulating wiretapping and surreptitious recording, in 1934, 1968, and 1986 — but owing to a mix of technological ignorance and "tough-on-crime" political rhetoric, each bill was narrow in scope and inadequate to reestablish a balance between privacy and surveillance. Thus, most of the parameters of surveillance were legislated on the state and local levels.

Alan Westin, who advised Congress throughout the 1960s and 1970s, notes that if privacy was "to receive its proper weight on the scales in any process of balancing competing values, what is needed is a structured and rational weighing process, with a definite criteria that public and private authorities can apply in comparing the claims for surveillance . . . with the claims to privacy."[13] To this end, the political system failed. By the close of the twentieth century, private surveillance went mostly unprosecuted on the federal level, and in many cases all government actors had to do to win legal and social approval was to point to a social problem and argue that surveillance would help alleviate it. There was always some bootlegger or immigrant agitator. Some communist, some gangster, some civil rights agitator, or avowedly militant antiwar radical. Rather than balance competing values, the United States merely established a series of weak qualifying procedures for a license to invade privacy. This is not to say that Americans were indifferent to these trends — physical surveillance became a key factor in the only resignation of a sitting president and played a major role in the unsuccessful impeachment of another.[14]

So it would be wrong to view the history of American surveillance from the postwar period to the internet age as some descent into an Orwellian power configuration or Foucault's "panopticon." Big Brother did not rise after World War II, nor did a central watchtower come to dominate the social and political landscape. It is, rather, a story about a society whose surveillance capacities grew at an exponential rate, eventually outstripping most legal and political efforts to keep pace with the social implications. But the Orwellian and Foucault metaphors that privacy advocates are so quick to draw

from do not adequately capture the varied reality. The power generated by surveillance flowed through a variety of channels, was harnessed by a host of actors, both public and private, for a variety of
reasons, and was all the while both condemned and applauded by
the public. Often at the same time.[15]

III

Americans have been spying on one another for some time. Not
long after Samuel Morse introduced the telegraph machine in the
1840s, people began figuring out ways to intercept the messages that
ran along its wires. The Union and Confederate armies tapped each
other's telegraph lines during the Civil War in hopes of gaining tactical edges. Confederate general J. E. B. Stuart even boasted about
having his own "wire man." Later, Gilded Age newspapers regularly
intercepted each other's wire transmissions to avoid being scooped.[16]

When the microphone and dictograph recorder were introduced
in roughly the same period, their potential for surreptitious use was
recognized almost instantly. Among the earliest appearances of a
"bug" was in the 1895 *Report of the Postmaster General,* wherein a
postal inspector is described as having secretly recorded a lawyer
(who had been using the mails illegally) confess his crimes and then
boast that he would deny having done so if ever brought to trial. The
inspector hid the small dictograph in his top hat.[17]

Telephones entered the public mainstream in the early twentieth
century, but because of technological and financial constraints, sub-
scribers, often several dozen at once, were looped into single service
networks called "party lines." By picking up the phone, a customer
could secretly listen in on the conversation of any other member of
his network, which happened quite frequently as there was no other
way to know whether the line was free. Operators as well had the
ability to listen in on any conversation. It's a testament to evolving
cultural norms that early telephone users never really had any reasonable expectation of privacy.[18]

As the twentieth century marched on, Americans came to desire
more privacy in their telephone conversations—and they were will-

ing to pay for it. The development of automated switching (operators just connect and terminate calls instead of staying on the line) proved to be a profitable venture for phone companies, and while it did not eliminate party lines completely it did pave the way toward an expectation of privacy for telephone communications.[19]

This development, however, cut both ways. New expectations of privacy on the phone meant that the information transmitted over them was suddenly more intimate and in many cases more valuable. It wasn't long before sinister characters found a way to capitalize. Direct splices into telephone wires and a good set of earphones permitted eavesdroppers to hear both sides of a conversation. Businesses, private individuals, and law enforcement were quick to take advantage of the benefits of eavesdropping on parties who believed they were speaking in private.[20] Conversely, the telephone allowed criminal enterprises to communicate over vast distances and coordinate their operations with increased sophistication.

And in 1928, it was a criminal enterprise that made the privacy problems associated with telephonic wiretapping a national issue. Roy "Big Boy" Olmstead was a rather successful bootlegger who presided over a Seattle-based operation that smuggled Canadian alcohol by sea for distribution throughout the United States. Investigators estimated the organization took in profits of around $2 million a year (in 1928 dollars). State and federal law enforcement agents used wiretaps installed outside Olmstead's home to build a case that resulted in the indictment of more than seventy people, including bookkeepers, secretaries, attorneys, salesmen, and a number of corrupt policemen. According to federal attorneys the wiretaps disclosed "a conspiracy of amazing magnitude" by revealing significant details of Olmstead's business transactions and those of his employees. Stenographers made notes of all conversations, and their accuracy was corroborated under oath by government witnesses.[21]

But the agents never obtained a warrant before installing those wiretaps, leaving a window for Olmstead's lawyers to appeal on Fourth Amendment grounds. The Fourth Amendment of the Constitution reads:

The right of the people to be secure in their persons, houses, papers, and effects, against unreasonable searches and seizures, shall not be violated, and no Warrants shall issue, but upon probable cause, supported by Oath or affirmation, and particularly describing the place to be searched, and the persons or things to be seized.[22]

Olmsted's appeal eventually reached the Supreme Court.[23] It posed a number of constitutional questions. Did the Fourth Amendment protect only property, such as a home or office, against searches? Was a wiretap that did not literally constitute a physical trespass a legal means for gaining evidence? Were wiretaps exempt from the warrant requirement precisely because they did not involve a physical trespass or seize tangible objects?

The gangster's attorney argued that without a warrant, the search constituted an illegal intrusion into Olmstead's home. This broad reading of the Fourth Amendment protected *all* activities that transpire within the privacy of the home, including telephone calls. Thus, because Olmstead made his calls from his home and under the belief that they were private, law enforcement agents had violated his privacy and his constitutional rights to be protected from unreasonable searches and seizures *and* self-incrimination.[24]

On the other side, federal prosecutors objected to extending Fourth Amendment protections to the telephone. They argued that telephone conversations were not inherently private because they were facilitated by "a franchised public carrier" and that every phone call involves at least three parties: the caller, the called, and the phone company. Also, because a wiretap was not a physical trespass, they argued, it was permissible without a warrant. Therefore no violations of constitutional rights had occurred.[25]

The Court, in a 5–4 decision, denied Olmstead's appeal. Writing for the majority, Chief Justice William H. Taft held that the Fourth Amendment "shows that the search is to be of material things—the person, the house, his papers, or his effects. The description of the warrant necessary to make the proceeding lawful is that it must spec-

ify the place to be searched and the person or *things* to be seized."
Taft could abide perhaps extending Fourth Amendment protections to the mails, for which there was considerable precedent, but
"the Amendment does not forbid what was done here. There was no
searching. There was no seizure. The evidence was secured by the
use of the sense of hearing, and that only."[26]

Taft didn't explicitly condone wiretapping. In fact, he dedicated
a paragraph to informing Congress that it would be well within its
rights to extend constitutional protections to telephone conversations. The chief justice's constitutional outlook, however, was rooted
in strict constructionism, and so until such legislation was passed
he refused to "attribute[e] an enlarged and unusual meaning to the
Fourth Amendment."[27]

As it happens, few people remember Taft's opinion. It was the
dissent, by Justice Brandeis, that lives on in law school classrooms
and history textbooks: a bold showcasing of ideas drawn from his
Harvard Law Review article on the right to privacy coupled with
cutting-edge liberal constructionist jurisprudence. Like he had decades earlier, Brandeis recognized the duty of jurists to find innovative legal solutions to the previously unthought-of conundrums
that inevitably accompany rapid technological change. When facing
down the instant camera, he looked to the law and found that all
the tools needed to protect the privacy of the individual were already there. All one needed was an inventive legal mind. Now, facing
down wiretapping technology, his mind remained unchanged. Brandeis noted that at the time the Bill of Rights was adopted, "force
and violence" were the only means by which the government could
compel self-incrimination. "Ways may someday be developed," he
prophesized, "by which the government, without removing papers
from secret drawers, can reproduce them in court, and by which it
will be enabled to expose to a jury the most intimate occurrences of
the home." "Can it be," opined the justice, "that the Constitution affords no protection against such invasions of individual security?"[28]

Brandeis argued that with the Fourth and Fifth Amendments the
founders endeavored "to protect Americans in their beliefs, their
thoughts, their emotions, and their sensations." They conferred "as

against the government the right to be let alone—the most comprehensive of rights and the right most valued by civilized men." And to protect that right, "every unjustifiable intrusion by the government upon the privacy of the individual, whatever the means employed, must be deemed a violation of the Fourth Amendment." The justice leaned heavily on the doctrine of "unclean hands," a concept often used in equity law whereby a court refuses to address a wrong committed on a person who himself has committed a wrong. By rejecting the claims of law enforcement, Brandeis saw himself as preserving the Court's decision from a kind of contamination.[29]

Brandeis's dissent in *Olmstead* remains one of the most widely read tracts in American legal history. Generations later the Warren Court would borrow heavily from its arguments when finally extending Fourth Amendment protections to wiretapping and also when rationalizing a constitutional right to privacy in matters of reproductive "decisional privacy." Brandeis had laid the groundwork for an entirely new approach to the Fourth Amendment by shifting the emphasis from *where* an alleged wrong took place (i.e., a property-based claim) to *how* it affected an individual. He was intent on provoking a larger conversation about privacy and due process.[30]

Interestingly, Olmstead's case also carried some larger economic considerations. During the trial, numerous telephone companies petitioned the Court to take a more restrictive position on government wiretapping. The companies held that the function of telephone networks "in our modern economy" was to allow private communication. "A third person who taps the lines," wrote attorneys for Pacific Telephone and Telegraph, "violates the property rights of both persons using the telephone, and of the telephone company as well." These petitions mark one of the earliest moments at which privacy was conceptualized as a commodity. With the advent of switchboards, the phone companies' profits became intimately tied to their ability to market private subscriptions as exactly that—private. "The wire taper [*sic*] destroys this privacy," they argued. "He invades the 'person' of the citizen, and his 'house,' secretly and without warrant."[31]

But *Olmstead* had not gone their way, so wiretapping by government agents and private individuals continued mostly unabated. The Depression era saw some spectacular moments, including the wiretapping of New York City Mayor Jimmy Walker's telephone in 1929, the discovery of numerous recording devices in the chambers of the Supreme Court itself in 1935, and the use of audio surveillance technology to record the private conversations of Philadelphia mayor Sam Wilson in 1938. In 1940 the governor of Rhode Island was found to have ordered the wiretaps on the telephones of his own attorney general.[32]

Six years after Taft suggested that Congress consider some kind of regulation on surveillance devices, it passed the Federal Communications Act of 1934. The bill covered a number of communications practices and, as legal scholar Robert Ellis Smith notes, "became the definitive scheme for regulating broadcasting and telecommunications." Section 605 addressed wiretapping specifically:

> No person not being authorized by the sender shall intercept any radio communication and divulge or publish the existence, contents, substance, purport, effect, or meaning of such intercepted communication to any person. No person not being entitled thereto shall receive or assist in receiving any interstate or foreign communication by radio and use such communication (or any information therein contained) for his own benefit or for the benefit of another not entitled thereto.[33]

The law reveals how little Congress knew about surveillance technology. It provided no mechanisms addressing the rapid pace of technological evolution, no reference was made to wiretapping in floor debates or the committee hearings, and the matter of police use was never raised. Legal scholars argue the bill was "never effective in limiting wiretapping by either law enforcement or private entities." It even failed to include any mention of "bugs" or other listening devices that were not connected to a telephone wire.[34]

But the biggest problems would come from a minor error in the bill's wording that did some real damage to privacy rights. The law specifically prohibited the intercepting *and* divulging personal communications—not *or* divulging personal communications. This essentially allowed federal law enforcement to continue using wiretaps in any instance they saw fit, as long as they didn't use evidence from those wiretaps in court. On the street, police would just "intercept" the private conversations of a suspect and wait for information that could allow them to obtain some other kind of incriminating evidence—like the location of illegal goods or the time and place of an illegal transaction.

IV

After World War II, the use of physical surveillance technology in the United States expanded at a rate that dwarfed any that came before it. This acceleration was facilitated by four key overlapping developments: new scientific breakthroughs in miniaturization technology; the rapid growth and professionalization of the private detective field; the aggressive commercialization and marketing of surveillance technology to the public and law enforcement; and the legitimization of surveillance as a popular component in pop culture.[35]

A sonic eavesdropping device, like a bug or a wiretap, is essentially a tiny radio station. Most of these devices have three functions: they absorb surrounding noises, they process and convert that sound into an electric signal, and they transmit that signal to a receiver. Bell Laboratories contributed a major breakthrough to audio surveillance in the late 1940s with the development of transistor technology (which replaced cumbersome vacuum tubes) and later the much smaller integrated circuits.[36]

The economic miracle that was post-WWII America was the perfect setting for these devices to mature and be disseminated. The country's unparalleled prosperity paved the way for new sectors of economic growth in science and technology and almost completely redrew the commercial landscape. America was never a stranger to large companies, but the size and sophistication of postwar corporations was something altogether new.[37]

Successful corporations thrive on information. Information

about shifting markets. Information about changing consumer preferences. And, of course, information about their competitors. It is, in no uncertain terms, a commodity. Thus, growing companies required ever more information, which in turn stimulated demand for the services of individuals with a knack for acquiring it. Enter the private investigator.

By the end of the 1950s the United States was home to more than 20,000 private detectives. Most were former law enforcement or military intelligence agents who had been trained in electronic eavesdropping techniques, and they often worked for corporations that required a conspicuous amount of information, such as insurance companies, credit agencies, and law firms.[38] As competition grew fiercer, investigators started flaunting their expertise in electronic surveillance when soliciting clients. Montclair Technical Services, for example, sent out letters to lawyers throughout Connecticut introducing the firm as "specializing in matters requiring the use of electronic listening and recording equipment" to an extent where they could "intercept and record conversations in virtually any situation." Attorneys would be comforted to know that Montclair kept all of its attorney and client lists confidential and never used them as references because "special care is taken to ensure privacy."[39] Advertisements from the Los Angeles–based Confidential Investigations showcased its staff of "competent investigators equipped with modern electronic and photographic equipment, portable listening devices, wireless transmitters, recorders, cameras, mobile two-way mirror units, etc. for any fact-finding assignment. Secret microphones installed."[40]

As the field grew throughout the 1950s and 1960s, it both aided and was aided by the drastic commercialization of surveillance technology. Surveillance tech was fast becoming a multimillion-dollar industry—and like any booming sector it employed aggressive and sophisticated marketing techniques. Year after year, at conventions such as the American Society of Industrial Security Officers, manufacturers filled display tables with gadgets and gizmos and put on demonstrations of their latest devices: microphones hidden in cigarette lighters, recording devices attached to handbag clasps, and palm cameras placed where no one except those "in the know" would see them. "The main reason I came," one private investigator told a *Star Journal* reporter, "was to see the latest in electronic devices."[41]

Ads filled the pages of mainstream periodicals by the early 1960s. The "Memocord" pocket recorder "lets you record conferences and interviews" with its "easily concealed tiny pin microphone." The "Bird," a stuffed parrot with a built-in tape recorder, allowed listeners to hear "what your company and friends say about you when you are gone." Geloso Electronics featured an "Attaché case Secret Recorder" with a variety of uses—"A Private Ear for Private Eyes and Others."[42] When the Continental Telephone Supply Company, a nationwide chain of spy stores, opened its Miami location, the national newspaper advertisement read:

> Big Brother is going to have its own department store. You are cordially invited to attend the opening of a unique new store designed to cater to members of our suspicious society. . . . This new retail outlet offers the very latest in telephone bugging devices, spy cameras, probes that can pick up voices through walls, lamps that are actually radio transmitters, disguised tape recorders and a host of other electronic privacy invaders.[43]

Popular culture, whether intentionally or not, contributed immensely to the retail surveillance craze. Spy tech made frequent appearances in some of the most successful films and television shows of the 1950s and 1960s. The widely popular James Bond films, *The Man from U.N.C.L.E.*, *77 Sunset Strip*, *Get Smart*, *Honey West*, *Mission: Impossible*, and a veritable army of spies, sleuths, and clever detectives all fueled a genre in which electronic surveillance gadgets were used to strike blows for truth and justice. In many cases these spectacular gadgets became franchise staples.[44]

Americans' viewing habits had a direct impact on the erosion of their privacy. The immense popularity of the spy/sleuth genre helped temper American mores against secret eavesdropping and fortified an image of surveillance technology as a necessary tool in a world where communists or other baddies were also developing advanced technology to serve sinister ends. Fans would be hard pressed to remember a time when their heroes secured a warrant for these devices, reflected on the privacy implications of their surveillance, or were chastised for illegal wiretapping.[45]

By 1960 the American public was experiencing a period of sensational surveillance commercialization. One particular revelatory moment came in 1959 when Hal Lipset, a charismatic San Francisco private eye, decided to turn a routine appearance before a Senate subcommittee into a theatrical demonstration of how far commercial spy tech had come. Lipset hid a miniature recorder in the committee chamber immediately before the hearings started. When called to testify later in the day, he patiently waited for questions pertaining to bug technology and responded by playing back the chair's opening remarks to a shocked room. The senators were far from amused by the gimmick, but they were also quick to express dismay at the lack of prosecutions for such practices and the weak state of the current laws.[46]

An issue of *Life* was dedicated entirely to the surveillance craze. The cover featured a beautiful woman pulling back her dress to reveal a small recording device taped to her back. "INSIDIOUS INVASIONS OF PRIVACY" was printed in block letters to her left, with the subheadings: "in business, in the home, by law enforcers, by the underworld, by anyone who's out to get you." The issue was filled with stories of professional sleuths eager to boast of the tools of their trade.[47]

The targets of postwar private investigators varied greatly. Among the more publicized episodes include the time detectives found wireless transmitters in the home and private office of the president of Schenley Industries, one of the "Big Four" American liquor distributors; the discovery of a cigarette-pack radio transmitter taped under a coffee table in a suite at the Mayflower Hotel in Washington D.C., where lawyers of the El Paso Natural Gas Company were discussing strategies for an upcoming hearing with the Federal Power Commission; and the case of the market speculator who paid a cleaning woman $2,000 to place a bugged pen and calendar set in the office of a rival.[48]

A number of businesses also used surveillance against their employees in a sort of Taylorism-meets-Orwell attempt to increase worker efficiency and prevent theft. Throughout the 1960s labor unions increasingly complained about employers using cameras and recording devices to check on production speeds. A Chevrolet plant in Baltimore drew the ire of the United Autoworkers Union when it installed closed-circuit cameras, enabling managers to observe workers from a centralized station. One UAW official reported that a foreman used an intercom system to listen to female employees working on assembly tables; he frequently cut in to tell them that he did not approve of their topics of conversation. And in 1965 the Communications Workers of America filed a grievance against a manager who installed surveillance devices in the air conditioning ducts of the ladies bathroom, ostensibly to discover who had been defacing the stalls and walls there.[49] In the mid-1960s a bug on a telephone used by labor organizers at the Southern Pacific Railroad was traced to the offices of a railroad superintendent. The union brought a $40,000 damage suit against the company and the official. Similarly, in Whittier, California, a private detective was caught tapping the telephones of the General Freight Company to overhear conversations between union organizers and employees. These practices were widespread enough that many private detective firms listed "union jobs" as part of their offerings.[50]

True to the cliché, many private investigators also earned a living by applying their surveillance skills to extramarital affairs. Alan Westin estimated that over 40 percent of the average private investigator's surveillance was done in "matrimonial cases." Given that most who step out on their spouses are secretive and self-conscious, the field was a ripe challenge for surveillance professionals.[51] In 1964 Alan Jay Lerner, the Broadway lyricist who had recently asked his wife for a divorce, was locked out of his townhouse after detectives hired by the missus found transmitters installed behind a stereo set. In 1958 the suspicious husband of Minnesota congresswoman Coya

Knutson went so far as to hire an investigative agency to bug her home and office, where her legislative and political affairs were frequently discussed.[52]

The congresswoman wasn't the only government official subject to private surveillance jobs in the postwar period. The mayor of Reading, Pennsylvania, confirmed press reports in 1964 that investigators hired by local racketeers had been operating in the city for months and were "believed to be listening in on conversations of local public officials, including the district attorney's office," to anticipate the tactics of an antivice campaign. In Delaware, a routine maintenance check in 1959 found that the private telephone line of the state's attorney general had been wiretapped. The following year a security officer at the Democratic National Convention discovered transmitters on the telephone lines of Adlai Stevenson's presidential campaign offices. This marriage of surveillance tech with political opportunism would bear only more fruit in the final decades of the twentieth century [53]

V

The proliferation of almost entirely unregulated private surveillance in the 1950s and 1960s presented a number of privacy problems. But the drastic expansion of *governmental* eavesdropping in this period highlights the much more pressing antidemocratic dangers inherent to a surveillance state.

By the early 1960s at least fifty federal agencies laid claim to some kind of investigative function, including the State Department, the FBI, army and naval intelligence, the post office, the Food and Drug Administration, and the Internal Revenue Service. These agencies eagerly embraced advances in surveillance technology and actively trained as many as 20,000 operatives in modern surveillance tactics.[54] This drastic increase in state-sponsored surveillance was conducted largely in secret; for more than a decade there was little to no public review of governmental surveillance practices. It wasn't until the 1965, following a series of congressional investigations, that the magnitude of surveillance was revealed and the issue became a subject of national concern.[55]

The first broad discussions about governmental surveillance took place a decade earlier when the House Judiciary Committee convened a series of hearings to address legal confusion surrounding the Supreme Court's ruling on Section 605 of the 1934 Communications Act. The confusion stemmed from a 1939 case, *Nardone v. United* States, in which the Court ruled that unwarranted wiretaps could not be submitted as evidence in a criminal trial, or used to develop leads in criminal cases, because such things were violations of the 1934 law. But the Court never said law enforcement had to stop using wiretaps altogether, and it was common knowledge that by the 1950s officers used these devices freely and then simply failed to mention doing so when a case came to trial, claiming instead that they developed their leads through criminal informants or anonymous tips.

Numerous groups and individuals testified in support of a total ban on wiretapping, including the American Civil Liberties Union, the American Federation of Labor, the American Jewish Congress, and the Philadelphia and Virginia Bar Associations. Representative Kenneth Keating (R-NY) summed up the arguments rather well when he declared that the law was presently inadequate to prevent "mere spying and fishing expeditions."[56]

But the current of anticommunism was strong in the 1950s, and the wiretapping issue had become entwined with the loyalty-security debates. Congress was rightly aroused by the growth of state surveillance, but the obstacles to action were powerful ones. Besides, the public wasn't exactly clamoring for reform—mostly because the rapid growth of government surveillance had been obfuscated by the fact that the rules governing such things were different in each state. Widespread disparities on the state level created quite a bit of legal confusion over wiretapping.[57]

Pennsylvania, for example, was remarkably progressive on the issue. By 1959 it had enacted a total ban on wiretapping by public and private parties (including federal agents) with penalties ranging up to a year's imprisonment and a $5,000 fine. New York State chose a different route, one that leaned heavily on the judiciary and mandated strict court-order procedures akin to the warrant protections outlined in the Fourth Amendment. In 1954 New York City approved wiretaps for roughly 1,000 telephone lines, which led to over 400 arrests, mostly for organized crime rackets such as larceny, gambling, and extortion.[58]

Yet most states remained locked in political stalemates over the appropriate use of surveillance by law enforcement. Illinois was the only other state to adopt a total ban, and only four other states adopted New York's model of heavy judicial oversight. In the early 1960s the legality of wiretapping was unclear in forty-three states.

This isn't to say that the 1950s saw no pushback on physical surveillance. FBI wiretaps took center stage in the sensational Judith Copland trials. Copland was Justice-Department-employee-turned-communist-spy caught red-handed transferring state secrets to a known KGB agent in 1949. She was indicted the following year for espionage and conspiracy, and convicted on both charges. But when it was discovered that the FBI had eavesdropped on Copland's conversations with her attorneys and then lied about it, those convictions were overruled. Embarrassed and defensive, Director Hoover himself declared that "the most violent critic of the FBI would urge the use of wiretapping techniques if his child were kidnapped and held in custody."[59]

Then there was the Supreme Court's decision in the 1957 case *Benanti v. United States*, which declared all wiretap evidence obtained by the New York police, even evidence obtained legally and with warrants, inadmissible in federal trials. The Court noticeably sidestepped questions about evidence gained through undivulged wiretaps, but the ruling was enough to influence Manhattan district attorney Frank Hogan to suspend all wiretapping evidence in state trials until the matter was clarified by the Court at some later date. The state's attorney was understandably furious, as the ruling forced the state to drop pending perjury charges against Teamster boss Jimmy Hoffa. It would've been a career case, but alas it was built largely on evidence gained through unauthorized wiretaps.[60]

Privacy scholar Frederick Lane notes that the 1950s could fairly be described as the "wiretapping decade," one that closed with the publication of a remarkable book—*The Eavesdroppers*—written by former Philadelphia district attorney Sam Dash, law professor Robert Knowlton, and engineer Richard Schwartz. The book was among the first to outline the vast expansion of surveillance practices. It offered readers chilling anecdotes describing the erosion of privacy in vivid detail, from the tapping of the Supreme Court chambers and other government officials throughout the 1930s and 1940s to recent technological breakthroughs. It did little to turn Americans against wiretapping, but the public could no longer say they weren't told.[61]

The true extent of secret government surveillance wouldn't be public until well into the 1960s. One of the earliest revelations came from a former FBI agent, Jack Levine, who after leaving the bureau alerted the Justice Department to the growing use of "improper practices." In his 1964 book *The FBI Nobody Knows*, Levine described the shockingly unregulated nature of FBI wiretapping practices. He described hundreds of agents operating in local field offices without any warrants or oversight, using advanced electronic surveillance to settle personal beefs and investigate misdemeanors. Levine also accused the FBI of lying to the attorney general and to Congress about how they used surveillance; he laid most of the blame squarely on Hoover and his obsession with conviction statistics.[62]

We now know that Hoover, as far back as 1949, understood that physical surveillance came with ethical concerns capable of evolving into bothersome political concerns. To cover his tracks, he ordered all investigative information obtained through "questionable electronic surveillance" that might "cause embarrassment to the bureau, if distributed" to be recorded in investigative files by using separate cover pages and *never* included with the official files kept in the bureaus archives. This way if FBI files were ever subpoenaed for trial, defendants would never know they were being surveilled and criminal cases would avoid the many pitfalls created by the unclear legal status of wiretapping.[63]

The invocation of "national security" typically gave the bureau as much surveillance latitude as Hoover desired. And when the fervor of anticommunism began to wane, federal investigators were able to justify the continued use of these tactics by pointing to a brand new threat: organized crime. Today Americans are thoroughly acquainted with the caricature of the calculating Italian mafia gangster. But for generations, organized crime thrived in cities that were largely ignorant of its presence. The process of lifting the veil began in a small town in upstate New York in 1957. A war between two downstate crime lords, Frank Costello and Vito Genovese, had finally come to a close after considerable bloodshed. Genovese emerged as victor and new head of the Luciano crime family (named for Charles "Lucky" Luciano). To consolidate power and solidify his legitimacy, Genovese called a meeting of mob leaders from across the nation at a country house in a quiet town called Appalachian.

But alas, after victory, some hard luck. Only hours into the meeting local state troopers became alarmed at the large number of fancy Cadillacs and Lincolns with out-of-state license plates parked outside the country house, so they started writing down plate numbers. The mobsters saw the troopers and panicked. Some ran into the woods. Others hid in the basement. All in all approximately sixty were detained and twenty charged with obstruction of justice for refusing to explain why so many of them had traveled to Appalachian (a few said they were there for a barbeque). None of the convictions stuck, but state law enforcement and the media were quick to announce the conspiratorial conference. The existence of a sophisticated nationwide organized crime network was clear; federal agencies had to act.[64]

Six years later former mob soldier Joe Valachi testified to Congress and a national television audience about the methods and organizational structure of *la cosa nostra*. Federal investigators argued, successfully, that they must be allowed to use every available tool to combat the growing threat, especially physical surveillance.[65]

Ultimately public opinion in the 1950s was ambivalent about the expanding surveillance state. On one hand, citizens expressed appreciation for the modern technological age and a fascination with devices that could manipulate sound and sight beyond the natural ability of their senses. They also recognized the many benefits surveillance brought to law enforcement, to individuals seeking valuable information for a variety of legitimate reasons, and to the private sector. On the other hand, the public was aroused by the increasing mention of surveillance devices in congressional hearings and the media. Few people were unaware of the potential dangers that came with unchecked surveillance power. Had they known the full extent of government surveillance, though, more might have demanded a complete public accounting of it.[66]

This ambivalence about government eavesdropping would endure. Americans' stance on privacy has never been monolithic. But in the 1960s the debate reached a tipping point. Revelations about the size of the surveillance state were met with powerful civic outrage.

VI

The critical turning point in public awareness, concern, and eventual consternation over physical surveillance technology came somewhere around 1963 and 1964. Media coverage of the sophistication of commercial surveillance technology ballooned in those years—both on television and in mainstream periodicals. They also saw the publication of two important books on the state of public and private surveillance that alarmed scholars and prompted discussion about how imperiled privacy had actually become. And finally, in those years all three branches of government started addressing the privacy problems of surveillance in hearings and courtrooms and public addresses. The activism of senators like Edward Long and bodies like the Warren Court, in particular on legal questions of criminal procedure and right to privacy, touched off a national debate about the appropriate function of law enforcement investigations and about the constitutional basis—if there was one—for privacy rights.

In the 1960s major outlets like *Life* and *Time* magazines, the *New York Times*, the *Wall Street Journal*, the *Chicago Sun-Times*, and the *Washington Post* began regular coverage of stories on surveillance. A widely read *Saturday Evening Post* feature "Big Brother is Listening" typified the formula used by most articles. It noted that "thanks to modern science, privacy is becoming rarer over the world. Even a child can send away for a $15 device that picks up sounds in a room across the street." Americans would need to protect themselves:

> There is, it turns out, a body of folklore on how to frustrate Big Brother. Some people rap the telephone with a pencil as they talk. Others run water, pound a table, or keep a radio or TV set turned on. . . . But the most sophisticated warriors keep a radio or television set turned on loud while they speak softly and continually face in different directions (which is the reason well-bugged hotel rooms and offices have a least four hidden microphones).[67]

Television could not resist the inherent entertainment value of surveillance gadgetry—nor could it keep from being shocked— shocked at what it found it could do. In May 1964 ABC aired a documentary uncreatively called "Big Brother is Listening" that featured an interview with Supreme Court Justice William O. Douglas, who would later go on to write the majority decision that recognized a constitutional right to privacy. NBC promoted its 1965 feature "The Big Ear" with ads showing a large photo of host Robert MacNeil standing on a street corner looking at his watch. Below the photo was a fun challenge:

> Robert MacNeil models three microphones and a wire recorder (all concealed on his person). . . . Can you spot the recording equipment?

> ANSWERS: Microphones: wristwatch, fountain pen, lapel button. They are connected by wires not to the attaché case (which could contain a tape recorder), but to a wire recorder MacNeil is wearing in a shoulder holster under his coat.[68]

Meanwhile, in academia, two seminal books published in 1964— Vance Packard's *The Naked Society* and Myron Brenton's *The Privacy*

Invaders—sent shockwaves through the community and helped legitimized surveillance as a scholarly concern. The incisive Packard noted that increased surveillance "breeds not only sameness but a watchfulness completely untypical of the exuberant, free-wheeling American so commonly accepted as typical of this land in earlier decades."[69]

All this momentum picked up considerable speed when the Senate tasked a special subcommittee with investigating surveillance activities by federal agencies. Chaired by Senator Edward V. Long (D-MO), the committee would play a decisive role in revealing the true extent of government eavesdropping and uncovering the secrecy and mismanagement that had facilitated the rise of the surveillance state in the 1950s.

As gifted investigators often do, Long began by following the money. Committee researchers combed the records of the General Accounting Office for all purchases of electronic equipment, identified the main suppliers, and subpoenaed them for information about their surveillance devices and their buyers. Long sent each agency detailed questionnaires about the specific uses of the surveillance equipment they purchased; he then followed up with personal interviews. Public hearings began with the manufacturers themselves, who were asked to display and explain their more sophisticated (and theatrical) products to the committee.

That showoff Hal Lipset snagged another fifteen minutes in the national spotlight here. This time he alerted staff members of his plans, and the senators agreed to play along. He planted a microphone inside a fake olive, put it in a martini glass, and then placed the glass on the witness table. When the committee chair finished speaking, Lipset played back his testimony to a (somewhat) shocked room. "The Bug in the Martini Olive" made national headlines and became a catch phrase for seemingly omnipresent surveillance technology.[70]

With a firm foundation established, the hearings then turned to the agencies themselves. Long was smart enough not to go gunning for the FBI immediately, so the Treasury Department was first. It's hard to imagine the public taking to the streets en masse to protest the mistreatment of IRS officials. Treasury's regulations had explicitly outlawed the use of surveillance technology in tax investigations—so strenuously that the prohibition was repeated in regularly issued directives from the 1940s through the 1960s. But under oath, witnesses from the IRS related colorful stories of widespread bugging and wiretapping to catch tax cheats, like the time agents bugged the public telephone booth in the lobby of their own building to obtain evidence against a woman suspected of running a private lottery. Many Treasury agents had issued outright denials of surveillance use right up until they were pinned down by the committee's data and the threat of perjury charges.[71]

After Treasury, the dominos started falling. Investigators from the Food and Drug Administration and later the Postal Service admitted to the use of peepholes, restroom surveillance (to prevent theft), mail openings, and correspondence tracking of specific "questionable figures." The fact that neither of these agencies had a particular stake in national security was frequently noted by committee members. Having built up some momentum, the committee believed it stood on firm enough ground to begin probing the details of FBI surveillance tactics toward the end of 1965. Amid the predictable tales of leasing lines from phone companies to bring down organized crime operations, numerous incidences of wiretaps for less severe crimes (sometimes misdemeanors) were also reported. What most disturbed the committee was the seemingly complete lack of proper oversight or clearly defined protocols during this drastic expansion of federal surveillance. That, and the fact that so many surveillance operations were being conducted by local field offices playing so fast and loose that they didn't even include their tactics in reports to the Justice Department.[72]

The Long committee hearings received ample news coverage throughout 1965 and 1966 and prompted scathing editorials from both the left and the right. Conservative champion William F. Buckley wrote that "more and more it becomes plain that privacy is the key to liberty ... [so] let us have yet another law. Rather, 50 state laws forbidding the sale or purchase or ownership of anti-privacy devices, with a penalty attached that will guarantee to any miscreant user thereof the privacy of a jail cell for a couple of months." Civil liberties writer Alan Barth charged that America was being overrun with "lawless lawmen." This commentary, of course, did little to dampen sales of surveillance technology in the private market.[73]

But thanks to all this new attention, private suits seeking damages from surveillance operations began to climb. An Illinois man sued his local phone company for furnishing his wife with a direct line to his answering service, allowing her access to conversations between him and his lawyer about their pending divorce proceedings. A California lawyer filed for $300,000 in damages when he discovered his offices were bugged by a rival firm. One of the more sensational cases of 1965 involved the Hamburgers of New Hampshire, who filed suit against their landlord when they discovered a microphone in a heating duct next to their bed. "It should not be necessary—by way of understatement—to observe that this is the type of intrusion that would be offensive to any person of ordinary sensibilities," affirmed a judge.[74]

While Congress was getting to the bottom of the pervasiveness of government surveillance, the judiciary began positioning itself as a bulwark against the many privacy concerns raised by law enforcement surveillance. The Warren Court is widely remembered as perhaps the most liberal collection of justices in the Court's history. The controversial rulings of its majority between 1953 and 1969 showcased judicial activism in a dramatic and often polarizing fashion. Lucas Powe succinctly summed up its political legacy when writing: "everyone seems to turn into a partisan when the Warren Court is mentioned," for it reminds us that "judges are aware of the political context of their decisions and are, like everyone else, influenced by the economic, social, and intellectual currents of American society."[75]

The Warren Court gave considerable attention to the rights of the accused, launching an aggressive expansion of individual civil liberties that teased out and clarified the legal nuances of the right privacy. Justice William O. Douglas, in particular, was vocal on privacy issues in multiple opinions. The bulk of this Court's privacy rulings centered on Fourth Amendment jurisprudence. In 1960 the Court prohibited the introduction of wiretap evidence in federal court by state officials (*Elkins v. United States*). The following year it banned the introduction of any evidence obtained by the use of penetrative "spike" microphones—foot-long rods usually drilled into a suspect's wall or heating ducts (*Silverman v. United States*). Justice Potter Stewart called spike mikes "the frightening paraphernalia which the vaunted marvels of an electronic age may visit upon human society."[76]

In one of their most controversial rulings, *Mapp v. Ohio*, the justices raised the Fourth Amendment to new heights with the establishment of the "exclusionary rule"—the legal principle that evidence obtained outside the proper scope of investigative procedure, however damning, could not be used as evidence in state trials. A bombshell ruling, *Mapp v. Ohio* provoked a loud response from law enforcement officials who said they were being "handcuffed" by the justices.[77]

Dollree Mapp ran a small numbers operation in Cleveland. She also had a history of altercations with law enforcement. Police arrived at her door one morning while looking for a fugitive wanted in connection with a bombing. Mapp refused to open the door and asked whether the officers had a warrant. They replied that they did not. Mapp then called her lawyer, who told her not to let anyone in without a warrant. The police left but were back within the hour (still no warrant) and kicked in Mapp's door. They did not find any fugitives but searched her apartment anyway for illicit materials. Mapp's lawyer arrived while the police were there, but the officers refused to let him in. Eventually police found four pornographic pamphlets and put Mapp in handcuffs. She was convicted under the state's obscenity laws and given seven years.[78]

In a 6–3 decision, the Court overturned Mapp's conviction. In the majority opinion Justice Tom Clark declared: "We hold that all evidence obtained by searches and seizures in violation of the Constitution [is] inadmissible in a state court. . . . Were it otherwise . . . the assurance against unreasonable . . . searches and seizures would be [meaningless]."[79]

The case's impact on search and seizure laws was monumental—

and an important step forward in the regulation of a positive right to privacy from unreasonable physical surveillance. Walter Signorelli notes that it "opened the gates to a flood of search and seizure cases." Prior to *Mapp* the New York City Police Department did not train officers in search and seizure laws. That changed after the ruling.[80] *Mapp* was a huge step forward for privacy. It was also, in hindsight, a logical precursor to the Court's eventual revisiting of the *Olmstead* case.

Charles Katz was a rather successful bookie who ran a sophisticated gambling operation out of Los Angeles with affiliations in Boston and Miami. A cautious man, Katz never conducted business over his home and office telephones, relying instead on public payphones. In time one particular payphone in a discreet location became his favorite. When the feds caught wind of Katz's operation, agents decided to install a recording device on top of the phone booth. They did so without a warrant but also without entering the booth; thus there was no "physical penetration" involved. Agents recorded Katz's side of conversations with other players in his operation. Once they had enough evidence, Katz was arrested, and federal prosecutors used the recordings to help convict him of transmitting illegal wagering information by telephone. Katz appealed, with his attorneys arguing that evidence against him was gathered in an unconstitutional manner. Eager to revisit the *Olmstead* ruling, the Warren Court agreed to hear arguments.[81]

Katz's attorneys essentially relied on the same arguments Olmstead's had, with a little help from Justice Brandeis's dissent. They claimed that the Fourth Amendment required a warrant for any federal surveillance operations, and that said warrant must state the probable cause for a search and names of the persons or things to be seized. In bugging the phone booth, the FBI obeyed none of these requirements. Moreover, they argued, a public phone booth becomes private when a person uses it for confidential conversations. As such, it becomes a "constitutionally protected area," just like a person's home or office. Therefore, *Olmstead* should be overturned.[82]

The state countered that in Katz's case no tangible property was searched or seized, so the Fourth Amendment did not apply. Besides, a telephone booth is a public place, and Katz made no effort to make it private. A phone booth, in short, is not a "constitutionally protected area."[83]

In a 7–1 decision, the Court overturned Katz's conviction and the *Olmstead* ruling along with it. In the majority opinion, though, Justice Potter Stewart rejected arguments from both sides about whether a phone booth was a "constitutionally protected area." Instead, he drew a *new* distinction noting that the Fourth Amendment "protects people, not places," and that "what a person knowingly exposes to the public, even in his home or office, is not a subject of the Fourth Amendment protection. . . . But what he seeks to preserve as private, even in an area accessible to the public may be constitutionally protected."[84]

Stewart concluded that if the FBI agents had sought advance authorization to bug the phone booth from a judge in the same way that they might have sought a search warrant, permission would probably have been granted because the agents followed the accepted procedures for a warrant. Katz was a criminal, after all, and the feds had probable cause to investigate him. But they didn't get a warrant. And in the United States "wherever a man may be, he is entitled to know that he will remain free from unreasonable searches and seizures. The government agents here ignored the procedure of antecedent justification . . . that is central to the Fourth Amendment and a constitutional precondition to the kind of electronic surveillance involved in this case."[85]

The lone dissenter was Justice Hugo Black. In many regards a liberal lion (and best friends with the privacy advocate Douglas), Black abandoned his usual liberal constructionist viewpoint, arguing that he could "see no way in which the words of the Fourth Amendment can be construed to apply to eavesdropping." Black noted that he would "willingly go as far as a liberal construction of the language takes [him]," but simply could not "in good conscience give a meaning to words which they have never before been thought to have and which they certainly do not have in common ordinary usage." Black refused to "distort the words" of the Fourth Amendment just to "bring it into harmony with the times." To do so would essentially make the Court "a constitutionally functioning constitutional convention."[86]

As with *Mapp*, the impact of *Katz* on law enforcement was tremendous. What the Court was really saying was that law enforcement—all law enforcement—didn't have the authority to make unilateral decisions concerning surveillance. Only judges—*scholars* of the law—have that right. From a constitutional standpoint it was a bold stroke by the judiciary. Ever since *Katz*, law enforcement personnel have had to apply for a court's permission to use electronic surveillance at the state and local levels, and those applications must be handled in the same way as applications for a search warrant. The judiciary must remain informed at all times.[87]

Stewart's phrase, "reasonable expectation of privacy," remains a cornerstone of privacy jurisprudence both in criminal and civil proceedings. Today, any charge of the violation of privacy is generally measured by that standard of reasonable expectation. It's the reason someone cannot claim a privacy invasion for being followed into a wireless store, but *can* if an individual tries to sneak a peek at the shopper's phone password while inside.

VII

Katz may have reined in law enforcement with its rigid warrant requirements, but government wiretapping remained a widespread phenomenon, and the nation still lacked comprehensive surveillance standards. Ironically, it was in this period that a strong attempt by the executive to rein in public and private surveillance backfired, accidentally legitimizing an expansion of the nation's surveillance apparatus.

This legitimization and expansion was due to a number of factors. The profit motive, of course, played a large role. During the military buildup for the war in Vietnam, surveillance-manufacturers-turned-military-contractors doubled their efforts to increase the sophistication of eavesdropping technology, just as the Department of Justice was making more federal funds available to state and local police forces for crime prevention. Privacy expert Robert Ellis Smith

smartly called this the "paint-it-blue syndrome," whereby contrac-
tors would develop new tech for the military, "paint it blue," and
then market that it to domestic law enforcement.[88]

"Paint-it-blue syndrome" flourished in a moment when the country was embroiled in both a fierce crime wave *and* a period of pronounced social upheaval. The nation's violent crime rate increased
126 percent between 1960 and 1969, just as the rise of rights consciousness emboldened antiwar dissidents, civil rights demonstrations, and race riots. These developments led congressional leaders
to allow law enforcement to use whatever tools they thought were
required to combat the increasing threats.[89]

Lyndon Johnson was not unsympathetic to the growing problem
with crime. Following his landslide victory in 1964, the president
appointed a Commission on Law Enforcement and Administration
of Justice and charged it with generating policy recommendations
that would allow Justice to start getting "tough on crime." Naturally,
wiretapping was a frequent topic of discussion among committee
members.[90]

Yet while the president was highly motivated to tackle the "war
on crime" head on, he also had a fierce ideological distain for eavesdropping technology. Less than a month after taking his strong position on the issue in the 1967 State of the Union, he requested passage
of his Right of Privacy Act—calling privacy "the first right denied
by a totalitarian system . . . [and] the hallmark of a free society."[91] It
was a bold course of action. Senator Long quickly introduced the
bill, proposing a total ban on all wiretapping and bugging except
when the president himself determined that national security was
involved. It would also prohibit the advertising, manufacturing, or
shipping of eavesdropping devices in interstate commerce.[92]

This was a critical moment in the history of American privacy.
Never had the country come so close to enacting such a strong measure to protect the privacy of its citizens from physical surveillance.
But while many in Congress agreed that some degree of legal standardization was required to regulate wiretapping, few believed that
an outright ban was desirable at such a troubling time. The crime
issue was simply burning too bright, and many in the Justice De-

partment were quick to express their reservations about limiting a useful crime prevention tool. One such figure, who wished to remain anonymous, argued that while he "might be old-fashioned," he thought "intellectual honesty is our best check and balance here [against government eavesdropping]. We must attract and train men of integrity. The courts still have the right to search and seizure. And the FBI doesn't prosecute or imprison people—they still have to go to court. That's another check."[93]

In response, a Justice Department official seemed rather insulted:

> Problems may arise when an agent is out of touch with the administration in some area, or when an area is vague or not understood. When you question the integrity of the individual agent, you're questioning the integrity of the entire administration. If you can't respect the integrity of the administration, who can you respect?[94]

It wasn't just the Justice Department that disagreed with Johnson's proposal. The president's own crime commission expressed reservations. In fact, the commission was about to submit a recommendation to Congress for legislation permitting electronic surveillance by all law enforcement, but backed down after Johnson's aides pressured them to stall. The result was a compromise between the president and the commission brokered by Under Secretary of State Nicholas Katzenbach, who saved Johnson from embarrassment by getting the group to agree not to oppose the administration's policies in its formal report if they were allowed to include a statement that electronic surveillance was a necessary weapon in the fight against organized crime.[95]

The final report, issued to Congress in February 1967, noted that "a majority of the members of the commission believe that legislation should be enacted granting carefully circumscribed authority for electronic surveillance to law enforcement officers." And so America's great moment for privacy was lost. The Right to Privacy Act of 1967 died in the Senate.[96]

Congress, though, seemed to be in step with public opinion. A national poll in 1966 asked respondents whether federal law should allow the FBI to use electronic surveillance to "catch spies and foreign agents"; 68.7 percent replied yes. When asked the same questions about "white slavers, dope peddlers, and riot leaders," the affirmative responses climbed to 70.1 percent. The only scenario in which less than half the responders agreed to wiretaps was in matters concerning the IRS (43.3 percent). This was still, after all, a nation born from a tax revolt.[97]

With Nixon on the rise, the Warren Court under siege, and violent crime still surging, Johnson's ban on electronic surveillance was proposed at a most inopportune moment. Perhaps the president tried to accomplish too much at once. Had he diverted his resources toward a ban exclusive to private eavesdropping or to nonfederal law enforcement bodies, things may have turned out differently.

On one side, law enforcement spokespersons and conservative "tough on crime" proponents asserted that certain types of crimes could simply not be solved without the use of wiretaps or bugs. They downplayed the sweeping power that surveillance practices give, and characterized agents as capable and qualified actors with commendable moral judgment that naturally check abuse. There was also the tactical reality that direct confrontation with criminals was dangerous and largely reactive, whereas listening to the phone calls and private conversations of suspects was a more elegant solution through which police could take the fight to the enemy by gathering evidence and choosing the most advantageous moments to make arrests.[98] Critics of wiretapping, on the other hand, some of whom were former law enforcement agents, argued that there was little evidence that electronic surveillance was necessary to catch criminals, whereas incidents of severe misuse were common and dangerous. Many cited Dash's *Eavesdroppers* and Orwell's *1984*. They called wiretapping the "lazy man's method," and charged that good police officers would never have to rely on such tools. The job could get done just as well without them.[99]

This debate was obscured by the lack of truly exhaustive data on the efficaciousness of electronic surveillance. That state and local law enforcement would not want to turn over such data is understandable, given the sensitive nature of such files and the potential dangers of being charged with improper surveillance use after the fact. Yet in the absence of such an investigation, all the public had to rely on was rhetoric and popular culture.[100]

The issue took another dramatic turn in the public eye in May 1968 when it was revealed that Martin Luther King Jr. had been the subject of extensive FBI surveillance throughout the 1960s.[101] The bureau initially monitored King under its Racial Matters Program, a series of investigations targeting organizations involved in racial politics. Then, in February 1962, Director Hoover, in pursuit of communists, deployed agents to find subversive materials and bug King's home and offices.[102] In a classic example of the privacy problems inherent to surveillance, the FBI did not find any evidence of communist infiltration, but the agency *did* uncover evidence that King was having extramarital affairs.[103]

The FBI went on to target King and other civil rights leaders in August 1967, with an operation against "Black Nationalist–Hate Groups." The FBI believed King might become a "messiah" capable of unifying black nationalists to start a full-fledged race war. According to a later Senate investigation, the impact of the FBI's efforts on King's credibility was "unquestionable."[104]

Before adjourning for the 1968 summer break, Congress devoted itself to the construction of a massive bill to address the growing crime rate and settle the surveillance question. Whatever impact the furor over the King wiretap revelations may have had on the pending bill was snuffed out with the assassination of Robert Kennedy on June 5. In such a climate, few were willing to speak against sweeping anticrime legislation. Emmanuel Celler (D-NY), chair of the House Judiciary Committee, warned that the Warren Court might hold much of the bill as unconstitutional if challenged, especially its lax surveillance provisions. These objections were quickly answered by House minority leader Gerald Ford, who fired back: "I refuse to concede that the elected representatives of the people cannot be the winner in a confrontation with the Supreme Court. Let this vote today be the battlefield."[105]

What ultimately became the Omnibus Crime Control and Safe

Streets Act was debated as Richard Nixon was securing the Republican presidential nomination with a powerful rhetorical thrust on the crime issue. Nixon was fond of referring to the United States as a "lawless society." The phrase was a cornerstone of his lengthy political tract, "Toward Freedom from Fear." With the Democrats floundering and the political right invigorated, proposals to severely constrain surveillance by law enforcement were easily painted as hampering the nation's quest to overcome lawlessness.[106]

With hindsight, we understand now that the skyrocketing crime rates of the late 1960s tapped into a complicated nexus of racial, gender, class, and generational anxieties. Many Americans felt the fabric of society was coming apart, which helped the law and order issue emerge at the forefront of political discourse. By 1968 law and order, according to Michael Flamm, "was the most important domestic issue in the presidential election and arguably the decisive factor in Richard Nixon's narrow triumph over Hubert Humphrey." Nearly twelve million voters had deserted the Democratic banner since 1964, many seemingly because they had come to believe that personal safety was a political priority.[107]

Johnson's War on Poverty and War on Crime were very much linked. Liberals insisted that the only truly effective way to fight crime was to attack root causes like poverty and unemployment. The argument helped to justify the War on Poverty in 1964, but soon left the Johnson administration vulnerable to conservative claims that the Great Society had worsened the epidemic of urban violence.[108] "Somehow, in the minds of most Americans the breakdown of local authority became the fault of the federal government," wrote a baffled Johnson in his memoirs. Implicit in his reflection was an acknowledgment that his administration had failed to convince many whites, particularly urban ethnic Democrats, that their fears and frustrations were being taken seriously.[109]

Conservatives, on the other hand, spoke with a clear "moral voice" on law and order. In the wake of Barry Goldwater's disastrous defeat in 1964, the issue helped to reunify the party. "In constructing a popular message with visceral appeal," notes Flamm, "conservatives maintained that the breakdown in public order was the result of three developments aided and abetted by liberals." First, the civil rights movement "had popularized the doctrine of civil disobedience, which promoted disrespect for law and authority." Second, the Supreme Court, in a series of decisions had been perceived by many as enhancing the rights of criminal defendants at the expense of law enforcement. Finally, the Great Society trumpeted by the White House "had directly or indirectly rewarded undeserving minorities for their criminal behavior during urban riots."[110]

By the summer of 1968, 81 percent of people polled believed that the system of law and order was broken. As one extreme example, most residents of the small and relatively peaceful community of Webster City, Iowa, listed street crime as their primary political concern despite their actual experience with crime being mostly limited to misdemeanors such as underage drinking.[111] This perception of crime as omnipresent hampered the search for an appropriate balance between privacy and law enforcement surveillance. The amorphous quality of crime, rights consciousness, and polarization gave cries for "law and order" an incredible potency. "Law and order," as a political platform, clarified a confusing assortment of dangers and disorder, explained their root causes, and implied a ready response.

Congress passed the Omnibus Crime Control and Safe Streets Act on June 19, 1968. It granted near blanket authority to federal and local law enforcement for electronic eavesdropping. Federal authorities were allowed to lean on wiretapping to investigate a wide variety of crimes outside the umbrella of national security, such as murder, kidnapping, narcotics, and racketeering. State and local police were provided with even more latitude. Physical surveillance on the local level was authorized for any crime deemed dangerous "to life, limb, or property, and punishable by imprisonment for more than one year." To privacy advocates, the contrast between the final bill and the original recommendations of the Johnson administration was absolutely startling.[112] Senator Hiram Fong (R-HI) lamented that the bill was "more appropriately described as the End to Privacy Act."[113]

At least the warrant controls imposed by *Katz* remained intact. Despite Ford's posturing Congress was not about to take such a brazen swipe at the judiciary. Title III of the bill provided:

> To safeguard the privacy of innocent persons, the interception of wire or oral communications where none of the parties to the communication has consented to the interception should be allowed only when authorized by a court of competent jurisdiction and should remain under the control and supervision of the authorizing court. Interception of wire and oral communications should further be limited to certain major types of offenses and specific categories of crime with assurances that the interception is justified and that the information obtained thereby will not be misused.[114]

There was some concern on the Hill that Johnson might veto the bill. He did not, but he warned Congress that it had taken an "unwise and potentially dangerous step" in allowing law enforcement to conduct surveillance "in almost an unlimited variety of situations." Indeed, he admonished:

> If we are not very careful and cautious in our planning, these legislative provisions could result in producing a nation of snoopers bending through the keyholes of the homes and offices in America, spying on our neighbors. No conversation in the sanctity of the bedroom or relayed over a copper telephone wire would be free of eavesdropping by those who say they want to ferret out crime. . . .[115]

On the surface, the law gave Johnson the ban he wanted on private sales of surveillance tech through interstate commerce. But it banned only devices whose "primary usefulness" was the surreptitious monitoring of conversations. This loophole merely required surveillance tech manufacturers to market their products—such as miniature recorders, transmitters, and pin cameras—as being "primarily useful" for less surreptitious purposes, such as home security or the safeguarding of one's professional holdings. In practice, this part of the act was rarely prosecuted. In the 1990s the average number of convictions for federal private surveillance violations was seven.[116]

The law was also silent on the very troubling rise of data-oriented privacy problems. As early as 1972, privacy scholar Arthur R. Miller called the Crime Control Act "a technological anachronism," an ill-conceived law that "completely ignores the reality of modern communications and computer science." We know that Miller's objections were right on the mark. The failure of the act to address the rise of "dataveillance"—the surveillance of individuals not through physical methods but by tracking the snippets of data they leave behind—showed a remarkable shortsightedness.[117]

Before signing the Safe Streets Act into law, the president was clear in his accompanying message to the republic that he would order the attorney general "to confine wiretapping and eavesdropping to national security cases only," regardless of what Congress wanted. But then Johnson would not remain president for very long.[118]

VIII

Richard Nixon's 1968 presidential campaign undoubtedly weakened US privacy protections at a critical moment. It is perhaps appropriate then that the events surrounding his eventual resignation from that office helped drastically reshape the public's perception of the surveillance state—especially operations undertaken under the guise of "national security." By 1974 surveillance technology found itself at the heart of a sensational and unprecedented constitutional crisis.

Like so many presidents who preceded him, Nixon, despite the folksy political veneer he was able to present to the public, was very much an intellectual. To preserve the details of his time in the White House for posterity, Nixon ordered the secret installation of numerous voice-activated recording devices throughout the building including the Oval Office, the cabinet room, most telephone lines, and even the Old Executive Office Building across the street. He was hardly the first president to record discussions in the White House. Franklin Roosevelt hid a microphone in his desk lamp, and nearly every executive since employed some kind of recording system for a variety of reasons—even after Nixon resigned. But it wasn't until Nixon that the public became aware of this tradition.[119]

Nixon believed the Constitution granted the executive unilateral authority to engage in electronic eavesdropping *outside* the White House whenever it identified a threat to national security. Upon assuming office he instructed Attorney General John Mitchell that regardless of the *Katz* ruling, warrantless surveillance of potentially "subversive" domestic groups was permissible under the Omnibus Crime Control Act and the "inherent powers" of the executive branch.[120]

The Supreme Court, noticeably offended, loudly rejected Nixon's approach in a 1972 case involving the bombing of a CIA building by white supremacists. In a unanimous decision the justices admonished the attorney general for failing to recognize that while unwarranted surveillance was not prohibited by the 1968 law, it most certainly was by the Fourth Amendment. The Court reminded the executive that unwarranted electronic surveillance was permissible only when combating "foreign" threats to the United States, and that regardless of any interpretation by White House counsel, the Bill of Rights still shielded all American citizens. The newest member of the Court, Nixon appointee William Rehnquist, felt quite differently about privacy rights than did his brethren, but he recused himself because while serving as assistant attorney general he had been the architect of Nixon's legal justification for unilateral surveillance.[121]

Two days before the Court sternly denied the existence of Nixon's "inherent power" to infringe on the privacy of whomever he wanted, operatives sent by the White House were arrested attempting to break into the offices of the Democratic National Committee at the Watergate Hotel. Their mission was to photograph confidential documents and install electronic surveillance devices to aid the president's reelection campaign. Seven men were convicted in short order, and while it took considerable time, Nixon's involvement in covering up the act brought about his downfall.[122]

The unraveling of the Watergate affair fell to the Senate Select Committee on Presidential Campaign Activities, known popularly as the Ervin committee—after its chairman, Sam Ervin (D-NC). The proceedings were a nationally televised media bonanza. After months of testimony, Nixon moved to neutralize the committee by citing "national security" considerations. This had been suggested by Nixon's senior advisors H. R. Haldeman and John Dean. When the president asked how he might hide their relationship with the Watergate operatives, Dean responded "you might put it on a national security basis," to which Nixon and Haldeman agreed. If they found themselves trapped, Nixon added, the response should be "the whole thing was national security." Dean agreed a second time, adding "I think we could get by on that."[123]

It wasn't enough. With help from Judge John Sirica and then special prosecutor Archibald Cox, the Ervin committee eventually got Dean to admit that several senior White House officials, the president included, attempted to cover up the break-in. The White House denied Dean's allegations, but when former White House deputy Alexander Butterfield admitted in open session that he was "aware of listening devices" installed in the White House, it didn't take long for *Eavesdroppers* author Sam Dash, acting as committee counsel, to realize that "there's a complete record of all these meetings" and nobody "had to draw a line to add it up."[124]

When pressed by Congress to turn over five tapes and specific documentation, Nixon reneged on a public promise not to invoke executive privilege and refused. The committee responded by producing a subpoena. The president wrote to the chief judge of the US district court that he had no intention of complying. Nixon's justification was something akin to that of Eisenhower when he faced off with Senator Joe McCarthy decades earlier. The executive branch certainly had a right to privacy because privacy is a necessary component of state function. But unlike the Eisenhower case, Congress could demonstrate a clear and compelling public interest in the materials they subpoenaed. They weren't just fishing, like McCarthy had been. Ultimately the Supreme Court rejected the president's claim to executive privilege and demanded, unanimously, that Nixon release all missing tapes. The president's political fate was sealed.[125]

As a privacy issue, Watergate placed eavesdropping technology at the heart of an unprecedented crisis of constitutional interpretation. Nixon's ideological position, like Rehnquist's, was that constitutional separation of powers bestowed upon the executive certain privacy rights or "privileges" that allowed it to withhold information from the other branches of government. Precedent dictated that this was especially true in matters where high-level communications were involved. Congress's position, on the other hand, ultimately that of the Court, conceded that the presidency had a well-established right to privacy, but that such a right was not absolute and could not be invoked to deny the judiciary access to evidence needed in criminal proceedings. Chief Justice Burger called attention to the damage that such a privilege could cause to citizens' constitutional rights:

> The Sixth Amendment explicitly confers upon every defendant in a criminal trial the right "to be confronted with the witnesses against him" and "to have compulsory process for obtaining witnesses in his favor." Moreover, the Fifth Amendment also guarantees that no person shall be deprived of liberty without due process. It is the manifest duty of the courts to vindicate those guarantees, and to accomplish that it is essential that all relevant and admissible evidence be produced.[126]

Watergate had structural and psychological impacts on American social and political notions of privacy. The nation may have been much more shocked by the president's intention to cover up his indiscretions than they were at the White House's attempts to eavesdrop on political opponents. Nixon was forced out due to his obstruction of justice, but wiretapping, while still weakly regulated under existing law, had also played a large role in that saga.

In many regards, Watergate was a new beginning in the larger national discourse on privacy and the surveillance state.[127] By the end of 1974, the public's association of Nixon's overtly duplicitous use of "national security" and "executive privilege" brought a vastly different political climate. More revelations of the extent to which the surveillance state had grown followed shortly.

In November 1974, over President Ford's veto, Congress added seventeen amendments to the 1966 Freedom of Information Act. Inspired by Watergate, these amendments "narrowed the exceptions accorded to federal agencies" and were based on the premise that executive secrecy was contrary to the national interest. Americans wanted less privacy in their government—and held that an informed citizenry was essential to the functioning of the political system. Perhaps the most drastic of these amendments authorized federal judges to review *in camera* information classified under "national security" and to rule whether this information should remain classified. Executive agencies could no longer, on their own, restrict public knowledge of their activities.[128]

Then, right before Christmas, with public interest in state surveillance still piqued, *New York Times* reporter Seymour Hersh alleged that the CIA, in violation of its congressionally mandated charter, had conducted a "massive illegal domestic intelligence operation during the Nixon Administration against the anti-war movement and other dissident groups in the United States." Ford ordered Secretary of State Henry Kissinger to report "within a matter of days" on the accuracy of the allegations. Kissinger delegated to CIA Director William Colby, who completed a comprehensive report before the year was up.[129]

Colby's report, shockingly, confirmed Hersh's charges. In response, Ford convened a commission, headed by Vice President Nelson Rockefeller. An invigorated press began digging into all aspects of the state's investigative functions, and soon a series of new surveillance abuses were uncovered. Details about the FBI's COINTELPRO, a program to harass and discredit "dissident" organizations, spilled out over 1975, as did revelations that FBI Director

Hoover had kept secret files filled with derogatory information on leading politicians and power players. Media outlets were justified in repeatedly asking: was privacy officially dead?[130]

These stories incensed many and increased congressional desire to learn more. State surveillance became a battleground issue in early 1975, which came to be known as the "Year of Intelligence." In January the Senate established a select committee (known as the Church committee) to investigate "intelligence activities carried out on behalf of the federal government." The end result was unsettling. In its hearings and publicized reports, the committee revealed a vast history of secret and often illegal surveillance activities stemming from essentially every investigative body of the executive branch. These abuses were hardly confined to the Nixon years but reached all the way back to the close of World War II.[131] Many were made possible through the invocation of executive privilege.[132]

Bombshell after bombshell was supplemented by an outpouring of documents released under the freedom of information and privacy acts, which in turn generated lawsuit after lawsuit, and then more bombshells during pretrial discovery procedures. Whistle-blowers and investigative reporting contributed additional troves of information.[133]

On August 17, 1975, Senator Frank Church appeared on NBC's *Meet the Press* and shared his views on intelligence gathering:

> It is necessary and important to the United States as we look abroad at enemies or potential enemies. . . . We must know, at the same time, that capability at any time could be turned around on the American people, and no American would have any privacy left. . . . If this government ever became a tyrant, if a dictator ever took charge in this country, the technological capacity that the intelligence community has given the government could enable it to impose total tyranny, and there would be no way to fight back because the most careful effort to combine together in resistance to the government, no matter how privately it was done, is within the reach of the government to know.[134]

Lock Johnson, a special investigator for the Church committee, recalls that "the Senate inquiry, and companion investigations by the House of Representatives and the presidential commission, rocked the intelligence bureaucracy like nothing before, even the humiliating defeat suffered by the CIA in the Bay of Pigs invasion of Cuba in 1961." Its leaders "spoke darkly of a struggle for survival."[135]

Frank Donner, who headed the ACLU's Project on Political Surveillance, observed that the reasons for the "attack on intelligence" are varied. "Certainly the self-questioning in the wake of the Vietnam War and Watergate contributed to the consciousness that the nation had betrayed the principles by which it had agreed to live as a people," notes Donner, "and the threshold exposure of the excesses of intelligence institutions, both domestic and foreign, in scope of targeting as well as in the use of illegal techniques, undermined the resistance to further investigation." In addition, FBI Director Hoover's death only a few years earlier, in May 1972, made it all the easier to call for sunshine and disinfectant.[136]

These developments, of course, had their detractors. Many believed the Senate intelligence investigation was an unwarranted exercise in self-flagellation, a witch-hunt leading to the destruction of the very intelligence capabilities that protected Americans' freedom and well-being.[137] Many leading media sources dismissed the Church inquiries as "witch-hunts." "In the zeal of some to reform and others to expose," concluded former president Nixon, "we have come very near throwing the baby out with the bathwater." Former CIA chief of counterintelligence James Angleton deplored the "now shaky and harassed CIA" and "the straitjacket Senator Church and the committee staff have brazenly tailored for it." The agencies "did engage in some illegal and ill-advised operations," admits Angleton, but "these are by no means altogether reprehensible when weighed in light of the national security considerations prevailing at the time." For David Atlee Phillips, the CIA had been, at worst, a "rogue mouse."[138] Some scholars also joined the counterattack. For these critics, the fashionable cry in the wake of the investigation was "unleash the CIA!"[139]

Yet intelligence officials *were* responsible for unlawful mail openings, break-ins, wiretaps, assassination plots, the interception of cables and telegrams, dubious covert actions, buggings, intelligence failures, and inefficiencies. "The Church committee did not invent these sad events," wrote Johnson, "horrors, in some instances. All too often some intelligence officials seem to consider themselves above the law."[140] In the view of historian Henry Steele Commager, "it is this indifference to constitutional restraints that is perhaps the most threatening of all the evidence that emerges from the findings of the Church Committee." The most important service of the committee was to enhance public awareness of the surveillance threat. This became the foundation of subsequent protective measures taken by Congress and the executive branch.[141]

Even more disturbing than the gigantic scope of the American surveillance state was its structure. There was little to no centralization and hardly any oversight. Surveillance was not a single mechanism that could be tweaked. Instead, it was a complicated and confusing realm filled with operatives who often acted on their own authority, choosing either to misinform or not inform their superiors, and with little to no accountability. This very obscurity had been the surveillance state's best defense mechanism; no one could protest what couldn't be shown.[142]

But none of this meant that surveillance tools would be dropped. As Donner writes, "intelligence as a means of containing movements for change, as a system of control, is simply too powerful a weapon in a highly conservative economic and social order lightly to be abandoned." Subsequent history has proven him correct.[143]

IX

Noticeably absent from most of the debates over wiretapping and bugs was discussion of the perils of visual surveillance. Visual eavesdropping technology, like closed circuit television cameras (CCTV), had been around since the 1940s, but early models were cumbersome and prone to glitches. It wasn't until the late 1960s that CCTV became a fixture in day-to-day life, and it would be decades longer before miniaturization made it ubiquitous.

CCTV technology was pioneered by the German engineer Walter Bruch in 1942, as monitors in Nazi V-2 rocket development. By 1949 small US government contactors began commercializing the technology for private security firms. In these early decades CCTV systems had limited range and low resolutions, required a dedicated monitor for each camera, and could broadcast only live feeds.[144] By the 1950s the commercial sector had found a host of uses for the "television eye." CCTV was used to check assembly line progress, guard warehouses, supervise prison cell blocks, watch gambling tables at casinos, prevent shoplifting, and punish employee theft. It *was* possible to record footage, but doing so was extremely cumbersome and required constant upkeep. The development of VCR technology in the 1970s provided a way to record and play back video footage with relative ease. By the end of the decade, most banks had CCTV cameras observing their customers and employees alike.[145]

The first incidence of law enforcement using CCTV as a crime fighting tool was in September 1968, in the small city of Olean, New York. In a bid to protect a Sears department store that had been recently robbed, the city installed eight cameras with overlapping views along its main business street, which then piped the images to the local police department. Within a year, more than 160 police chiefs from around the country visited Olean to inspect the system, along with a colonel from the US Army Weapons Division; Donald E. J. MacNamara, a professor of criminology; representatives of the Israeli Defense Force; and Major General Somjai Jenyavanija, head of Thailand's national police force.[146]

"The *New York Times* came here twice," said Mike Arnold, who came up with the idea and facilitated the installation. "They thought people would rise up and scream about it because of what they called 'Big Brother syndrome.' But the reporter was here for two weeks and he couldn't find anyone who was against it."[147]

Five years later the New York City Police Department installed CCTV in Times Square. While various studies have disagreed over the precise impact of public CCTV usage and crime *prevention*, few dispute the direct correlation between a proliferation of urban CCTV networks and the ability of police to more effectively prose-

cute criminal offenders. During the 1980s video surveillance prolif-
erated across the nation's public areas, as many municipalities saw
it as a cheaper way to deter crime than expanding police departments. But growth was much more pronounced in the private sector. CCTV cameras soon became a staple of the consumer experience. Whether pumping gas, shopping groceries, depositing money
in the bank, or picking out a dress, Americans were being surveilled.
A 1998 study by the ACLU of New York City counted over 2,300
surveillance cameras in Manhattan alone, "trained on public streets,
sidewalks, buildings, and parks."[148] By the end of the century few
bothered to take notice anymore.[149]

The presence of CCTV in public spaces serves as much to communicate the *image* of safety as it does to prevent crime. Retail
spaces, malls in particular, often make their cameras conspicuous
to consumers—in many cases customers are able to see themselves
entering a store on overhead monitors. Christian Parenti observes
that "this public display of surveillance deters theft by producing
correct and useful types of fear (fear of authority)."[150]

By the early 1990s CCTV and digital visual surveillance technology was welcomed into the home with the growing popularity of
the "nanny cam." As the duality of the name implies, parents could
position these cameras so that they could either observe their children while attending to other tasks (the camera *as* nanny) and/or
surreptitiously observe "the help" (the camera *watching* the nanny).
This technology gave rise to webcams, which enabled tens of thousands of people to turn the surveillance dynamic around completely
by broadcasting their own lives over the internet.[151]

The main reason Congress had failed to include any provisions
for video surveillance in the 1968 Omnibus Crime Control Act was
because no legislator, despite considerable evidence and a veritable
tidal wave of pop culture references, anticipated that video equipment would ever mature to a point where it would be small enough
and inexpensive enough to be used widely by individuals. Not until
the arrival of the actual year of 1984 did lawmakers begin addressing
in any meaningful way the privacy problems inherent to CCTV. That
year, privacy expert and US circuit court of appeals Judge Richard

Posner argued from the bench that "television surveillance is identical in its indiscriminate character to wiretapping and bugging." He said that the court would "think it a very good thing if Congress . . . [brought] television surveillance within its scope."[152]

After more feet dragging, Congress provided the bare minimum of regulation in 1985 by declaring that CCTV use required a warrant *only* if the video included audio recordings. Beyond that, television surveillance without sound remained beyond the reach of any congressional statute well into the twenty-first century. Prohibitions have been structured state by state, and most protect only areas in which people have an unequivocal "expectation of privacy" such as bathrooms, locker rooms, fitting rooms, and similar spaces.[153]

Congress did do a lot more to keep up with the evolution of audio communication technology in the 1980s. The Electronic Communications Privacy Act of 1986 amended the Omnibus Crime Bill to include warrant protections for cellular telephones, pagers, email, and data-line voice communications. These protections did not, however, apply to pen registers—the electronic devices that record all numbers called from a particular line (so people can check their phone bills for accuracy)—and so no warrant is required for law enforcement to procure records of whom citizens contact on these devices and when. We now call this information *metadata*.[154]

By the early 1990s it was becoming increasingly clear that the nation was careening toward an unprecedented communications revolution. The break-neck pace of technological evolution found federal law enforcement agencies feeling uneasy about their inability to eavesdrop on a host of new mediums such as conference calls, voicemails, integrated digital networks, and internet chat rooms. Toward the end of the George H. W. Bush administration, the FBI began pushing a "digital telephony" proposal that would allow it unfettered access to these forms of communication. The proposal was initially met with fierce resistance from civil liberties groups and Congress, but a version was eventually shepherded into law in large part because of strong support from the Clinton White House. There was very little in the way of constructive debate.[155]

The sweeping Communications Assistance for Law Enforcement

Act of 1994 was the first eavesdropping law to actively preempt the establishment of any communications technology that federal law enforcement could not access at will. It also gave law enforcement access to all "caller identifying information" including digits that a caller punches *after* making a phone call such as a voicemail password, an extension, or bank PIN. Each telecommunications carrier needed to "ensure that its equipment, facilities, or services [are] capable of isolating and enabling the government . . . to intercept, to the exclusion of other communications, all wire and electronic communications." As Robert Ellis Smith notes, the telephone companies initially balked, but when Congress and the Clinton administration authorized $500 million to offset retooling expenses, "the telephone companies swallowed hard and went along with the idea."[156]

The intellectual precedent established by the bill—that no digital communications should ever be impenetrable to governmental wiretapping—is one of the foremost challenges facing privacy advocates in the twenty-first century.[157]

X

When taken as a whole, the history of physical surveillance in the twentieth-century indicates that the American people have always regarded eavesdropping with a large degree of ambivalence. This is understandable, given the dialectical nature of surveillance and the related interplay between privacy and curiosity. But ambivalence is not the same as polarization. Few Americans have ever supported an outright ban on surveillance, and fewer still have agreed that eavesdropping should proceed unrestricted. There have even been times when Americans were united in their opinions regarding surveillance despite larger partisan fissures.

The Clinton-Lewinsky scandal of the late 1990s is a good example. While the nation and Congress were fiercely divided over the president's right to lie about a secret sexual encounter, the public's condemnation of Linda Tripp (who had secretly recorded phone conversations in which Monica Lewinsky revealed lurid details of Clinton's indiscretions) was significantly less split. Tripp's actions violated established societal norms, in that she recorded intimate private telephone conversations without informing her friend *and* transmitted those recordings to a larger audience. In this extremely polarizing moment, most Americans could agree that Tripp was in the wrong.[158]

It is no great revelation that Americans tend to prefer a semblance of balance between the competing values of privacy and surveillance. Among the larger obstacles toward achieving this balance has been the absence of any definite criteria that public and private actors could apply when comparing claims for disclosure with claims for increased privacy. What we have has come mostly from the judiciary, but only through vague legal terminology such as "probable cause" and "reasonable expectation of privacy."

Given the revelations of the mid-1970s, it is clear that more regulation was needed at the federal level, though Congress has largely failed to provide it. But perhaps it is wrong to view legislation as the key to achieving equilibrium. Bureaucracies certainly foster and profit from the flow of information yielded by surveillance, and so it is logical to think that a democratic society could leverage the popular vote to force those bureaucracies to rein it in. But privacy, as a societal phenomenon, extends well beyond the legal and political realms. And so the criteria required to balance it with the societal benefits of surveillance should encompass more than just politics. A social movement might work just as well.

One such solution would place a strong cultural emphasis on fostering a civic-minded consciousness about privacy and surveillance. Most private and government surveillance conducted in the 1950s was done in secret, but when Americans began talking openly about privacy from a variety of perspectives in the 1960s they were more likely to question the circumstances surrounding it, and those conducting it were more likely to be challenged.

Another solution might be to better channel the profit motive to the benefit of privacy and those who want to protect their communications. Scientific countermeasures to surveillance like "scramblers" and radio frequency "jammers" were a rather underdeveloped commercial market in the twentieth century, despite the public's desire for privacy. Laws passed in the mid-1990s constrained them even further. This conversation seems to be changing in the twenty-first century with the increasing popularity of privacy-enhancing technologies.

But we should not be too optimistic. Westin, writing in the 1960s, argued that science and privacy together "constitute twin conditions of freedom in the twentieth century." Thirty years later public and private surveillance had become a fixture in daily life. People have grown largely apathetic to being watched. And legally speaking, a license to invade privacy is rather easy to qualify for. And so the history of American surveillance in the twentieth century is ultimately a story about a society whose surveillance capacities grew at an exponential rate—grew so fast that its regard for privacy couldn't keep pace.

5

BIG IRON AND THE SMALL GOVERNMENT

Privacy and Data Collection, 1933–1988

I

In early 1963 a crew of workers contracted by the federal government installed an IBM model #7074 computer inside a "starkly antiseptic 40-foot room" just east of Martinsburg in the rolling West Virginia hills. The machine was a rental, leased at a hefty $4,000 per day. IRS chief Mortimer Caplin was confident the increased efficiency it brought to tax collection would far outweigh the cost.[1]

But when news spread that the IRS was upgrading from paper files to computers, cartoons in the press began depicting bleak Orwellian scenes of taxpayers being spied upon by mechanical brains, while domineering machines with long eerie tentacles weaved in and out of living rooms, banks, and the US Treasury. *Popular Science* reported that "as far as the IRS is concerned, your personality, history, and spirit . . . will be reduced to magnetic specks on a single reel about the diameter of an LP record," and predicted that soon large corporations would also plug into "Big Brother 7074." *Time* magazine kept the *1984* theme rolling months later, lamenting that "today's Americans are a submissive lot" compared to previous generations who would have "shrieked with rage" as these new "big grey machines in Washington" took the nation a step closer to "computerized Big Brotherhood." Amid the clamor, many probably found themselves agreeing with the sentiment expressed two years earlier by Representative James Oliver (D-ME), who when asked about the growing use of computers in government statistics responded simply: "it's my impression that these machines may know too damn much."[2]

II

Privacy's next counterweight—large-scale data collection or "Big Data"—dates back to the earliest years of the republic. In Article I, Section II of the Constitution, the framers made America the first nation to legally demand a *regularly* scheduled enumeration of citizens. Counting people wasn't a new idea, of course. Nations have acquired, refined, and made use of data about those they govern since antiquity—rarely without some measure of difficulty. But it was two later developments—the introduction of mainframe computers in the 1950s (known affectionately as Big Iron) and the expansion of the New Deal welfare state—that are most responsible for elevating the privacy problems of Big Data to a position of overwhelming social, cultural, and political concern.

As the bureaucratic structure of the federal government expanded throughout the twentieth century in the interest of public welfare, the amount of information it collected naturally grew exponentially. In some instances, all a federal office required of its applicants was a name, date of birth, and current address. But in most cases, to engage with the state also meant relating more personal details like financial information, criminal history, marital status, medical history, and level of educational attainment. By the late 1930s, almost every taxpaying American had a government issued number that was exclusive to them.

Prior to the widespread use of computers, federal offices like the Internal Revenue Service, Social Security, and the Department of Education and Welfare each maintained its own catalog of records. Big Iron made it possible to streamline this data. Made the data much easier to access, cross-reference, and share. Very quickly, people in the tech community grew excited by the wondrous possibilities Big Data had to offer and began considering the creation of a centralized national "data bank grid," where each American would have a single comprehensive "digital dossier," to be a foregone conclusion. "It is as inevitable as the rail, telephone, telegraph, and the electrical power grids that have preceded it," wrote one statistician in the late 1960s.[3]

They were right. And it is here, in the late 1960s, where the history of Big Data starts to accelerate. The first proposals for a national data center reached Congress as early as 1965. Supporters argued that the digitization and centralization of government records would make social welfare more efficient, less expensive, and therefore more effective. But others expressed fears that such a center would mark the end of privacy and give rise to the age of the "computerized man." Opponents painted those in favor as dangerous technocrats who ignored human values in pursuit of efficiency. The Senate, politically cautious and technologically naïve, rejected the idea.[4]

But the victory proved a hollow one for privacy advocates. The commercial sector had begun to see the potential of Big Data—not just the increased efficiency it could bring but also the profits targeted marketing could yield. As information technology grew more sophisticated, federal agencies continued to collect data and began sharing their files more openly among themselves and with private companies. Yet in the wake of Watergate, concern over data sharing turned to shock while a number of public and private organizations began investigating the precise nature of public and private recordkeeping. What they uncovered was quite troubling: over a thousand databanks were sharing and storing information about the private lives of millions. Worse, oversight of them was disturbingly unclear. All agreed that existing law was wholly inadequate to protect privacy rights in the face of rapid technological change.[5]

Public and private interests that engaged in data collection fought back. Increased privacy protections and oversight, they argued, would inhibit efficiency and be economically wasteful. They were remarkably effective, even as Congress passed the Privacy Act of 1974, which defined the rights of access to information held by federal agencies and placed restrictions on the collection, use, and disclosure of personal information. Problem was, lawmakers failed to conceive of privacy as something beyond an "individual right." As a result, the Privacy Act offered minimum protections for information privacy and was rife with loopholes and ambiguous language. Also, while certainly providing *some* protections for data privacy, the law instilled into the American consciousness big data's growing permanence in our daily lives.[6]

In subsequent years federal offices exercised one of these loopholes and began a series of welfare fraud investigations using Big Iron to audit government records and search for irregularities. This practice of computer matching, or "data mining," took different forms but generally involved cross-referencing millions of names and social security numbers from one agency with those of another to identify inconsistencies that might suggest fraud. Hundreds were prosecuted as a result; agencies estimated that they had saved taxpayers millions of dollars.[7] Advocates of computer matching gained a powerful ally in President Reagan, who from his earliest days in office trumpeted data mining as a powerful tool to eliminate waste and inefficiency across "big government."

But data mining also lacked balance and proper safeguards, and the process soon encumbered thousands of Americans who were not swindling their government. Cases of mistaken identity were quite common and led to wrongful arrests, unwarranted employment terminations, obliterated credit scores, and the accidental refusal of medical benefits to eligible citizens. Numerous privacy problems and constitutional questions arose. Claims of Fourth Amendment violations were frequent, as were charges that individuals had almost no dominion over information about them, had limited access to it, and could therefore not challenge its accuracy or limit its dissemination. These arguments almost always incorporated Orwellian imagery — asserting, as one writer put it, that the "technology of privacy invasion" had moved "from the realm of science fiction into the world of public policy."[8]

The big lesson to be learned from all this: the aspirations of New Deal liberalism and the welfare state played the greatest role in the unprecedented expansion of data *collection* in the United States, and attempts by fiscal conservatives in the 1970s and 1980s to rein in "big government" and the "nanny state" that brought the greatest increase in the *aggregation, processing,* and *sharing* of that data. The conservative ascendency of the 1980s, particularly the Reagan administration, expanded the practice of information collection that began with the liberal triumphs of the 1930s. Computer matching was done in the name of efficiency, free enterprise, and "small government." From there, powerful private interests who benefited from access to government data aided the effort considerably.[9]

Large-scale data collection changed over the second half of the twentieth century as access to sophisticated data processing technology was increasingly democratized. The earliest computers were so expensive and so cumbersome to maintain that only large organizations with vast resources could maintain them — government agencies, banks, telecommunications companies, and the like. As computers became more and more affordable, large-scale data collection became much more inclusive — putting greater pressure on privacy. Because the democratization of data was messy, confusing, and tricky to regulate, privacy advocates found it increasingly difficult to establish clear and effective protections against the improper circulation and misuse of personal information. In the absence of all-inclusive "omnibus" privacy laws that were embraced by most other countries, the legal system settled for sectoral or "patchwork" remedies.

The privacy debates of the 1980s did yield some valuable compromises, but even implementing privacy protections has been problematic since regulating computer matching effectively legitimized it. America soon had a de facto national government database and the weakest privacy protections of all the advanced democracies.[10] And this was before the internet changed everything, aggregating impossible volumes of personal information in ways that still aren't completely understood. As America stood on the cusp of the internet age, it was wholly unprepared for what would come next.

III

One of the funnier stories to come out of America's first census is the tale of Roger Waite, the calamity-prone census taker from Vermont who was brought to a boil by the unforeseen hardships of his post. His letter of resignation was succinct, but the fellow had a head for imagery: "Sir: I beg to report that I have been dogbit, goose-pecked, cowkicked, briar-scratched, shot at, and called every 'fowel' that can be tho't of. I have worked 12 days and made $2. I have had enough and I beg to resign my position as census taker for Crittenden Township." In 1790 Waite had to ask only six questions on behalf of the new republic, all of them purely demographic. But despite the absence of any financial inquiry, many perceived the census as an affair linked to taxation, and sporadic pockets of resistance quickly formed throughout the nation. Some went with the silent treatment, some gave false names, others opposed on religious grounds. A census taker in rural Pennsylvania was killed.[11]

It would be wrong to call the public's opposition to the first American census a movement. It was more an uncoordinated series of knee-jerk reactions employed in a variety of places for a variety of reasons. The young government, fulfilling its constitutional obligation, successfully collected and processed information regarding almost four million of its citizens. And again, nations have acquired, refined, and made use of data about those they govern since antiquity—usually with some measure of difficulty.

The founding fathers understood that if their experiment with representative democracy was to function correctly, the United States would need some understanding of its numbers. Beyond measuring representation for the states, the government was mostly interested in assessing its potential military and industrial strength. Placing a census requirement in the first article of the nation's Constitution speaks to their sense of urgency. With Article I, Section II, America became the first country in history to require a regular periodical enumeration of its inhabitants.

Exactly how to do a census fell to the first Congress, which appointed marshals across several districts with instructions to start counting on the first Monday in August 1790.[12] The marshals' assistants, America's first census takers, asked six questions: name of the head of the household; number of free white males older than sixteen; number of free white males younger than 16; number of free white women; number of other free persons; and number of slaves. They were paid $1 for every 150 persons counted in country districts or every 300 persons in cities and towns. Any marshal failing to file his returns with the government by September 1, 1791, would be severely fined. The final number came in just shy of four million inhabitants.[13]

Washington and Jefferson both expressed skepticism at that figure, suspecting that many people had "understated to the deputy marshals the number of persons in their families."[14] They had reasons to be suspicious. The original census rosters included such unlikely citizens as Joseph Came, Peter Went, and John Sat, as well those alliterative delights, Comfort Clock and Constance Cathole. Joining them on the roster of blatantly phony appellations were hundreds of others, including Joseph Crackbone, Ruth Shaves, Web Ashbean, Sarah Goosehorn, Moses Rainwater, Mercy Cheese, Unity Tallowback, Lookinbill Barnthistle, and Sussannah Beersticker.[15]

However frustrating (and hilarious) this was, a proper census has strong implications for the public good. Alexander Hamilton noted that the census ought to provide "an opportunity of obtaining the most useful information for those who should hereafter be called upon to legislate for their country," which would "enable them to adapt the public measures to the particular circumstances of the community."[16] Hamilton wasn't alone. Only months before the 1800 census was to begin, President Jefferson lent formal support to a brief presented to Congress by the American Philosophical Society that advocated making the enumeration "a vehicle for ascertaining sundry facts highly interesting and important to society." The proposal called for a significant increase in the number of questions to create "a more detailed view of the inhabitants of the United States under several different aspects" in order to "ascertain more completely the causes of which influence life and health, and to furnish a curious and useful document of the distribution of society." The ambitious plan was largely ignored by Congress, but the official questionnaire did expand to thirteen questions.[17]

With few exceptions, every successive census has asked more questions than its predecessor. In 1850 the federal government created a centralized bureau to make the process more efficient. In the process it greatly expanded the scope of its inquiry to include the name of every free person living in a household as well as information concerning agriculture, education, commerce, manufacturing, and other topics to gain, as Congress put it, "a full view of the pursuits, industry, education, and resources of the country."[18]

For the first sixty years of the census, all of its information had been publicly posted to give people a chance to correct errors. But in 1850 there was too much information—as well as widespread reports of census takers misusing the information for personal and professional gain. The secretary of the interior, Thomas McKennan, was forced to issue a statement warning of legal repercussions for any assistant marshal who participated in the unnecessary exposure of private information "with reference to business and pursuits, and other facts relating to individuals, merely to gratify curiosity, or the facts applied to the private use or pecuniary advantage of the assistant."[19]

The census hit a methodological brick wall in 1880 when the famous Gilded Age surge in immigration swelled the population by almost a third. Gathering and processing information about fifty million inhabitants took almost eight years, at exorbitant cost. As waves of huddled masses continued to come, many in Congress began to fear the 1890 census could not be finished before it was time for the 1900 count.[20]

The bureau's salvation came in the form of technological innovation. Months before the 1890 census, Herman Hollerith—civil engineer, mathematician, graduate of the Columbia School of Mines, and recent hire of the census bureau—began developing an electric counting machine capable of processing information collected on punch cards. According to privacy scholar Frederick Lane, Hollerith was inspired by the "design and operation of a mechanical weaving system developed by Joseph Jacquard, a French silk waver and inventor," and also by "railroad conductors using a similar method to keep track of which passenger was supposed to be sitting in each seat." To keep freeloaders in check, the conductors would punch holes in tickets to indicate qualities like gender, build, hair color, and other distinguishing physical characteristics.[21]

Hollerith's contraption was essentially a mechanized feeding device that relied on a series of strategically placed pins. As the pins fit through various combinations of holes on the individual cards, they touched off a small amount of mercury that sent an electrical charge to a corresponding counter and tabulated the information. The census board recognized the machine's potential almost immediately and instructed its deputies to gather census information on customized punch cards. The new machine finished the 1890 census in just under three years. Though distrusting press outlets claimed accuracy had been trumped by speed, Hollerith's invention became the government standard for processing of large amounts of data. The bureau later claimed that "through the adoption of this system a much more complete presentation of the statistics of population was made than any preceding census."[22]

Hollerith had such faith in his invention that he decided to go into business for himself, founding the Tabulating Machine Company (TMC) in 1896. TMC received the contract for the 1900 census and was also approached by various foreign governments, including those of Russia and much of western Europe, for their own enumerations. Then, in 1905, Hollerith's relationship with the census bureau turned sour. He stubbornly refused to make improvements on his original design, and when the bureau tried to manufacture its own machines he sued, citing breach of patent. When the lawsuit was ultimately dismissed years later, Hollerith decided to sell TMC to a New York business firm in 1911 for a seven-figure profit. He soon became head of a new organization, the Computer Tabulating Recording Company (CTR), which after Hollerith's retirement in 1921 fell under the management of Thomas J. Watson. Watson renamed the company the International Business Machines Corporation (IBM).[23]

IBM's meteoric rise was largely due to the federal government's increasing need for data processing as it expanded the welfare state. As the New Deal was creating a slew of new federal agencies, the government became one of the company's best customers. The Social Security Administration in particular kept almost all of its information on punch cards, and by 1943 it had acquired almost 100 million records. IBM remained at the forefront even as the technology for large-scale information collection continued to evolve. Punch cards gave way to magnetic tape in 1946 with the advent of the mainframe computer. Memory capacity swelled. Processors clocked speeds previously unthought-of. Eventually workers hauled filing cabinets out of government offices, to be set out for garbage collection.[24]

IV

The vast storage and processing needs of the postwar federal government made it a pioneer in the development of electronic data processing. In 1951 the first commercial mainframe computer, the UNIVAC I (developed by an IBM competitor), was installed in the Census Bureau. In the early 1960s Big Iron created for the Department of Agriculture a sophisticated and centralized personnel recordkeeping and reporting apparatus dubbed MODE. That machine was responsible for cutting checks to more than 100,000 employees. Next came the Veterans Administration, which installed a centralized personnel system called PAID to handle various tasks such as paying benefits, keeping employee records, and searching for redundancies. By 1966 twenty-two agencies had installed mainframe computers to store and access information on the public and approximately 1.5 million federal employees.[25]

While there was little public apprehension over the influence of computers on personal lives in the 1940s and 1950s, that changed in the early 1960s. Voices in the technology community began to voice concerns over a lack of privacy safeguards. Two books, Vance Packard's *The Naked Society* and Myron Brenton's *The Privacy Invaders*, both published in 1964, were among the earliest attempts to call attention to the unchecked expansion of computerization. Packard argued "the expectation that one has a right to be let alone—the whole idea that privacy is a right worth cherishing—seems to be evaporating among large segments of our population."[26] Nevertheless, the more popular argument was that government recordkeeping needed *greater* coordination and efficiency. Ironically, even as the nation was becoming embroiled in bitter struggles over rights consciousness on numerous fronts, computerization was paving the way for new and enticing kinds of analysis that promised a more comprehensive picture of exactly how inequality played out along lines of race, class, age, and gender.

Alan Westin, a pioneer of privacy studies, authored two books that paid special attention to data collection. Westin defined privacy as "the claim of individuals, groups, or institutions to determine for themselves when, how, and to what extent information about them is communicated to others." He advocated moderation and pragmatism, noting that while privacy was important, the Orwellian imagery used by its advocates was largely inappropriate as most who supported computerization were not tyrants but well-meaning actors caught up in an "exciting challenge" to "know more about the factual universe than had ever been possible before." He also noted that data collection clearly required some kind of regulation in the face of technological development, but that the role of policymakers must be to provide a *balance* between privacy and computerization.[27]

In their zeal for social justice, many academics began to complain that government recordkeeping wasn't as efficient as it might be. Data were scattered across dozens of agencies, collected on an inconsistent basis, and largely inaccessible to any single group of researchers. Because cross-referencing data took weeks if not months, statisticians felt the lack of centralization was an unnecessary obstacle that stifled Big Iron's true potential. In 1965 a three-year study of federal data management by the American Economic Association advocated creating a centralized national data center, drawing on the records of the Census Bureau, the Bureau of Labor Statistics, the Internal Revenue Service, and the Social Security Administration.[28] Opposition was fierce and immediate. A special subcommittee of Congress was tasked with investigating the privacy problems that could be raised by such a center.[29]

The first House subcommittee hearing dealing with the computer and invasions of privacy convened in 1965 and dug in on the national data center proposal the following year. As concerned as they were about privacy, they were a bit dazzled by the technology too. "Today the computer is a central figure of our society," opened Representative Frank Horton (R-NY), "the increasing rate at which it will change our lives exceeds the imagination, exceeds even the imagination of the computermen who foster it." The first witness called was author and sociologist Vance Packard. "Consider how many 12-digit numbers can be added in 20 seconds," testified Packard, getting to the heart of the matter. "With a pencil, the answer is two. With an adding machine, 10. With a computer, 160 million. The rate of change is astronomical. This change is upon us already. It is here."[30]

Advocates for the data center launched their arguments from a number of flanks. Some argued the proposal wasn't really that revolutionary; the government already collected, organized, and published vast amounts of data in response to both state and public demands. Most leaned heavily on the notion of *efficiency*, citing the "inadequacies [of an] over-decentralized statistical system" that corresponded to obsolete methods and wasted millions of federal dollars. Statisticians argued that the center would secure important historical records and improve the general quality of government files.[31]

Others positioned themselves as champions of the public good, noting that it was "becoming increasingly difficult to make informed and intelligent policy decisions on such questions in the area of poverty as welfare payments, family allowances, and the like, simply because we lack sufficient 'dis-aggregated' information." John Macy Jr., chair of the US Civil Service Commission, argued that for proper decisions to be made on the public welfare, his agency would "require the use of information across departmental boundaries," which would then free his staff from mundane data-related tasks and "liberate the manager to give his mind to greater scope of creativity."[32]

Despite the array of persuasive arguments, the data center's supporters were simply outgunned. Opponents raised a number of poignant and effective privacy objections that drew heavily from the well-established symbols of popular literature and science fiction. Central to many was the image of the "Computerized Man."

The metaphor was so powerful and so readily apparent that, in 1966, subcommittee chair Cornelius Gallagher (D-NJ) used it to open proceedings, describing a protagonist "stripped of his individuality and his privacy. Through the standardization ushered in by technological advance, his status in society would be measured by the computer, and he would lose his personal identity. His life, his talent, and his earning capacity would be reduced to a tape with very few alternatives available."[33] One sociology professor later showcased the metaphor:

> 1984 is only 18 years away. My own hunch is that Big Brother, if he ever comes to these United States, may turn out not to be a greedy power seeker, but rather a relentless bureaucrat obsessed with efficiency. And he, more than the simple power seeker, could lead us to that ultimate of horrors, a humanity in chains of plastic tape.[34]

The *1984* image is certainly engaging but also, at its core, an inadequate simplification. The more substantive arguments from privacy advocates moved away from the realm of fiction toward concerns about the permanence of the data collected, the lack of context associated with a computer printout, and the dangers of an inescapable past.[35]

"As we pass through life we leave a trail of records, widely distributed and generally inaccessible—except with a great deal of effort and diligence," noted Paul Baran, a computer expert from the Rand Corporation. He and others tried to draw attention to the privacy problems associated with information *aggregation*. Information gathered in small scraps and later assembled into a single file generally doesn't include each piece's context. Thus, a subject may be revealing more than intended, even as a later interpreter is seeing more than is actually there. "Human beings" argued Baran, "by their day-to-day need to make decisions using totally inadequate evidence are prone to jump to conclusions when presented with very thin chains of inferred relationships." A Yale Law professor put it another way:

> Information gets less reliable the further away it is from the source. . . . If somebody wants to come and talk to me about a

student, inside of 10 minutes they get an idea of what I'm like and they get an idea of the way in which I talk about people. But a machine does not know those things. So when I say "unsatisfactory" because the man talked back to me, the machine only knows that this man is unsatisfactory. It does not know anything about me. Maybe it is I that is unsatisfactory and not the student.[36]

Representative Horton thought "pigeonhole" was the best verb to describe the phenomenon. Packard, when he testified, preferred alliteration and dehumanization: "Most of us applaud the automated processing of peaches. But does it follow that we should applaud the automated processing of people? I think not."[37]

Privacy advocates made the most of the dangers of automated knowledge. Some witnesses spoke of the machine's inability to make allowances for early errors or indiscretions. One testified about a friend's son who was unable to get a job at several department stores, despite character references from his minister, scoutmaster, principal, and chief of police, because his name was in a file of known lawbreakers. It turned out the young man had been caught stealing a $2 fishing line when he was thirteen.[38]

In this case and others, Reich made a similar argument about the effects of automation on hiring, claiming that anybody smart enough to be hiring others in a great organization would likely reject any job application that came with a computerized report showing *unsatisfactory* in any regard. Without any context, most employers would see a computer's negative assessment and simply move on.[39]

Other witnesses predicted economic hardship for the millions of people whose credit status was shaped by computerized data collection. Packard testified about an acquaintance who discovered, by accident, that his local credit bureau listed him as having been the target of three lawsuits for failure to meet financial commitments. The first was a "five dollar scare suit back in the 1930s over a magazine subscription he had never ordered." The second was a disagreement over legal fees that was amicably withdrawn. The third was a lawsuit he himself had filed — and won — against a client for nonpayment of services.[40]

The ACLU's John Pemberton continued this line by taking aim at the frequency of inaccurate information in digital dossiers. "The great bulk of information about an individual is not gathered as the result of inquiries by skilled Government security investigators," he wrote to the subcommittee. "Rather, it is often acquired by Government employees of poor judgment, by private agencies, credit unions, insurance companies, and businesses. . . . Once an unreliable bit of information makes its way into a file it forms an indelible mark."[41]

Privacy advocates stressed that there was an inherent *moral* component to the idea that a person's history, fragmented sloppily across digital tape, could never die. The notion of an inescapable past was somehow un-American. Cornelius Gallagher (D-NJ) argued that information collection "strikes at the core of our Judeo-Christian concept of 'forgive and forget,' because the computer neither forgives nor forgets." Others drew from popular historical memory: "America's frontiers were largely settled by people seeking to make a fresh start. . . . The Christian notion of the possibility of redemption is incomprehensible to the computer."[42]

V

Let's unpack once more. Orwellian predictions aside, many of the opponents of the data center demonstrated an excellent command of the privacy problems at play. Foremost was the problem of *aggregation,* the understanding that information collected in snippets over time can be reassembled to present an image of an individual that is grossly inaccurate and potentially damaging. Aggregation has little respect for context, just facts, and as Solove is fond of noting, "the whole is greater than the sum of its parts." Aggregation run amok, especially if the information gathered is somewhat inaccurate, can have a significant impact on one's job prospects and creditworthiness. It can also make one a prisoner of his or her recorded past.[43]

Others called attention to *secondary use,* the unethical sharing of information that was handed over for one purpose but used for another without approval. Information isn't merely out-there or not-out-there. People share specific pieces of information with some that they choose not to share with others. *Dehumanization* was also invoked quite frequently. The idea that increased data collection and processing on a massive scale would reduce the multifaceted reality of what it means to be alive—the full spectrum of human emotion and interaction—to a sort of digital dossier. Individuals would have less control over their own self-narratives. If taken to a logical conclusion, there would eventually be two entities for every individual: the flesh-and-blood citizen and the digital citizen that exists wholly as a composite of decontextualized snippets of information.[44]

The data center's opponents were not Luddites. They knew it was foolish to ignore the trend toward centralization, and they knew that technology only ever follows one trajectory. But they also knew that until very recently, privacy's strongest safeguard had been fragmentation. They desired a balance between technological developments that made sharing easier and the privacy of individuals. But the eighty-ninth Congress rejected the motion for the data center mainly because they still didn't know enough about the privacy problems it raised. Most believed that real protections would be achieved only through a coordinated effort by industry professionals, not Congress, an idea articulated by Senator Sam J. Ervin the following year: "The computer industry, the data processing experts, the programmers, the executives—all need to set their collective minds to work to deal with the impact of their electric systems on the rights and dignity of individuals."[45]

VI

Privacy advocates won the day, but the practice of collecting and sharing personal information nevertheless grew exponentially in the late 1960s and early 1970s in both the public and private sectors. Corporations used data gleaned from government agencies and other companies to make direct marketing campaigns more sophisticated. Insurance companies and investigative employment firms actively pursued every bit of data they could get to make informed assessments. And government agencies continued to lean on Big Iron to manage their records.[46] One especially visible manifestation of the growing power of big data came with the rise of the credit card industry.

The rise of the credit card industry is generally attributed to the organizational foresight of Frank McNamara, who founded the Diners Club Charge Card Company in 1950 as a way to spare people the embarrassment of not having enough in their wallets to cover a dinner check. For a $5 annual fee (and a charge between 4 and 7 percent to merchants), subscribers could leave their cash at home and just say "charge it" at hundreds of restaurants, car rental companies, hotels, and florists in the New York and Chicago areas. The Diners Club Card also appealed to businesses looking for a more efficient way to tabulate expenses. It was an almost instant success, spawning an entire industry of competitors.[47]

Credit bureaus had been around since the early twentieth century—established by banks and merchants to determine terms with new borrowers. But it wasn't until the 1950s and the rise of the credit card that bureaus assumed a central role in day-to-day life. Each of the approximately 2,000 bureaus at that time was only as good as the information it held about its consumers, and data collection and processing procedures varied greatly among them. Most relied on public records such as civil and criminal cases along with basic residential and employment histories, but each company interpreted its information and the creditworthiness of its subjects differently. Privacy scholar Frederick Lane notes that in 1953 one bureau claimed it used its information to organize its files of delinquents into categories that included "loaders," or "women planning a divorce who stagger their husbands' accounts with a ten years supply of lingerie and jewelry."[48]

At its core, data collection is about "discrimination in determining precisely what actions are warranted to each member among large populations," according to privacy expert James Rule. With proper data, organizations can discriminate "who is worthy of credit, and how much credit should be extended" or discriminate between "individuals more or less dangerous to the public order," or as to "who is liable for tax assessments or social insurance benefits, and to what extent." In the private sector the reward for effective discrimination is profit.[49]

By 1960 consumer debt in the United States had risen to over $51 billion — almost ten times what it had been at the end of the war. With so much on the line, credit bureaus began relying on computers to access and share information in the hopes of identifying potentially bad investments. Throughout the decade, the bureaus bought and exchanged consumer information with insurance companies, investigative firms, private companies, and the government — all with little to no oversight. Data processing expanded from the late 1960s into the 1970s through the increased *sharing* of aggregated data among interested commercial entities and government agencies. Public and private organizations facilitated symbiotic relationships across multiple sectors. Bank account information is of interest to credit card companies. Medical information is of interest to insurance companies. Tax returns are of interest to mortgage lenders. But as we have seen, not all information is good information. As the sector grew, more and more reports arose of reporting errors that brought disastrous consequences and alleged invasions of privacy.[50]

In March 1969 Mike Wallace of CBS News capitalized on the climate. He established a dummy corporation, printed up letterhead, rented a mailbox, and requested reports from twenty credit bureaus on people selected at random from the telephone book. Ten of them provided full reports without question. On the air, Wallace contrasted this information with footage of the executive director of the Associated Credit Bureaus of America stating that "credit reports were available only to legitimate grantors of credit who were checked by credit bureaus if they were not known to the agency."[51]

The outrage was proper and loud. Congress soon passed the Fair Credit Reporting Act in 1970, the country's first information privacy legislation. The law required credit agencies to let consumers check their personal reports for errors and established penalties for the unauthorized disclosure of information. A first step, but far from a solution. Many in the media and other public figures balked at the law's ineffectiveness. Sheldon Feldman of the Federal Trade Commission (FTC), which was tasked with enforcing the law, remarked that the legislation was rather "fuzzy."[52]

Despite the Fair Credit Reporting Act, insurance companies routinely checked with their customers' neighbors for information about perceived drinking habits, home life, and leisure activities. Private investigators and employment firms checked arrest records, tax history, and car payments. Credit bureaus sought out every financial transaction made by their subjects. And sales divisions pored over data to better identify prospective buyers. The overwhelming majority of the information collected was held and processed by Big Iron. And because it is cheaper to share information than to reproduce it, data continued to be exchanged and reassembled at an unprecedented rate.

Reports of privacy abuses remained frequent in the early 1970s, and the media began to expand their coverage of the problem. One Washington newspaper ran a story on the Retail Credit Company of Atlanta, which boasted over 38 million reports and was "to insurance credit investigations what General Motors is to the automobile." A number of former employees had just testified to Congress that they often used unverified records or concocted information that was placed in customer files. That information was then sold to credit agencies and other commercial entities who in turn shared it with the government.

The article told the tale of Mahlon Barash and his lovely wife Leah, who upon moving to the Arlington area were visited by an overly friendly woman who said she represented the neighborhood's welcoming organization. "The woman gave them free gifts and told them about local churches, schools, and stores," says the article, "she also managed to ask them about their income, estimated expenditures, number of credit cards, and occupations." It wasn't until twenty minutes later that Leah spotted the name "Credit Bureau Inc." (a Retail Credit Co. subsidiary) on a brochure the woman had. "My wife would never have let her in if we knew who she was," fumed Mr. Barash. "I got pretty hot about it the more I thought about it." When asked for comment, the FTC said it had already brought a cease and desist order against Credit Bureau Inc. after receiving similar complaints.[53]

Then there was the Medical Information Bureau (MIB), used by life insurance companies to determine an applicant's eligibility and premium. According to its executive director, MIB had almost 11 million files and was averaging 2.2 million new ones every year. In most cases, the data came unwittingly from consumers who had permitted a life insurance company to gain access to their medical records. The problem was, "seven hundred insurance companies pool such information with MIB. If they have found evidence that the consumer has alcoholism, sexual depravation, psychiatric problems, or a criminal record in his past history, that information is likely to go to the MIB." The piece mourned for a time when "people used to have control over those who felt the need to gather such data. . . . But those days are gone forever."[54]

Another report from the *New York Daily News* centered on a man it called "Brian McGraw," who in 1968 applied for a job at a large cosmetics firm. After the initial interview and testing, the sales manager informed him enthusiastically that he scored higher than any applicant ever and immediately offered Brian the job. He accepted, but was approached weeks later by a superior who told him to "come clean about the information on his job application." McGraw didn't know what the man was talking about, and the man offered nothing. Six months later Brian quit upon realizing he had somehow become the office pariah.[55] Two years later McGraw was about to accept another job when the company suddenly said someone had made a mistake. McGraw asked to look at all information they had that he didn't provide himself. The company refused. McGraw threatened litigation and was finally able to see that a credit reporting company had reported that McGraw had been dishonorably discharged from the navy and had been arrested for assaulting an old woman in her home. In fact, McGraw had an honorable discharge, and in the case of the woman, all charges had been dropped. Nevertheless, absent context he was a violent offender who preyed on the elderly.[56]

In the early 1970s books like Charles Fried's *An Anatomy of Values* and Arthur R. Miller's *The Assault on Privacy* contributed to a growing body of literature that looked to educate the public about the vast expansion of public and private databases in recent decades. Between the data center proposal and 1974, there were twelve hearings in the Senate, fifteen in the House of Representatives, and two joint hearings in Congress on privacy and data collection. One 1971 Senate subcommittee identified 858 databanks used by 54 federal agencies operating with little to no oversight.[57]

In 1973, Miller helped author a substantial report by the Department of Health, Education, and Welfare (HEW) that declared that "under current law, a person's privacy is poorly protected against arbitrary or abusive record-keeping" and that there existed an urgent "need to establish standards of record-keeping practice appropriate to the computer age."[58] This report is an important document in the history of American data collection. Strikingly prescient, it expressed a number of concerns, not the least of which came in its conclusion that a "common language" already existed to a considerable extent in the use of an individual's social security number as a "standard universal identifier."[59]

The social security number. Because almost every American had one, it was much more reliable as a universal identifier than, say, a person's given name or driver's license number. Social security numbers were originally conceived during the New Deal exclusively to meet the organizational needs of the Social Security Bureau, but the federal government was instrumental in expanding its use of social security numbers in the decades that followed as identifiers of workers, taxpayers, students, servicemen and -women, and pensioners—to name a few. As Igo points out, few Americans were concerned about the potential for government intrusion when the social security program began. "Never simply a means of tracking citizens," she writes, "the social security number, by remapping the population via exclusions and benefits, helped to produce a specific kind of national citizenship, one that carried substantive privileges." The HEW report rebuked the establishment of any standard universal identifier in the United States "now or in the foreseeable future" and recommended "against the adoption of any nationwide, standard, personal identification format, with or without the SSN, that would enhance the likelihood of arbitrary or uncontrolled linkage of records about people, particularly between government or government supported automated personal data systems."[60] But that identifier already existed.

The report concluded with a number of legislative recommendations. Packaged as a "Code of Fair Information Practice," it rested on certain basic safeguard requirements:

- the prohibition of secret data-based record keeping systems,
- a clear process through which individuals could access their own records and correct errors,
- a means for individuals to prevent secondary use or information obtained for one purpose being used for other reasons without the subject's consent
- and a requirement that any organization engaging in information collection take appropriate measures to prevent the misuse of the data they hold.

Again and again the report made the point that the law was simply not keeping pace with technology and that legislation would be required to regulate the practice of recordkeeping.[61]

The report was among the first of a handful of government statements that looked to define informational privacy protections on a broad level. It shows that lawmakers and policy advisors were aware of the threats posed by data collection, and the principles they outlined clearly defined certain "nontrivial" privacy interests. This is significant when we consider the United States, unlike most nations, never adopted an omnibus information privacy law that applied to the private sector. But the report also never questions the purposes for which data are collected; neither does it provide an adequate explanation for when and how individuals might be able to simply "opt out."

The unfolding of the Watergate scandal heightened the public demand for tougher privacy legislation. Congressional consideration of privacy issues continued. In many ways the Watergate scandal was about transparency or a lack of privacy concerning institutions. But when Americans learned that the Nixon administration sought personal data collected by federal agencies to track and harass political enemies, many also came to believe that while big data was likely a permanent aspect of what it meant to live in a computerized world, some regulation of that data was required to prevent abuses of power.

Hearings on five separate privacy bills were convened in the House and the Senate in 1974. In them, most privacy advocates raised concerns similar to those voiced in the HEW report. They also summoned the familiar barrage of problems associated with information aggregation, insecurity, secondary use, and the growing reality of an inescapable past. Unlike the data center hearings in the mid-1960s, privacy advocates were able to draw from an array of boots-on-the-ground privacy invasions thanks to newspaper stories and descriptive complaints submitted by congressional constituents.[62]

One anecdote submitted to the Senate illustrated perfectly the dangers that lay at the intersection of private and public data collection. An army intelligence agent was ordered by a superior to investigate the bank, arrest, and court records of a private citizen. He later learned that the investigation was a personal favor for an executive of a private company with whom the private citizen was employed. After the agent reported the incident to a Pentagon official, the superior was disciplined. It was too late to help the subject of the search, though, who by then had already been fired. "What people writing to Congress fear most is the uses to which this technology may be put by men of little understanding but great zeal," argued the *Columbia Law Review*. "They know that, applied to unlawful or unwise programs, computers will merely absorb the follies and foible of misguided politically-minded administrators."[63]

Many also said that if the Senate really cared about protecting privacy, it would establish a federal privacy board with authority to enter public and private spaces where information was held, hold hearings on potential violations, exercise subpoena power to compel the production of stored files, and have the power to order an organization to cease and desist information practices the board deemed unwarranted.

By 1974 the political climate over privacy was too conspicuous to ignore—Congress would need to act with some form of national legislation. And while both chambers debated the bill that would eventually become the Privacy Act of 1974, those who profited from data collection also had their say. And their arguments proved remarkably effective. Many argued the dangers of data-related privacy invasions were too vaguely defined and that Congress was essentially gearing up to legislate on a problem it still didn't understand. This line of attack was complemented with claim after claim that too much restrictive legislation would inhibit government efficiency and create an undue financial burden on private businesses.

Interests like the American Life Insurance Association (representing 367 companies and accounting for over 90 percent of the legal reserve life insurance in the United States) pressured Congress to recognize a distinction between public and private information collection and stressed that any restrictions passed by Congress should apply only to government agencies. Like most of their allies, they argued the Fair Credit Reporting Act had already addressed the privacy problems of private sector firms and that "the proposed controls on private information systems" were entirely unrealistic— "so broad as to cover virtually every information practice and procedure that is a part of almost every business transaction," and that their effects would be "extremely burdensome . . . not only unfair, but unworkable."[64]

The American Mutual Insurance Alliance (speaking for more than 100 property and casualty insurance companies) seconded these claims: the Fair Credit Reporting Act was entirely adequate, and the new bill "would impose many rigid, novel, and complex requirements which are inappropriate to the conduct of business . . . and would thus create severe difficulties." Another association of 256 credit executives argued "the regulations being proposed to protect each individual's right to privacy are very extensive and we suspect they will be extremely costly to administer" and were clearly unwarranted "based on the very limited consideration which has been given to personal information systems in the private sector." Two hundred and sixty literary publishers, who routinely shared mail-order "book club" subscriber information, argued that unless direct mailing companies and mail-order book clubs were explicitly exempted, "the impact on the publishing industry could be devastating." The California Bankers Association noted a lack of proper scope, claiming the proposed bill would "apply to the 'mom and pop' corner grocery store as fully as it does IBM."[65]

Perhaps surprisingly, government agencies were just as quick to take up arguments of efficiency and undue hardship. Carle Bakke of the Department of Commerce recommended that the business community be exempt "on the basis of but meager knowledge of the cost and consumer service effects of so wide a sweep." He also called for a number of exemptions for government databanks and strongly rejected the proposal for a federal privacy board in the name of avoiding a "top-heavy government." The comptroller general argued that restrictions on government data sharing would create an organizational nightmare and "adversely affect the audit work of the General Accounting Office." The Department of Defense, unsurprisingly, asserted that any privacy bill would need to include a number of exemptions in the interest of national security and to prevent "heavy administrative burdens" within the Pentagon. Even the HEW opposed a privacy board on grounds that it "would be extremely complicated, costly, and might uselessly impede desirable applications of computers to recordkeeping."[66]

When the dust settled, both houses of Congress agreed on a compromise measure that became the Privacy Act of 1974. The law gave individuals rights of access and correction to computerized federal files and placed restrictions on the collection, use, and disclosure of personal information by federal agencies. Congress punted the question of restricting commercial interests by establishing a Privacy Protection Study Commission to investigate the issue more thoroughly. The act didn't apply to records kept by state and local governments or those of private companies, and no federal privacy board was established.[67] This was, some might say, an unsurprising and aggressively American solution.

The 1974 Privacy Act was inadequate in many ways. Priscilla Regan, among the foremost experts on American privacy legislation, believes it "encompassed the minimum protection that was advocated at the time" and "would not have been seriously debated and passed in 1974 without the Watergate revelations." Igo notes that while it was "designed to empower citizens, the Privacy Act would wind up stoking fears that the United States had become a full-fledged surveillance society in which individuals were outmatched from the outset" largely because of their inability to identify exactly who had their information and what it was being used for. The law's failure to create a privacy board bogged down its implementation. Despite a provision intended to regulate the use of social security numbers, it did little to curtail their use as a common universal identifier. It also contained a rather large loophole with a "routine use" exemption, which allowed the disclosure of personal information by federal agencies if the purpose was compatible with the purpose for which it was collected. A 2006 survey by the Department of Justice found that "the Act's imprecise language, limited legislative history, and somewhat outdated regulatory guidelines have rendered it a difficult statute to decipher and apply." All in all, a poor response to one of the most significant—and growing—dangers to privacy.[68]

So why was the final bill's reach so limited? The arguments of the data interests were certainly effective, but a lot of the blame falls on the privacy advocates themselves. By framing privacy again and again as an "individual right," they ignored larger social considerations and left themselves exposed to charges of myopia. This is perhaps understandable given the tendency of postwar American activism toward rights-based individualism. Mary Ann Glendon argues that "our individual rights—laden public language . . . tend to be presented as absolute, individual, and independent of any necessary relation to responsibilities." Privacy advocates failed to position privacy as a larger societal right essential to the progress of any free civilization. Regan aptly regards this limited conceptualization as a chief detriment to the formulation of effective privacy law:

> An individualistic conception of privacy does not provide a fruitful basis for the formulation of policy to protect privacy. ... [We need] a logic for a new way of thinking about privacy — not solely as being important to an individual but also as having broader social importance. This social importance derives from the fact that privacy is a common value in that it is shared by individuals, a public value in that it has value to the democratic political system, and a collective value in that technology and market forces make it increasingly difficult for any one person to have privacy unless everyone has a similar minimum level of privacy.[69]

Again, in the short time between the data center debates and the 1974 Privacy Act, information processing systems were becoming more democratized and information itself more mobile and profitable. When lobbying against the data center in the mid-1960s, privacy advocates were essentially squaring off against an archetypal force that was singular and identifiable. As such, they were operating within well-established social and cultural parameters. But by 1974 privacy advocates were facing a much more varied array of interests. The rhetoric employed by these interests, particularly their economic arguments, complicated the terms of the privacy debate and proved simply too much of an obstacle to overcome.

The shortcomings of the Privacy Act are, in a way, quantifiable. A decade after its passage (in 1984!) incidents of data sharing between federal agencies reached into the billions—thanks largely to the advent of federally sanctioned computer matching and the Reagan administration's pursuit of "small government" under the banner of bureaucratic efficiency.

VII

Data mining compares two or more sets of digital records, typically in search of points of overlap. Some prefer the term *cross-referencing*. This could, in theory, be done manually with paper records, but that is burdensome if not impossible with a large number of files. Only Big Iron is capable of processing millions of files on a reasonable timeline.

As one example, in 1976 an agency checked federal employment records against welfare records in the Chicago area. An agent keyed in the parameters of the search on a mainframe, which soon spat out what those in the matching business call raw hits. This case produced 4,600 raw hits—government employees who were potentially receiving welfare benefits improperly. Checks for errors and other mitigating factors cut this list in half. Perhaps someone transposed the digits in a social security number. Perhaps a federal employee adopted a child with a physical impairment and is eligible for welfare benefits to cover medical expenses. Those still on the list are dubbed solid hits, and in this case their contact information was passed on to the FBI. Hundreds of state and local prosecutions followed. Some were exonerated for reasons not found in the initial vetting. Many were caught swindling the system and convicted of fraud.[70]

The success of that investigation gave rise the following year to the first major computer matching program at the federal level. Dubbed Project MATCH, the search ran federal payroll files against the welfare rolls of eighteen states, New York City, and the District of Columbia. Invoking the "routine use" exemption of the Privacy Act, the goal was to identify government employees who were fraudulently receiving Aid to Families with Dependent Children (AFDC) benefits. In a few months Project MATCH, under the direction of HEW Secretary Joseph Califano, identified 7,100 potentially suspect individuals. After vetting, most offenders were simply informed that they would no longer be receiving payments. Searches in DC alone saved taxpayers more than $330,000 in wrongful payouts. Criminal indictments were brought against fifteen HEW employees. Five had their cases dismissed, four had their charges reduced to misdemeanors, and six pled guilty to felony charges. None served prison time.[71]

Project MATCH had as much to do with rooting out administrative waste as it did with rooting out fraud. The HEW office reported that only 21 percent of the losses from AFDC were attributed to blatant deception. Opponents charged that the matching program was clearly inconsistent with the Privacy Act's "routine use" exemption and labeled it a dangerous "fishing expedition." Not an entirely farfetched idea given that Project MATCH generated so much information that agency officials didn't have the manpower to follow up every lead.

Califano hailed Project MATCH a success and quickly advocated more matching programs at the federal level as well as in the private sector. Numerous figures at all levels of government were very receptive to the idea. In 1979 Congress required the states to conduct wage matching for all AFDC recipients. The practice gained a reputation as a money saver that enhanced bureaucratic efficiency, and throughout the 1980s states implemented their own matching programs for a variety of purposes. Over time, the searches started bringing private institutions into the fold—particularly large employers and banks.

Computer matching meshed well with the Reagan administration's policy rhetoric and proved a useful weapon in its crusade to eliminate bureaucratic waste and the "cancer" of inefficient "big government." Amid the 1980 campaign Congress had passed the Paperwork Reduction Act, tasking the Office of Management and Budget with promoting the effective use of information technology in the federal government and data sharing among federal agencies. Soon after moving into the Oval Office, Reagan established the President's Council on Integrity and Efficiency (PCIE) to support both objectives. The council pushed hard for the establishment of a long-term computer matching project and began developing a federal inventory of computer matching software packages.[72]

On the surface it might appear that data matching suited supporters of "big government" as well as it did fiscal conservatives. It was, after all, making the welfare state more efficient and less prone to fraud. But it's important to understand the social and political ideologies of those who were most responsible for this implementation. Data mining was promoted largely by a political movement that made dismantling federal social welfare a cornerstone of its legislative agenda. The New Right, as some call it, was hardly uniform. But overall, Republicans of the 1980s campaigned on drastic cuts in public assistance, food stamps, environmental agencies, and taxes, calling for a "New Federalism" that would reduce the size and scope of the federal government and devolve regulatory authority to the states. "Government," President Reagan said again and again, "is not the solution, it's the problem."[73]

From 1980 to 1984 federal and state agencies conducted over 533 computer matches that touched on more than 7 billion individual records. In that span, the frequency of searches nearly tripled.[74] As the practice grew more frequent, computer matching secured an air of legitimacy. In 1982 Reagan formed the Private Sector Survey on Cost Control (widely known as the Grace Commission) to study federal management problems and recommend ways to eliminate waste. The commission concluded that the federal government had "significant deficiencies from managerial and operating perspectives, resulting in hundreds of billions of dollars of needless expenditures." The methodology it used certainly drew heavy fire from Democrats, but a majority of those in Congress embraced the findings and responded by passing the Federal Managers Financial Integrity Act of 1982 and later the Deficit Reduction Act of 1984. The first act required periodic evaluations of federal programs to reduce fraud, waste, abuse, and error; it was instrumental in encouraging information sharing. The second act required states to establish information systems containing wage and income information from employers to verify an individual's eligibility for welfare and other benefits. The Office of Technology Assessment (OTA) later noted that that particular law "called for the most far-reaching data sharing at both the state and federal levels."[75]

One of the larger computer matching programs of the Reagan years was the ominously named Project SPECTRE,[76] which matched social security benefit payments against Medicare death records. The HEW reported the search led to $7.5 million in recovered social security funds and a total of $25.3 million overall. Of the original 8,300 raw hits, 5,263 people were found to have been improperly collecting dead people's benefits. Most payouts were simply terminated. Criminal indictments were brought against sixty-two individuals suspected of willful deception, of whom twenty-four received felony convictions. Another HEW search later that year uncovered 47,000 people who had been receiving federal employee disability compensation but were in fact working other jobs, which should have made them ineligible for the benefits.[77]

As 1984 loomed, numerous press outlets began running stories about computer matching and its privacy implications. Those with an eye for irony were quick to note that a vast expansion of federal information practices was being conducted under the banner of "small government." A new series of congressional hearings to address the privacy concerns of computer matching convened with numerous privacy advocates on hand. Senator Cohen of Maine, addressing a 1982 subcommittee, argued the purpose of the hearings was "not to reject matching as a concept or the computer as a management tool for discovering fraud, mismanagement, and waste," but to question "whether we are going to fall down and pray to a false god in a sort of idolatry."[78]

The arguments raised by privacy advocates again took a variety of lines. Cohen expressed concern that "in matching there has been a focus upon the low-income scale of our society and none on some of the more major fraudulent practices involving hundreds of millions of dollars that also take place." The OTA noted there were "numerous procedural guidelines for computer matching, but little or no oversight, follow-up, or explicit consideration of privacy implications," and that "Congressional actions seem to be contradictory" in "placing restrictions on agency disclosure of personal information" while subsequently endorsing computer matching. A number of opponents also raised Fourth Amendment objections. Priscilla Regan points out that while the Supreme Court has interpreted the amendment as prohibiting searches that are overly inclusive in nature — like dragnets — "many people who have not engaged in fraud or are not actually suspected of criminal activity are subject to the computer search. This raises questions about the presumption of innocence, as reflected in Fourth and Fifth Amendment case law." There is also the question of computer matching's potential conflict with the equal protection clause "because categories of people, not individual suspects, are subject to computer matches."[79]

John Shattuck of the ACLU was particularly vocal in a 1982 Senate hearing on governmental affairs, decrying the perils of information sharing:

> The sad fact is, Mr. Chairman, that once a computer match has taken place, any person whose name appears as a raw hit by virtue of turning up on two unrelated computer tapes is often presumed to be guilty of the wrongdoing that is under investigation.[80]

Shattuck related a number of anecdotes to illustrate the potential dangers of information sharing to the individual citizen. One involved a middle-aged New Yorker who was denied a taxi license because a computerized report showed that when he was thirteen years old, in Massachusetts, he had been temporarily placed in a mental institution. What the files did not show was that he was an orphan and the institution was the only home that state authorities could find for him due to overcrowding.[81]

Then there was the Massachusetts woman who had her Medicaid benefits terminated while in a nursing home after a computer match of welfare rolls and bank accounts revealed that she had an account above the Medicaid assets limit. It turned out the woman's bank account contained a certificate of deposit for a local funeral director, to be used for funeral expenses, which should have been recognized as an exempt resource under federal regulations. The computer match did not reveal this fact. "In the last 5 years," argued Shattuck, "I think the [Privacy] Act has been so thoroughly circumvented by the executive branch that, frankly, it can no longer be seen as an effective safeguard against computer matching abuses."[82] Other privacy advocates attacked the efficiency argument by calling attention to the fact that many state and federal agencies used confusing methods to measure the savings yielded by computer matching—the actual fiscal benefits were still unclear. A 1986 OTA report did indeed find there was "no firm evidence . . . to determine the costs and benefits of computer matching." Measuring the cost-benefit analysis of computer matching has always been a murky business, in part because agencies never operated under uniform standards of fiscal measurement.[83] These sentiments, however widespread, did little to curb the expansion of federal computer matching between agencies and the private sector. The *efficiency* line proved markedly effective while the privacy problems, however legitimate, were too vaguely formulated to register as a pressing societal concern.

One reason the efficiency argument was so enduring is its common sense. Even now, tech companies that facilitate the centralization and cross-referencing of data held by commercial organizations are immensely profitable because they can root out redundancy, streamline day-to-day operations, and save millions. So when government figures like Richard Kusserow, the inspector general for the Department of Health and Human Services, testified that Project SPECTRE had saved $44 for every $1 spent on investigations, or that California's investigation of AFDC payments cost $6,000 but yielded $200,000, many saw no reason not to take him at his word.

Advocates of computer matching could make the case for a larger societal good that privacy advocates had failed to. For every taxi driver denied a license, proponents of matching pointed to droves of welfare cheats—people who undermined programs that were enacted in the spirit of the public good. Cases of government employees who were delinquent on child support payments, doctors who received Medicaid and Medicare payments after defaulting on their federal student loans, and people who claimed social security benefits in the name of dead relatives became useful symbols in the Reagan administration's political rhetoric of waste, small government, and "welfare queens" in "gold Cadillacs." In their own way, those offenders legitimately caught by computer matching contributed to weakening privacy and undercutting the tangible benefits of social welfare.

The 1980s were not an entire loss for privacy advocates. Congress passed the Computer Matching and Privacy Protection Act (CMPPA) in 1988, which required "agencies to formulate procedural agreements before exchanging computerized record systems" for purposes of computer matching and established data integrity boards within each agency to serve as a checks on program supervisors. But many privacy advocates view the law as a sort of a Trojan horse. Computer matching was finally regulated, but the law mainly reflected issues of cost-benefit, due process, and administrative efficiency—not privacy. Also, while the CMPPA required agencies to obtain at least two pieces of proof before cutting benefits and to notify people whose records were being matched, it also effectively legitimized computer matching as desirable, institutionalized the routine sharing of information between agencies, and created the de facto national data center that the Senate once rejected and that privacy advocates had been opposing for decades.[84]

VIII

The story of poor Roger Waite the census taker is charming because most of us, on some level or another, can sympathize with his molesters. Perhaps we would have treated him with a bit more compassion, but we also can't help but smirk at the success of these Americans who considered even the most basic aspects of their personal lives to be none of their government's damn business. Whatever our political views, our historical memory often frames the American Revolution as a story about the pursuit of limited government. We revere the founders in part because they created a system that was inherently distrustful of itself—inherently distrustful of powerful actors who would involve themselves too much in the quotidian affairs of citizens.

By the early 1990s, as the internet age loomed—an age in which the sheer volume of personal information collected and shared dwarfs everything that came before and has yet to be completely understood—the United States had failed to articulate the concept of information privacy in a way that might have led to effective policies and protections.

One large misstep can be found in the privacy advocates' improper use of symbols and metaphor. Orwell's *1984* is about a surveillance society. The story is indeed powerful, culturally resonant, and valuable when taking on issues of police surveillance and the freedoms of speech and association. But *1984* is inappropriate when discussing the actual privacy problems arising from information collection and data sharing. Some scholars of data mining say that a more apt metaphor is Franz Kafka's 1924 novel *The Trial*, wherein one Joseph K. is arrested by two warders "one fine morning" and finds himself up against a bureaucratic labyrinth impossible to navigate, in a powerful state that "uses people's information to make important decisions about them, yet denies the people the ability to participate in how their information is used."[85]

The tendency in the late twentieth century to lobby from a platform of rights-based individualism also played a large role in the overall failure of privacy advocates. By repeatedly positioning privacy as an *individual* right, privacy advocates unwittingly restricted their ability to package privacy as something essential to the greater good of society. This limited conceptualization left privacy weakened in the face of arguments that stressed the greater societal benefits of nationwide bureaucratic efficiency. As Solove points out, "when the law protects the individual, it does so not just for the individual's sake but for the sake of society. Privacy thus shouldn't be weighed as an individual right against the greater social good. Privacy issues involve balancing societal interests on both sides of the scale."[86]

Data collection, in its purest form, examines large groups of people. And so arguments designed to rein it in are best packaged not by focusing on individual harms but by calling attention to the common privacy rights shared by the entire group being examined. Every member of such a group is entitled to a minimum standard of protection to keep his or her information from being collected and processed in ways that the larger society deems inappropriate.

Establishing what, exactly, is an appropriate flow of information and what minimum standards should thus be applied is the responsibility of lawmakers *and* a vocal electorate. Again, the societal value of privacy is well established. It allows for meaningful participation in the democratic process not only for individuals but for political organizations and religious groups as well. It protects consumers from unfair discrimination in the marketplace—something that can have tremendous consequences over the course of a lifetime—by pushing against the larger trends of dehumanization that accompany the boiling-down of groups to a series of disparate facts and figures that have little regard for the capacity of individuals to grow and change. And it reinforces the foundational premise of American law that one must first be rightly suspected of wrongdoing *before* one becomes the subject of an investigation.

The privacy protections enacted by Congress throughout the twentieth century worked more to enhance the extension of data collection than they did to constrain it. By the 1970s most Americans had come to believe that the tide was simply too powerful to stop. Making data collection systems more open and more accountable in the interest of balance and fairness tends, according to James Rule, to "disarm public objections and streamline[] acceptance of the underlying practices . . . by establishing that any 'purpose' or 'need' for personal information justifies such monitoring." Indeed, privacy codes often "open the floodgates for unlimited extension [of these practices]." Privacy protections achieved through legislation, say some legal scholars, have largely served to "smooth the bumps and brush aside obstacles en route to a vastly less private world."[87]

The many wondrous benefits of data collection are well established. It allows governments and businesses to function more efficiently and effectively. It allows consumers greater personalized access to items they both want and need. It provides citizens with greater access to social welfare. And it allows social scientists—statisticians in particular—to achieve a greater understanding of the larger trends and obstacles present in American society. These benefits, and hundreds more, are what make data collection such a powerful competing interest to privacy.

The privacy advocates of the 1960s gained a measure of success largely because the threat to privacy was the familiar threat of those in positions of great power. As databases become more and more democratized, advocates came to face not just the government but a host of commercial entities with varying aims and practices, which made privacy problems more confusing, harder to articulate, and more difficult to address with policy initiatives. A powerful sense of helplessness had set in. So did a sense of inevitability. As big data became more and more profitable, the forces privacy advocates opposed were less and less grounded in familiar social and political traditions. Privacy advocates also found themselves in conflict with free-market ideology in general. This is still the case today—but then things are changing.[88]

6

SEX, MORALITY, AND REPRODUCTIVE CHOICE

The Right to Privacy
Recognized, 1961–1992

I

The word *privacy*, as a point of fact, does not appear in the Constitution. *Private* does. But only once. In the Fifth Amendment. And not even in the section on self-incrimination, which would seem logical, but at the very end where it says the government cannot take away a citizen's "private property" without just compensation.

Regardless, in 1965, after a decades long fight, the Supreme Court deemed that absence irrelevant when it overturned an arcane nineteenth-century statute prohibiting the distribution of contraceptives to any and all persons in the state of Connecticut—even if the recipients were married or could demonstrate a clear medical need. That the law would seek to regulate the behavior of married couples in their most private interactions was an idea so repellant to the justices of the Warren Court that it pushed them to declare that "specific guarantees in the Bill of Rights [contained] penumbras, formed by emanations from those guarantees that help give them life and substance," and that those guarantees "create zones of privacy." Any attempt to penetrate the privacy of the marital bed, according to the justices, conflicted "with a right of privacy older than the Bill of Rights—older than our political parties, older than our school system." The case was *Griswold v. Connecticut*.[1]

For all the various ways privacy has captured the attention of the public, whether from problems inherent to photojournalism, or public interrogation, or surveillance, or data collection, it was ultimately problems raised in context of *sexual reproduction* that inspired the justices of the Supreme Court to explicitly recognize the existence of a constitutional right to privacy.

II

Griswold was understandably a benchmark in the history of American privacy. By applying constitutional protections to what legal scholars would eventually call "decisional privacy" in sexual reproduction, the ruling pushed the limits of constitutional theory and laid the groundwork for the legalization of abortion in *Roe v. Wade* eight years later, and with it all the social and political backlash that followed. *Griswold* was not a contest between adversely aggrieved individual parties. It was the result of a carefully orchestrated litigation campaign that spanned decades. A focused undertaking designed to facilitate broad social change. Like other such legal campaigns it originated in a social movement, was a struggle passed down over generations, and often benefited from momentum generated by political forces that it did not entirely control.[2]

The ruling was a major victory for American privacy, but the campaign behind that victory was not waged by privacy advocates. It was waged by feminists and medical professionals. And so to understand the power behind this crucial moment, *Griswold* must be seen as part of a larger social and political discourse about two overlapping developments: the women's rights movement and sexual morality laws.

Gender-specific notions of privacy date to the early industrial age. As hundreds of thousands of artisans abandoned their home-based workshops to labor in factories, driven out by the cold economic realities of technological progress, the establishment of distinctly public and private "spheres" took hold in American society. In the nineteenth century, discussions of female privacy were rooted in understandings of feminine norms and peaceful seclusion in the private home or "woman's place." What Barbara Welter famously called the "cult of true womanhood." A century later that same discussion largely rejected the home as the domain of women and embraced reproductive rights, with a woman's "privacy" evoking a freedom to use contraception or have an abortion. It is no coincidence this transition occurred in the context of a new rights consciousness and the sexual revolution.[3]

The right to decisional privacy established in *Griswold* and *Roe* extends well beyond reproductive issues. Access to birth control helped to create new powers, new norms, and new expectations of self-determination among American women. "Decisional privacy," according to legal scholar and leading privacy expert Anita Allen, "must be recognized as one of the important remedies for the problem of sexual inequality and women's lack of meaningful privacy."[4]

The language of the "home" was crucial to this discourse. On the path to *Griswold* and *Roe*, feminists aligned the benefits of decisional privacy in contraception and abortion with women's ability to reject the traditional private sphere and morality laws imposed by patriarchal societies. By choosing not to have children, they argued, women could achieve more meaningful privacy in the home because they were freed from their traditional roles of nurturer and caregiver and "subjugation through confinement." When combined with the goals of employment and pay equality, decisional privacy could transform the home into a place where women could find the same comforts as men—a place that served as a haven with reliable opportunities for solitude, self-reflection, and selected intercourse with others.[5] In other words, they envisioned a full-fledged sexual revolution.

It is tempting to see this convergence as a classic historical example of how the social can inform the political: America's rapidly changing sexual norms influenced the decisions of the Supreme Court. There is further possible evidence: in the seven years between *Griswold* and *Roe* the Court also struck down state-level bans on obscene literature, overruled prohibitions against interracial marriage, and extended *Griswold*'s contraception rights to unmarried couples.

But we shouldn't overreach. A closer look at exactly *how* these cases were argued and decided, *Griswold* and *Roe* included, reveals that each was significantly anchored in heteronormative rationales. The crusaders, by design, argued in conservative terms. They may have achieved liberal victories, but the language and structure they used hardly embodied the rhetorical essence of sexual revolution. The most compelling evidence of this well-planned incrementalism is the Court's failure to explicitly recognize a right to "sexual privacy"—only "decisional privacy" in certain aspects of sexuality.[6]

Griswold and *Roe* undoubtedly established a legal bulwark for privacy in the United States. And for that alone they are significant. Yet, rather strangely, very little of the fierce social and cultural debates that followed *Roe* ever engaged the right to privacy on its own terms. Opponents of abortion, galvanized by a political right in transition, focused instead on "right to life" issues and grounded their rhetoric in terms of declining moral standards, fetal viability, and the rights (other than privacy) of the unborn. Abortion advocates, in response, began conflating decisional privacy with larger notions of liberty in constructing their "pro-choice" platform. Over time, pro-choice supporters spoke much more about their "freedom to choose" than they did their right to decisional privacy. When the abortion issue reached the Court again at the height of the culture wars in *Planned Parenthood v. Casey* (1992), both the public and the judiciary largely repackaged the issue as one of "liberty" rather than privacy. And so while the right to privacy ignited one of the most contentious issues in American social and political history, it strangely spent relatively little time at the center of that debate.[7]

III

One of the earliest American "invasion of privacy" cases ever brought before a court of law concerned a woman giving birth. In 1881 one Mrs. Alvira Roberts brought suit in a Michigan court against her obstetrician, Dr. John H. Lemay, and his associate, Mr. Alfred B. Scattergood. In attending to Mrs. Roberts while she was in labor, Lemay brought with him the "young unmarried" Scattergood to carry his lantern and instruments. Roberts and her husband assumed the young man was a medical assistant; he remained at their house for the duration of the labor and witnessed the delivery. At one point Scattergood reportedly took Mrs. Roberts's hand and restrained her "during a paroxysm of pain." When the couple learned later that Scattergood was a man "utterly ignorant of the practice of medicine," they were incensed that the doctor would allow an outsider to witness such a private affair in their home.[8]

The judge agreed. Finding for Roberts, he declared that "the occasion was a most sacred one and no one had a right to intrude unless invited because of some real and pressing necessity which it is not pretended in this case." Mrs. Roberts, he held, had "a legal right to the privacy of her apartment at such a time, and the law secures her this right by requiring others to observe it, and to abstain from its violation."[9]

While the right to privacy was slow to develop in American jurisprudence, state legislatures began passing laws to criminalize abortion as early as 1821. Prior to that, courts typically followed the centuries-old standards of English common law, which permitted all forms of abortion before "quickening" (the moment a mother could feel a gestating fetus move), typically around the sixteenth week of pregnancy. Early statutes were not primarily designed to make abortion a crime but to limit unsafe practices such as the use of poisonous elixirs, dangerous rituals rooted in superstition, and other types of quackery.[10]

The law was rarely used to enforce any sexual norms in antebellum America. Morality laws were few. And sexual expression was relatively fluid and flexible. Only after 1840 did laws prohibiting abortion began to get broader, become more restrictive, and grow teeth. Some, like those passed by New York in 1845, made abortion punishable at any time during pregnancy. The impetus for this expansion did not come from a desire to legislate morality but from a growing nationwide movement toward medical professionalization. As antebellum doctors pushed hard for improved professional standards and the elimination of unqualified practitioners, they sought to more fully regulate medical practice itself.[11]

By the late 1850s an interstate coalition of physicians launched a veritable crusade on the subject of abortion. Advances in biology and physiology had enlightened doctors to the reality that a fetus develops gradually. This changed the moral calculus of abortion for some doctors, but most still saw in abortion an issue that could unite physicians, strengthen professional societies by giving the field a clear goal, and legitimize their influence in the political sphere. These physicians were motivated, organized, and remarkably successful. By 1860 twenty of the thirty-three states had anti-abortion statutes. After 1880 abortion was illegal in every state except Kentucky, with some states imposing punishments not only for the abortionist but for the patient as well.[12]

It was here, in the Gilded Age, when legislation that denied reproductive decisional privacy took on a distinctly moralistic character and began to cover contraceptive devices. Much of the blame for this new infusion of morality can be pinned on the period's growing nativist movement. As cities began to swell with European immigrants, the social character of abortion and contraception changed. Many middle- and upper-middle-class white women used abortion to limit family size. "In the eyes of many contemporary physicians," writes political scientist Eva Rubin, "the acts of these upper-class women were inexcusable. They not only did not appreciate the seriousness of what they were doing, but by failing to have the proper number of native American offspring, they were allowing immigrants from Ireland and Eastern Europe to populate the country with their teeming families."[13]

By 1880 morality was a powerful aspect of the anti-abortion movement. Prosecutors were increasingly finding that judges and juries were more willing to convict in abortion cases than they had been. Most states allowed some form of abortion if there was compelling evidence that a mother's life was endangered by pregnancy, but many maintained outright bans. Connecticut, one of the most stubborn states, forbade even the advertising of any abortion or contraceptive device.[14]

Of course, abortions continued despite the proliferation of these statutes. The pressures faced by the newly pregnant are as old as humanity and do not easily relent before the law. Whether to address family size and spacing, health reasons, financial concerns, or a host of other concerns, many women still sought ways to free themselves from unwanted pregnancy. Reliable data on the frequency of abortion in the period between the Gilded Age and *Roe* are difficult to compile for obvious reasons. Estimates have ranged from two hundred thousand to more than one million a year. An influential study in 1962 estimated that approximately one million illegal abortions were performed annually in the United States. Another survey five years later estimated that an abortion was performed in America every ninety seconds.[15]

Whatever the true figure, illegal abortions, often performed by amateurs, led to a marked decline in medical standards and caused a significant amount of pain and suffering (so much for the drive for medical professionalization). Self-abortion, home remedies sold by amateurs and con artists, and back-alley abortions were all widespread and difficult to constrain. And abortion was not a subject on which most women could speak openly. The operation had become associated with sexual misbehavior and a lack of spiritual and personal character.[16]

In the broader history of infamous figures who wielded the law in their crusades against birth control and sexual immorality, a special place must be reserved for Anthony Comstock. Born, appropriately, in rural Connecticut in 1844, Comstock moved to New York City in the late 1860s. A devout protestant, the young man grew increasingly appalled by the sexual permissiveness he saw in the city's streets after sunset. It seemed to him that New York was teeming with prostitutes and pornography and that only a concerned and properly emboldened citizenry could stem the tide of its damnation.[17] Comstock began supplying the police with information for raids on sex trade merchants and, in the process, came to prominence with his anti-obscenity crusade. Comstock was particularly offended by explicit advertisements for birth control devices. The man said often, and loudly, that the availability of contraceptives alone promoted lust and lewdness. If he could stifle the contraceptive industry, he believed, he could bring about the city's moral salvation.[18]

Just shy of his thirtieth birthday, Comstock became the head of the New York Society for the Suppression of Vice (NYSSV). Established in 1872, the organization was financed by some of the wealthiest and most influential figures in New York society. "The power of these censorship organizations originated in the wealth and prestige of their members," notes historian Nicola Beisel. "More than one-quarter of the anti-vice supporters in Boston and New York were in the *Social Register* or were millionaires, while virtually all the rest were businessmen or professionals."[19] The moral crusader used their money to lobby the state legislature for laws criminalizing vices such as premarital sex and adultery. He also used it to lobby Congress.

In 1873 Comstock got his wish. Congress passed an act for the "Suppression of Trade in, and Circulation of, Obscene Literature and Articles of Immoral Use." Known popularly as the "Comstock Law," the statute's central purpose was "to prevent the mails from being used to corrupt the public morals." In practice the law cracked down on the distribution of information about or devices that caused abortion or contraception. Within a few months the term *Comstockery* entered the parlance as a synonym for prudishness.

Historically, morality campaigns often wrap themselves in rhetoric centering on the protection of children from sexual deviants. The era of Comstock was no different. Clinton L. Merriam, the New York congressman who introduced the anti-obscenity bill, appealed to the need to shield America's babes from obscene materials. "I am sure that this American Congress will not only give all the aids of legislation for the annihilation of this trade," he argued, "but that the outraged manhood of our age will place, in the strongest possible manner, its seal of condemnation upon the low brutality which threatened to destroy the future of this Republic by making merchandise of the morals of our youth."[20]

Comstock was appointed special agent to the US Post Office and given a broad range of powers to enforce the statute. He would hold the position for the next forty-two years. Comstock mostly targeted easy prey: mail-order services and low-rent shops that sold cheaply produced photographs of nude women. The defendants were typically poor and uneducated, and they often failed even to present a defense. At the twilight of his life, Comstock claimed to have successfully prosecuted more than 3,600 defendants and destroyed more than 160 tons of obscene literature.[21]

Comstock's impact on American morality law was unmistakable. By the turn of the century, twenty-four states had enacted versions of the Comstock Act, many of them more stringent. Over the years these Comstock Laws evolved and were repackaged multiple times, and prosecutions continued even as Americans became increasingly diverse and tolerant. *Griswold*, among other things, is credited with being among the final coffin nails for these outdated laws.[22]

But we mustn't be too quick to dismiss nineteenth-century censors simply as prudish Victorians. The issues they addressed — pornography, contraceptives, abortion, the corruption of children by indecency in art, literature, and popular culture — are enduring political concerns. The rhetoric employed in anti-vice crusades was powerful and, like many moral reform movements, drew heavily from claims that children were threatened by a sharp decline in national moral standards. Some of the more outlandish aspects of these claims remained powerful and recurrent well after the Victorians were all dead, as seen in the shameful use of "save our children" rhetoric throughout the anti-homosexual crusades of the late twentieth century.[23]

Comstock's conjoining of contraception and sin was instrumental toward galvanizing the women's movement. In 1916 Leta Hollingsworth argued that anti-obscenity laws, by forbidding the circulation of information about or devices that caused abortion and contraception, were "intended to force women to remain in their traditional roles of wives and mothers by compelling them to bear and rear children." The desire to curtail sexually explicit material was a natural outgrowth of the "separate spheres" ideology holding that the private realm, inhabited by women and children, needed protection from the public realm. But by obliterating any distinction between instructional literature and pornography, Comstock also enabled the movement to produce its first generation of birth control martyrs, whose imprisonment served as a powerful symbol that would embolden a counter-reform movement.[24]

IV

Resistance to Comstockian ordinances came in multitudes, perhaps none of them more aggressive than that of nurse/writer/educator/ suffragette Margaret Sanger, who debuted her crusade for reproductive choice in 1914 with the illegal publication of a monthly newsletter, *The Woman Rebel*. Sanger was actively picking a fight, hoping the newsletter would generate enough controversy to provoke a federal case. It didn't take long—her wish came true that same year, when the New York State's attorney charged her with four counts of violating the Comstock statutes. Ever smart and stylish in her defiance, in place of a legal defense Sanger wrote a sixteen-page pamphlet outlining her views and instructing women on proper methods of contraception gleaned from her professional medical experience.[25]

"There is no need for anyone to explain to the working men and women in America what this pamphlet is written for or why it is necessary that they should have this information," it opened, "they know better than I could tell them, so I shall not try." On its surface the tract was more medical than political; most of its pages outlined popular usages for vaginal douches and condoms and attacked popular superstitions about conception. But it was a political act and, as such, contained requisite rallying cries: "The working women can use direct action by refusing to supply the market with children to be exploited, by refusing to populate the earth with slaves," it proclaimed. "Pass on this information to your neighbor and comrade workers. . . . Spread this important knowledge!"[26]

Rather than stand trial Sanger fled to England, leaving behind a growing popular movement supporting birth control education. Indecisive prosecutors eventually dropped the charges against her, allowing for her return.[27] But neither this nor the granting of women's suffrage in 1920 put the political conundrums at hand to rest. Sanger opened her first clinic in 1921; established the American Birth Control League (ABCL), which changed its name to Planned Parenthood in 1942); and tied ideas of birth control to larger notions of feminine liberation and sexual equality. Sanger's ideas crystalized as "Voluntary Motherhood," an ideology that implied "a new morality—a vigorous, constructive, liberated morality. That morality will, first of all, prevent the submergence of womanhood into motherhood. It will set its face against the conversion of women into mechanical maternity and toward the creation of a new race." Freedom from unwanted pregnancy was packaged as a freedom to experience all of life's blessings. The right to "decide how many children she will have and when she shall have them will procure for her the time necessary to the development of other faculties. . . . She will give play to her tastes, her talents and her ambitions. She will become a full-rounded human being."[28]

The New York Police Department made periodic raids on Sanger's clinic, and the movement was quick to turn these to its advantage. On April 15, 1921, eight officers arrested two attending physicians and three clinic nurses and seized all of the clinic's medical and patient records. Sanger, incensed, argued that the "clinic had been minding its own business and hoping that its powerful ecclesiastical neighbors would mind theirs." Officers returned the records four days later, but not before many doctors had spoken furiously to the press about the state's invasion of doctor-patient confidentiality. The impact was so distasteful that the police commissioner issued an apology.[29]

By the end of the 1920s individual ABCL chapters were sprouting up across the country. In the face of local conditions, many chapters were forced to separate the contraception and abortion issues. Sanger herself began gravitating toward a contraception-centered public agenda as the organization matured into the 1930s.[30]

The immediate origins of the *Griswold* case were in Waterbury, Connecticut, approximately thirty years before it reached the Court. There, in October 1938, the Connecticut Birth Control League (CBCL) quietly opened a weekly clinic in the ethnically diverse and heavily catholic downtown.[31] The opening attracted attention in Waterbury's Catholic-friendly newspapers, and the clergy at the Immaculate rectory published a forceful condemnation: "We hereby urge our Catholic people to avoid contact with it and we hereby publicly call the attention of the public prosecutors to its existence and demand that they investigate and if necessary prosecute to the full extent of the law."[32]

In the words of the distinguished historian David Garrow, whose book *Liberty and Sexuality* remains the definitive text on *Griswold* and *Roe*: the League was "quietly ecstatic at their success in extending to poor women the same medical advice that privately was available to those who could afford family physicians."[33]

The CBCL pushed back, arguing that the clinic's purpose was being misunderstood. Dr. William Goodrich, a physician at the clinic, looked to minimize the birth control angle when he claimed that "out of 250 women who come to such clinics yearly, an average of perhaps 15 come for birth control advice. They get the same advice that women who can afford personal physicians get from their own physicians." A lawyer for the CBCL then pointed out that prohibiting the distribution of birth control information ran counter to the public health laws of the state.[34]

The state's attorney, William B. Fitzgerald, a graduate of Holy Cross College, did not agree. After procuring a warrant from Judge Frank McEvoy, a fellow member of the advisory board of Father Cryne's Diocesan Bureau of Social Service, two officers were dispatched to the clinic and confiscated "several bags and boxes of articles," including contraceptives and literature on birth control. Both were illegal under the state's particularly harsh Comstock statute, so the judge ordered the clinic closed until the CBCL could justify its use of these materials in court.[35]

The case worked its way to the Connecticut Supreme Court by 1940. CBCL's lawyer Warren Upson argued that contraception was the "antithesis of abortion," and that "the power to commence a pregnancy is one of the inalienable rights of the citizens . . . [and] if the people of Connecticut have any natural rights whatsoever, one of them is certainly the right to decide whether or not they shall have children, and to this natural right, the right to use contraceptive devices is a natural concomitant." Upson also echoed arguments found in a similar legislative battle in 1935, when the *New Haven Journal-*

Courier noted that there had never been an actual prosecution under the Comstock law because "its enforcement would require a police surveillance over the intimacies of family life," and that "whether such advice can be forbidden under the state and federal constitutions is a question requiring settlement."[36]

The learned justices were unconvinced, ruling against the CBCL, 3–2. Writing for the majority, Justice George Hinman noted that

> it is not for us to say that the Legislature might not reasonably hold that the artificial limitation of even legitimate childbearing would be inimical to the public welfare and, as well, that the use of contraceptives would be injurious to public morals . . . considering that not all married people are immune from temptation or inclination to extra-marital indulgence, as to which risk of illegitimate pregnancy is a recognized deterrent deemed desirable in the interest of morality.[37]

Defeated and deflated, the CBCL closed its clinics and announced that "since this organization is responsible and law abiding, there will be no further service." This would remain the case for more than two decades, apart from one rather impactful exception.[38]

V

The relationship between privacy and gender, or the distinct ways in which the genders both perceive and experience privacy in different ways, predates America's conversation about reproductive rights. The industrial revolution had a considerable impact on the creation of distinct "spheres" of social experience. Throughout the nineteenth century, as the artisan was forced to abandon his workshop, which was often attached or located very close to his home, and began daily trips to a factory, popular conceptions of what was considered private and what was considered public changed drastically. Men more commonly went off to work in the morning and returned home to their wives in the evening. The home, or the "private sphere," grew increasingly synonymous with the norms of seclusion that separated the "household" from the larger social world—the "public sphere." With these changes, privacy began to assume distinctly feminine connotations.

The dominance of industrial capitalism meant that many women, particularly in the middle and upper classes, were confined, either alone or ideally with their children. This position made them both legally subordinate to and economically dependent on their husbands. Men, on the other hand, both shaped the outside world through their labors and political participation, *and* structured the private sphere as heads of the household who determined how women's time and resources should be used.[39]

Allen Westin categorized these developments and others associated with the modern industrial age, such as "urbanization and the anonymity of urban life, mobility in work and residence, weakening of religious authority over individuals" as things that "all provided greater situations of physical and psychological privacy." Westin's analysis is certainly accurate when interpreting the increase in physical and physiological privacy of men, but he errs when extending those privileges to women.[40]

The privacy of the home, that kind of privacy one receives from that special kind of existence generated within the nuclear family, is often a very different experience for women than it is for men. A traditional man was often able to find a degree of *meaningful* privacy—the kind that facilitates relaxation, recovery, self-reflection, and self-actualization. A traditional woman, charged with childcare and domestic responsibilities, rarely experienced the same benefits from the private sphere.

In her wildly important 1966 academic article "The Cult of True Womanhood," Barbara Welter examines magazines, gift annuals, and religious literature and shows how the nineteenth-century women is perhaps better categorized as "the hostage in the home." The true "woman's place," writes Welter, "was unquestionably her own fireside—as daughter, sister, but most of all as wife and mother." Scripture reenforced this social pressure, for "'St. Paul knew what was best for women when he advised them to be domestic,' [said one magazine writer]. 'There is composure at home; there is something sedative in the duties which home involves. It affords security not only from the world, but from delusions and errors of every kind.'"[41]

Welter's impact on the field of gender studies cannot be understated. It inspired legions of gender historians (many who went on to perform wondrous deeds) to examine how the cult of true womanhood structured the worlds of private and public, the home and the workplace, the family and the professions, and helped to maintain class- and race-based hierarchies of power that justified women's exclusion from participatory democracy.[42]

The establishment of the home as a distinctly private sphere to be preserved entirely by noble wives and mothers presented middle- and upper-class women with two problems. First, it severely constrained their ability to overcome powerful social and economic inequities that substituted confinement to the home for *meaningful* privacy in the outside world. A woman's role as guardian of the home was a large obstacle to her attaining that kind of privacy that is actually useful to a person. Second, women faced the problem of how then to best seek out and enjoying meaningful privacy without being viewed as having sacrificed their noble feminine ideals to brash and selfish individualism. A woman who shunned her role as a caretaker to achieve meaningful privacy was not, in the eyes of many, a "true woman."[43]

"The ideals Welter uncovered in her analysis of nineteenth-century prescriptive literature, novels, diaries, and correspondence did not simply *codify* modern notions of women's place," according to historian Nancy Hewitt. Rather, in response to dramatic economic and political upheavals, they *constructed* white, middle-class true women as "the gladiators at the gate, fending off the evils that accompanied the pursuit of wealth and power by bourgeois men and the expansion of cities, factories, and plantations that fed their success." Among the so-called weaker sex, "intellect was geared to her hymen, not her brain."[44]

The feminists of the Progressive Era were quick to call attention to the fact that motherhood, family life, and housekeeping duties typically entailed that a true woman sacrifice a good deal of her own meaningful privacy. Charlotte Perkins Gilman certainly understood the nuances of *meaningful* privacy; she wrote in 1898 that "such privacy as we have at home is family privacy, an aggregate privacy; and this does not insure—indeed, it prevents—individual privacy." Any attempt by a woman to achieve privacy in the home, noted Gilman, "any tendency to withdraw and live one's own life on any plane of separate interest or industry is naturally resented, or at least regretted, by other members of the family." This situation affected women more than men "because men live very little in the family and very much in the world."[45]

Two decades earlier, Elizabeth Cady Stanton spoke of "the solitude of the self" as the basis for why women deserved equal rights, holding that "the strongest reason for giving woman all the opportunities for higher education, for the full development of her faculties . . . a complete emancipation from all forms of bondage, of custom, dependence . . . is the solitude and personal responsibility of her own individual life." No matter how much women "prefer to lean, to be protected and supported, nor how much men desire to have them do so, they must make the voyage of life alone." Only with equal rights would a woman's "solitude at least be respectable."[46]

But we should not just blindly wedge males and females into the public and the private spheres and leave it at that. Historians are still debating the suitability of the public/private lens for analyzing gender oppression. Inspired by a political vision, early second-wave feminist historians often promoted many historical and comparative accounts of the changing sources of gender inequality. Nevertheless, "the shared conclusion of gender historians," according to Joan Landis, "is that it remains an indispensable framework for gender analysis."[47] For one, economic status drastically determined women's experience of the home. The poor certainly have an equal need for meaningful privacy, but most were compelled by economic necessity to accept smaller, crowded, and more thinly walled accommodations than their middle-class counterparts. And even those women who, out of economic necessity, joined the public sphere by working outside the home frequently found themselves coming home to the physically taxing housekeeping and caretaking roles prescribed by the gender norms of their time—roles that limited their ability to enjoy meaningful privacy in the homestead in the way many of their husbands did.[48]

For feminists of all stripes, as the twentieth century marched on, the idea of the private sphere as the man's "castle" and the woman's "place" was increasingly identified and increasingly challenged. Under this arrangement, men were entitled to make almost all of the important decisions that had bearing on the families' well-being and were able to view the home as a place from which to retreat from the social world and find repose—a place to find meaningful privacy. Women, on the other hand, because of their housekeeping and caregiving obligations, from which they made little in the way of important household decisions, were never quite able to find a similar space from which to escape the pressures and responsibilities of their day-to-day lives.

By the 1960s, challenging the idea of the private sphere as the man's "castle" and the woman's "place" had become a centerpiece of the women's movement. The ideological underpinnings of this resistance to the private sphere was most famously encapsulated by Betty Freidan's description of women living in suburban homes as prisoners in "comfortable concentration camps . . . dependent, passive, childlike . . . suffering a slow death of mind and spirit." The book sold more than two million copies before the decade ended.[49]

This strain of liberal feminism, or "second-wave" feminism, the one that fought for and eventually won reproductive *decisional* privacy in *Griswold*, was the outgrowth of multiple factors. Reflecting on the early days of the movement, Catharine MacKinnon noted that

for women the measure of the intimacy has been the measure of the oppression. This is why feminism had to explode the private. This is why feminism has seen the personal as the political. The private is public for those for whom the personal is

political. In this sense, for women there is no private, either
normative or empirically. Feminism confronts the fact that
women have no privacy to lose or to guarantee.[50]

Supporters of second-wave feminism looked with favor on decisional privacy in the context of contraception and abortion because they viewed it as a tool through which women could achieve
autonomy. Autonomy to enjoy sexual intercourse without fear of
unwanted pregnancy. Autonomy to actively pursue fulfillment as a
mature sexual being. Autonomy to thrive in the economic sphere
without being interrupted by conception. Decisional privacy to
choose whether to bear a child also affords fertile women a valuable
degree of control over the personal privacy they have at home.[51]

The contraception and abortion questions had resurfaced in the
1950s under pressure from both feminists and a new generation of
physicians who were beginning to realize that antiquated laws were
hindering their ability to provide patients with the highest level of
care. Many of these doctors also believed that the American Medical Association (AMA), not the law, should have the final word on
appropriate standards of medical practices.[52]

Americans were talking more openly about sex in the mid-
twentieth century, particularly after the publication of Alfred C.
Kinsey's 804-page *Sexual Behavior in the Human Male* in 1948 and
his companion piece on females five years later. Kinsey's landmark
work showed Americans for the first time, in cold scientific detail,
that masturbation, premarital sex, extramarital affairs, and homosexuality were all on the normal spectrum of sexual behavior. At the
same time, new birth control technologies, such as IUDs and the
pill, were introduced worldwide.[53]

Also, by the 1950s the American legal community was growing
increasingly concerned about the widespread disregard of abortion
laws. A national conference on the issue was sponsored by Planned
Parenthood and the American Academy of Medicine in 1954, quickly
followed by an impactful study by legal scholar Glanville Williams.
In 1959 the American Law Institute (ALI) proposed changes to abortion law nationwide and published a draft of a model state-level law

that would have allowed abortion under certain conditions. By the early 1960s bills based on the ALI model were passed in Colorado, California, and North Carolina.[54]

Then the epidemic of German measles (a popular term for rubella) between 1962 and 1965 brought the contraception and abortion debates to the fore. The disease was particularly dangerous for pregnant women and was known to increase the likelihood of fetal heart disease, blindness, and mental retardation. Perhaps 80,000 pregnant women who contracted German measles sought abortions and were turned down in this period, and as many as 15,000 children were born with birth defects as a result. Hospitals throughout the country, notably in California, began ignoring anti-contraception and abortion statues.[55]

Meanwhile, back in Connecticut, the CBCL sensed that perhaps the time was right to reapply pressure to the state's contraception statute.

VI

The path to *Griswold* was paved with a series of test cases in the late 1950s and early 1960s aimed at pushing the contraception issue onto the docket of the Supreme Court. Some of these ran aground due to legal technicalities. The most crucial of these pre-*Griswold* defeats was *Poe v. Ullman*, a joint venture by the ACLU and Planned Parenthood in concert with the CBCL.

Poe centered on two women, both of whom experienced serious health problems during previous pregnancies. Their physician Dr. Buxton, a Connecticut practitioner and friend to the CBCL, gave his professional medical opinion that both women would face health risks if they became pregnant again, and that the safest treatment for them would be consistent use of contraceptives.

The women and Dr. Buxton, as petitioners, knew the state's attorney would likely enforce the 1879 statutes, as he had in the past. In three separate cases, the petitioners sued on grounds that the law violated the equal protection clause of the Fourteenth Amendment, and that the statutes deprived them of life and property because their doctor was unable to provide them with advice about contraceptives without fear of prosecution. The Connecticut Supreme Court dismissed the appeals, as predicted, after which the Supreme Court consolidated the cases and agreed to hear oral arguments in 1961.[56]

Arguing for the birth control league, hailing from Yale Law School, was the fiercely capable civil liberties purist Fowler Harper. He had fought for the termination of the House Committee on Un-American Activities. He had fought for the repeal of the McCarran Act. He had fought against the death sentences of the Rosenbergs. And he opposed most legislation that allowed wiretapping. In his brief to the Court, Harper cited a national poll in which 72 percent of respondents believed that information about contraceptive devices should be available to the public. He then shifted to logic grounded in privacy, arguing that while his clients did not hold that the right to privacy was directly protected by the Fourteenth Amendment, "their privacy is mercilessly being invaded by these laws and that, this being so, it is a highly important factor for this Court to consider in weighing the hardship upon individuals against the theoretical, if not entirely fictitious, advantages of the laws as promoting public morality."[57]

Harper leaned heavily on privacy rights. "The normal and voluntary relations of spouses in the privacy of their homes is regarded as beyond the prying eyes of peeping Toms, be they police officers or legislators," he argued. The Connecticut statutes "invade the privacy of the citizen," violate the "privacy of the home," and "regulate the private sex life of all married people." Channeling Brandeis with his phrasing, he concluded "that these spouses want to be let alone in the bedroom," and that the current law "interferes mercilessly with the most intimate and sacred experiences of life."[58]

Alas, in the short term, *Poe* was doomed to failure. The Court ducked overturning the contraception law case on the grounds that no crime had actually been committed and that there was no indication the 1879 statute would ever be enforced. In the eyes of the majority, the procedural merits simply weren't there because the appeal did not satisfy a "case or controversy requirement," and so it was dismissed. The Court preferred not to deal in hypotheticals.[59]

Justices Douglas and Harlan took the opportunity to pen caustic dissents castigating the contraception statute while affirming the importance of privacy jurisprudence. Douglas felt that the rights of the "Poes" were unequivocally violated under the terms of the equal protection clause; he expressed outrage that the Connecticut law "reaches into the intimacies of the marriage relationship" and, if enforced, would "reach the point where search warrants issued and officers appeared in bedrooms to find out what went on." Any possible enforcement "would be an invasion of privacy that is implicit in a free society," a thing that "emanates from the totality of the constitutional scheme under which we live." Douglas's dissent previewed the line he would eventually take on a constitutional right to privacy. "Liberty," he explained, "is a conception that sometimes gains content from the emanations of other specific guarantees [in the Constitution] or from experience with the requirements of a free society." In short—the Constitution has ample room for the recognition of higher truths, and privacy was one of them.[60]

Harlan, also incensed, wrote his own dissent. He began by quoting at length from Brandeis's *Olmstead* dissent, arguing that the "privacy of the home in its most basic sense" was certainly "a most fundamental aspect of *liberty*." Not just in the Fourth Amendment, "the Constitution protects the privacy of the home against all unreasonable intrusion of whatever character."[61]

Poe was technically a loss, but there was cause to be hopeful. The dissents showed that the issue was far from settled and could be interpreted, as intended, as an invitation to try again. The language used by Douglas and Harlan contributed to a constitutional roadmap that allowed for the eventual overturning of the Connecticut law *and* for a further expansion of the birth control struggle that few could have anticipated at the time. Planned Parenthood for America (PPA) adeptly interpreted the dismissal as evidence that victory was close at hand. "We welcome the recognition by the Court that the law has in fact become a nullity," read the PPA's official statement.[62]

In Connecticut, Estelle Griswold of the PPA local office (PPLC) told reporters that since, in the eyes of the highest Court in the land, the law was unenforceable, she and her associates would open a new clinic in New Haven no later than September 1961. The clinic would administer advice and contraceptive devices of all kinds, and should anyone take issue she "would of course welcome prosecution by the state" under its "absurd and antiquated" statute.[63]

Griswold was picking a fight, and she got one. She and Dr. Buxton opened their clinic, and police raided it ten days later. Officers recalled that "Mrs. Griswold stated that although she welcomed arrest and a chance to settle the question of the . . . statute's legality, she would refuse to be pictured and fingerprinted, feeling that she had not committed any crime, would not accept bail, and would physically resist and repel any effort . . . to seize medical records." With that, Griswold and Dr. Buxton shook hands with the officers, who promptly left. Official charges were filed in the coming days. And after predictable outcomes in the Connecticut courts, the Warren Court agreed to hear the case in 1965.[64]

With Fowler Harper hospitalized with terminal cancer, PPA approached his longtime Yale colleague, Thomas Emerson, to argue for Griswold. To most observers victory was a foregone conclusion. Emerson predicted that the final ruling would be 7–2 in favor. It wasn't all bluster and bravado. Legal scholar Lucas Powe notes that by the mid-1960s even Catholic leaders knew the law had to go — "the South was an outlier on segregation; the Northeast on contraception; and the Court was tolerating no outliers." Also, the Court had already been fleshing out aspects of the right to privacy in other cases concerning the Fourth and Sixth Amendments.[65]

Emerson's brief was structured around two core arguments. First, that the 1879 statute "contravened the liberty protected by the [due process protections] of the Fourteenth Amendment." Second, that the law's application to Griswold violated her First Amendment right to freedom of speech. Emerson inserted the privacy argument into his equal protection claim:

The Connecticut statutes violate due process in that they constitute an unwarranted invasion of privacy. Whether one derives right of privacy from a composite of the Third, Fourth, and Fifth Amendments, from the Ninth Amendment, or from the "liberty" clause of the Fourteenth Amendment, such a constitutional right has been specifically recognized by this Court. Although the boundaries of this constitutional right of privacy have not yet been spelled out, plainly the right extends to unwarranted government invasion of (1) the sanctity of the home, and (2) the intimacies of the sexual relationship in marriage. These core elements of the right to privacy are combined in this case.[66]

According to Emerson, the First (privacy in one's freedom of association), Third (no soldiers may be quartered in private homes in peacetime), Fourth (protections from unreasonable searches and seizures), and Fifth (protection from self-incrimination) Amendments, when taken together, "embody a general principle which protects the private sector of life." Additionally, "the interest of married spouses in the sanctity and privacy of their marital relations involves precisely the kind of right which the Ninth Amendment was intended to secure." Ultimately, "the sanctity of the home and the wholly personal nature of marital relations" together formed "the inner core of the right to privacy."[67]

Four additional amicus briefs were filed in support of Griswold. One from Robert Fleming for the Catholic Council on Civil Liberties emphasized that the right of privacy was situated firmly "within the liberty protected by the Fourteenth Amendment." The ACLU's brief concurred, arguing that "marriage and the family" were "the ultimate repository of personal freedom," and included "the wife's right to order her childbearing according to her financial and emotional needs, her abilities, and her achievements."[68]

Arguing the other side was Connecticut's assistant prosecutor Joe Clarke, who met the privacy argument by simply arguing "there has been no invasion of anyone's privacy in this case." Clarke, not quite as eloquent as his opponents, thought it best to rely on the inclusion of his own moral philosophy, chiding that the idea that "single people should be allowed to use a contraceptive device is so contra to the American experience, thought, and family law that it does not merit further discussion."[69]

Oral arguments in the case began March 29, 1965, at 1:30 p.m. Standing before the justices, Emerson smartly positioned Griswold's case as one of "due process in the basic sense." The Connecticut statute was "arbitrary and unreasonable, and in the special sense that it constitutes a deprivation of right against invasion of privacy." He held that the broad language of the Ninth Amendment was "the basis for the right of privacy" because it referred to the presence of additional rights that could be "retained by the people." The Ninth spoke of higher truths, according to Emerson, and "if there is any right that you would think would be reserved by the people and which the government should not interfere with, it would be this right."[70]

Oral arguments bled into the following day whereupon Justice Black, ever prescient, broke into one of Emerson's rebuttals by asking whether his "argument concerning these things you've been talking about relating to privacy invalidate all laws that punish people for bringing about abortions." The lawyer responded that it would not, as that conduct "does not occur in the privacy of the home . . . the conduct being prohibited in the abortion cases takes that conduct outside of the home, normally. There is no violation of the sanctity of the home."[71]

Justice White, perhaps sensing that Emerson was getting backed into a corner, suddenly asserted himself into the discussion, noting "abortion involves killing a life in being [*sic*], doesn't it? Isn't that a rather different problem than contraception?" To which Emerson replied, "Oh, yes, of course."

But Black wasn't finished: "Are you saying that all abortions involve killing or murder?" "Well, I don't know that you need to characterize it that way," replied Emerson, "but it involves taking what has begun to be a life." That was all the justices had to say about the abortion issue for the time being, and oral arguments for both sides concluded shortly thereafter.[72]

Emerson was right about the 7–2 margin. But he could not have predicted the scattered composition of the Court's decision. The justices were aligned on who should win, but explaining why required one majority opinion and *three* concurring opinions. Justice

Douglas, writing first for the majority, was impressed more with Emerson's privacy justification than with the claims to substantive due process. In many ways he rehashed his *Poe* dissent, demonstrating first that a right to privacy was textually based and, second, that the contraception issue was covered by that right.[73]

Douglas's opinion stands as the most important affirmation of the right to privacy's relationship with the Constitution. It acknowledges that "the association of husband and wife is not mentioned in the Constitution nor in the Bill or Rights." But regardless, the Court had previously recognized that "specific guarantees in the Bill of Rights have penumbras, formed by emanations from those guarantees that help give them life and substance. Various guarantees create zones of privacy. . . ." *Griswold* involved "a relationship within the zone of privacy created by several fundamental constitutional guarantees," which no state had the right to invade.[74]

In a series of concise sentences Douglas started with the First Amendment right to association affirmed in cases such as *NAACP v. Alabama*, then moved to inherent protections of the Third Amendment against soldiers being quartered in homes, followed by Fourth Amendment search and seizure protections, and finally the Fifth Amendment right against self-incrimination. These amendments facilitated specific "zones of privacy" in the Constitution and were surely open to liberal interpretation because of the implication of higher truths mentioned in the Ninth Amendment. These zones, according to Douglas, could also be legally extended to the individual states thanks to the Fourteenth Amendment.[75]

His concluding remarks turned to the contraception law directly and included a rather ironic defense of the marriage institution considering the man was thrice divorced:

> The present case, then, concerns a relationship lying within the zone of privacy created by several fundamental constitutional guarantees. And it concerns a law which, in forbidding the use of contraceptives, rather than regulating their manufacture or sale, seeks to achieve its goals by means having a maximum destructive impact upon that relationship. . . . We deal with a right

of privacy older than the Bill of Rights—older than our political parties, older than our school system. Marriage is a coming together for better or for worse, hopefully enduring, and intimate to the degree of being sacred. It is an association that promotes a way of life, not causes; a harmony in living, not political faiths; a bilateral loyalty, not commercial or social projects. Yet it is an association for as noble a purpose as any involved in our prior decisions.[76]

Justice Goldberg's concurring opinion, which Warren and Brennan joined, spent most of its time tying the privacy argument to the Ninth Amendment. Goldberg quoted approvingly from Harlan's *Poe* dissent and the "traditions and collective conscience of our peoples to determine whether a principle is 'so rooted there as to be ranked as fundamental.'" For him, marriage was simply "an essential and accepted feature" of the American experience.[77]

Justice Black, however, could not bring himself to agree with Douglas and Goldberg's free-wheeling interpretations of the Constitution. Although he and Douglas were famously close, Black abhorred his colleague's theories on the right to privacy, citing that it engaged "no less than six Amendments to the Constitution, but does not say which of these Amendments, if any, it thinks is infringed by the Connecticut law." Black rejected the privacy argument outright—noting "with all deference" that he could "find no such general right of privacy in the Bill of Rights, in any other part of the Constitution, or in any case ever before decided by this Court."[78] Drawing to a close, Black jabbed, "I think this is an uncommonly silly law. . . . I like my privacy as well as the next one, but I am nevertheless compelled to admit that government has a right to invade it unless prohibited by some specific constitutional provision." Fortunately for privacy, the brethren disagreed.[79]

In the larger story of American privacy *Griswold*'s importance was, of course, that it gave the concept a firm constitutional grounding. But even more significant was that it tied privacy to the centuries-old bedrock of American political theory. The constitutional recognition of a right to privacy was an acknowledgment that privacy was implicit in America's liberal democratic traditions and inherent in its culture of individualism and its sense of notional exceptionalism. Although the right *Griswold* established was described only in terms of "marital" privacy, it formed a basis for the future refinement of privacy as a larger aspect of constitutional legal theory and the political realm.[80]

"Viewed as an episode in the history of privacy—rather than the history of reproductive freedom or women's rights," notes historian Sarah Igo, the Court in *Griswold* used the concept to "resolve an issue that almost no one at the time associated closely with privacy. Undoing a morals regulation that affected fewer Americans by the year, it addressed neither the actual harms of policing intimate life nor the deeply contested issues around individual privacy that by 1965 begged for attention." Nevertheless, it was also "a clear statement that there were tangible places and situations where privacy continued to reign in a modern society, where individuals' lives would be sealed off from an insistently knowing society."[81]

In the larger story of American feminism and reproductive rights, the "marital" privacy affirmed in *Griswold* laid the groundwork for the eventual legitimization of "decisional" privacy in *Roe v. Wade* a few years later. Justices Black and White both noted in oral arguments that contraception is not the same as abortion and that each have significantly different moral and legal dimensions. But there are overlaps, and for proponents of reproductive choice those overlaps proved to be enough.[82]

On the surface *Griswold* largely affirmed the privacy of the home—or at least the marital bed—condemning the fictional image of policemen bursting into homes late at night to search nightstands for diaphragms and condoms. But in practice laws against contraception also prevent sexually active young women from reducing the number of persons whom they are forced to provide for. That is, they limit opportunities for meaningful privacy.[83]

And so the argument for reproductive liberties, to whatever degree it was or wasn't explicitly condoned by the Court in *Griswold*, was not only that the exercise of free choice belonged to women as a requirement of moral justice but also, as Anita Allen put it, that "the privacy called for by moral concern for the quality of individual and group life depends upon the ability of women to determine when and if they have children." By recognizing the existence of a constitutional right to *marital* privacy in reproductive choices, the eventual recognition of a right to *decisional* privacy (packaged as "freedom of choice") was a logical next step.[84]

VII

Public reaction to *Griswold* was generally positive. Even Hartford's archbishop Henry O'Brian conceded that "Catholics, in common with our fellow citizens, recognize this decision as a valid interpretation of constitutional law." Of course, this amiability would soon crumble once the case was reinterpreted through substantive due process to justify abortion in *Roe v. Wade*.[85]

Reactions from the legal community was predictably mixed — divided between liberal constructionists who applauded Douglas's acumen and imagination, and strict constructionists who thought the ruling was dangerously vague and an irresponsible parlor trick of constitutional law. Legal scholar Robert Dixon quickly questioned the implications of the ruling for larger problems of informational privacy. "Information relevant to married people's lives is what *Griswold* comes down to," argued Dixon, "unless some kind of information access theory is recognized as implicit in *Griswold*, then it stands as a decision without a satisfying rationale."[86]

Griswold set the Court on the path to *Roe* precisely when the sexual revolution was swelling. The National Organization of Women (NOW) initiated a strong push for abortion law reform in the mid-1960s, despite its initial reluctance to take on the issue for fear that its broader goals of political and economic equality for women would be less impactful if muddled by conversations about sexual taboos and procreation. Even Freidan did not initially see the issue as a viable rallying point. But the younger and more radical elements of the women's movement were uncompromising on abortion rights and threatened organizational mayhem. And so to preserve unity, NOW made the issue a cornerstone of its platform in

1967 and included the "right of women to control their reproductive lives" in its "women's bill of rights."[87]

In February 1969 Freidan addressed the First National Conference on Abortion Laws, calling for a "new stage" that would no longer seek reform of existing abortion laws—"reform is something dreamed up by men"—but outright repeal. Friedan told the delegates:

> My only claim to be here, is our belated recognition, if you will, that there is no freedom, no equality, no full human dignity and personhood possible for women until we assert and demand the control over our own bodies, over our own reproductive process . . . Women are denigrated in this country, because women are not deciding the conditions of their own society and their own lives. Women are not taken seriously as people. Women are not seen seriously as people. So this is the new name of the game on the question of abortion: that women's voices are heard.[88]

Dignity. Personhood. Control. The rhetoric of second-wave feminism stressed these things because they were perceived as necessary requirements for self-realization. As necessary requirements for freedom and equality. Choosing privacy rights as the legal and political avenue through which they would pursue these demands made perfect sense because all of them, in some form or another, fit under the umbrella of that multifaceted concept. The Supreme Court had already said as much.

Protests and demonstrations began springing up nationwide. Guerrilla theater troupes performed scenes on city streets. The activist Redstockings disrupted a New York State legislative hearing on abortion where a panel of fifteen experts, fourteen men and one nun, were giving testimony. "We are the experts!" shouted the protesters before hastily organizing their own open meeting in which dozens of women spoke about their own experience with abortion. Actresses and female musicians began speaking of abortions in news conferences and magazine articles. These, and a slew of other public spectacles helped dramatize the abortion controversy and broadened discourse in the public forum. By the early 1970s the atmosphere of guilt and shame that had for so long prevented new consideration of anti-abortion statutes was disintegrating.[89]

These changing standards of sexuality seemed to be mirrored by the Judiciary. In the eight years between *Griswold* and *Roe* the Supreme Court handed down five significant rulings striking down laws designed to constrain sexual behavior or sexual expression. Understandably, this behavior has led many to believe that the Court was influenced by the larger currents of the sexual revolution. It is important not to take this categorization too far.[90]

Morality laws, which seek to regulate activities considered anathema to public standards, are almost always the purview of state legislatures. Before 1965 these laws regulated a considerable range of sexual expression, such as pornography, miscegenation, oral and anal sex, prostitution, homosexuality, incest, and birth control, and they prompted censorship of local television, newspapers, and radio.[91]

Historically, libertarians and social progressives both tend to have a problem with laws designed to preserve public morality. Both political philosophies profess that individuals should be able to decide for themselves what is moral and what is not—that larger claims of a "public morality" have no regard for individual choice and are often ripe for exploitation by an overzealous minority. They stress the difference between the public and private spheres: while they can understand why certain things may be banned in public, the law oversteps when it starts infringing on practices done in the privacy of one's home or that are considered particularly intimate.

Yet for all its interest in privacy, the Supreme Court's pattern of overturning such laws in the 1960s and early 1970s should not be misconstrued as support for increased sexual expression or even sexual privacy. A closer look at these rulings reveals that the justices embraced a sexual rights doctrine that wasn't broadly libertarian or egalitarian; instead, as historian Marc Stein points out, it "affirmed the supremacy of adult, heterosexual, marital, monogamous, private, and procreative forms of sexual expression." The doctrine of the Warren Court was quite heteronormative.[92]

During oral arguments in *Griswold,* most of the justices either commented or suggested that that laws against homosexuality, fornication, and adultery were constitutional. Even Douglas made it clear that he was refereeing only to the privacy rights of "married persons" and "married couples." *Griswold* did not establish a literal sphere of sexual privacy in the home or even the bedroom; instead, it created a "quasi-literal and quasi figurative sphere in which married people have certain privileges that unmarried people do not have." Seven of the justices suggested that laws against nonmarital sex were constitutional, and the other two (Douglas and Clark) did not voice any disagreements.[93]

A year later the Court ruled in *Memoirs v. Massachusetts* (nicknamed *Fanny Hill*), after publishers challenged that state's banning of an eighteenth-century English novel on grounds that it was obscene. The justices overturned the ban, citing experts who claimed the work had "a modicum of literary and historical value." On the surface, *Fanny Hill* also seemed to be an endorsement of free sexual literary expression. But the majority opinion refers frequently to the fact that the protagonist, a prostitute who describes in graphic detail her many sexual encounters, is ultimately redeemed through marriage and a rejection of her previous lifestyle. The decision privileged normative sexual expression but was clear that the banning of certain works that speak "only to the prurient interest" and were without "any redeeming social value" was constitutional.[94]

There's a larger lesson here about the tactics of successful litigation campaigns. That the details of these cases happened to fit certain heteronormative criteria was no coincidence. The actors waging these campaigns knew full well that victory depended on their being able to cherry-pick cases that the Court would not find too offensive. That's why Estelle Griswold announced that the New Haven clinic would be giving advice to *married* couples. It is why the appellant in *Memoirs* chose a book whose ending applauded monogamy. Symbols are important when the stakes are high, and therefore must be chosen carefully. Change is made in such incremental ways. The fact that these litigators chose to package their cases thus is evidence they understood the justices were no crusaders for sexual rights.

The presence of a heteronormative standard is why when the ACLU finally brought an anti-miscegenation case in *Loving v. Virginia* (1967), it made sure to present a white man illegally married to a black woman, and not the other way around. Once again, the justices expressed consternation for the laws they were overturning (the decision was unanimous) but did so, according to Stein, with language that affirmed the status of marriage and "the special rights associated with adult, monogamous, heterosexual relationships," which could not be denied on grounds of race.[95]

The ACLU was cautious not to stray too far from this heteronormative doctrine when it began looking for test cases to challenge anti-miscegenation laws in the 1950s. Its legal director, Rowland Watts, encouraged attorneys to search only for cases that met a specific favorable criteria, and noted that "a white husband and nonwhite wife combination is better than vice versa" and that "a white-Indian or a white-Oriental combination is better than a white-negro combination." He also asked attorneys to consider couples "with a standing in the community" and suggested that "a case from a Western state or a border state is better than a case from the deep South."[96]

The Court finally decoupled marriage and procreation when it granted birth control access to unmarried couples in *Eisenstadt v. Baird* (1972)—its last sex/reproduction case before *Roe*. In many ways the ruling was the logical outgrowth of *Griswold*, but again, the justices did not come close to establishing a right to "sexual privacy."[97]

Eisenstadt took on a Massachusetts law that prohibited the sale of vaginal spermicidal foam to unmarried individuals. Sensing an opportunity to extend the gains it made in *Griswold*, the ACLU began prepping the case in 1971. On advice from his legal director Mel Wulf, ACLU attorney John Robertson grounded his brief in "the fundamental nature of the right to privacy in the context of intimate sexual relationships." Robertson stressed that the public mood and decisions by lower courts were increasingly reading *Griswold* "as establishing a right of sexual privacy which extends to both married and single men and women" alike. Jabbing at the problems of enforcement, he comically noted that "newlyweds face the peculiar dilemma of having to see a doctor after their wedding and before their wedding night."[98]

The Court agreed. Justice Brennan, writing for the majority, struck down the Massachusetts law by noting that

> in *Griswold* the right of privacy in question inhered in the marital relationship. Yet the marital couple is not an independent entity with a mind and heart of its own, but an association of two individuals each with a separate intellectual and emotional makeup. If the right of privacy means anything, it is the right of the *individual*, married or single, to be free from unwarranted governmental intrusion into matters so fundamentally affecting a person as the decision whether to bear or beget a child.[99]

Naturally, critics of these rulings see them as facilitating a sharp decline in moral standards and a rise in sexual indecency and godlessness. They say the Court gave its explicit blessing to the sexual revolution. But in reality the Court still heavily endorsed a doctrine of heteronormative supremacy as it inched closer to an expansion of sexual rights.[100]

A good indicator of the heteronormativity of the Court even after *Roe* was its decision to uphold state sodomy laws in *Bowers v. Hardwick* (1986). Critics interpreted the case as a conservative departure from the Warren Court, but Stein and others see it as "a logical culmination of the comments about sex the Court had been making since 1965."[101] Upheld 5–4, Justice White's majority opinion rejected the notion that the privacy protections established in *Griswold*, *Eisenstadt*, and *Roe* could be applied to same-sex couples and denied these precedents on grounds that they were designed to protect "family, marriage, or procreation," and did not have "any resemblance" or "connection" to "homosexual activity." As for privacy in the home, White argued "it would be difficult to limit the claimed right to homosexual conduct while leaving exposed to prosecution adultery, incest, and other sexual crimes . . . committed in the home." Justice Blackmun dissented, claiming that the heart of the issue was what "Brandeis called the right to be let alone."[102] He was eventually vindicated when *Bowers* was overturned in *Lawrence v. Texas* (2003).

Historical memory can be a tricky thing. The justices of the Warren and Burger Courts had no interest in being standard bearers for the sexual revolution. Even the most liberal among them, when one looks closely at their words and deeds, were uncomfortable straying too far from traditionalist standards regarding sex. But how the public perceives a Court decision can be even more important than what the Court itself decided. There can be no question that these rulings, however limited, aided in the liberalization of sexual norms. And there is also no question that while the Court never explicitly condoned a right to "sexual privacy," the eight years bookended by *Griswold* and *Roe* remain a sort of golden age for American privacy jurisprudence.[103]

VIII

By the time *Roe* reached the Court in 1973, the makeup of its bench had changed. Of the nine justices who had decided *Griswold*, only four remained.[104]

This is a tale most are familiar with. In 1970 Norma McCorvey was an unmarried and pregnant resident of Texas seeking an abortion. But Texas law made it a felony to abort a fetus unless a doctor insisted it was the only way to save the life of the mother. Linda Coffee and Sarah Weddington, two recent graduates of the University of Texas Law School, helped McCorvey, under the alias Jane Roe, file suit against Henry Wade, the district attorney of Dallas County, to challenge the statute outlawing abortion on grounds that she had a constitutional right to privacy in her reproductive choices and that the state was violating that right. The case was argued before the Supreme Court twice, first in 1971 and again in 1972 with a companion case from Georgia, *Doe v. Bolton*.[105]

Advocates for the state made three core arguments: that they had a duty to protect prenatal life, that life is present at the moment of conception, and that the unborn are people and as such entitled to protection under the Constitution. The Texas law, they claimed, was "a valid exercise of police powers reserved to the States in order to protect the health and safety of citizens, including the unborn" and was therefore constitutional. They understood that the cases would test the strength of *Griswold*'s right to privacy.[106]

Within two weeks of the Court's announcement that it would hear *Roe*, Planned Parenthood's Harriet Pilpel invited a number of abortion activists to a dinner meeting to discuss preparation of amicus briefs. The question was how much emphasis to place on the right to privacy established in *Griswold* versus arguments about fetal "personhood" and the applicability of the Constitution to the unborn. Both approaches had advantages and drawbacks.[107]

They would need doctors on their side, and many were willing. Roy Lucas of the James Madison Constitutional Law Institute authored the main briefs for *Roe* and *Doe*, and immediately secured the endorsement of the American College of Obstetricians and Gynecologists, the American Medical Women's Association, and the American Psychiatric Association. The individual signatories totaled 178 prominent medical leaders.[108] Lucas's brief spent the first two-thirds of its 145 pages addressing procedural issues and emphasizing the scope of support from the legal community for the legalization of abortion nationwide. The final third was dedicated to the right to privacy located in *Griswold* and affirmed by *Eisenstadt*.[109]

There were seven additional briefs. Harriet Pilpel wrote one, arguing that "the right to abortion must be viewed as a corollary of the right to control fertility which was recognized in *Griswold*." The Planned Parenthood Federation of America brief quoted from an article by former justice Clark, supporting the notion that "the right of a women to choose whether or not to bear a child is an aspect of her right to privacy and liberty." Pilpel was relentless in her invocation of *Griswold*, much more so than Lucas, emphasizing that "the right to contraception implicitly includes the right to choose whether or not to become a parent."[110]

The first round of oral arguments for *Roe v. Wade* began a few minutes after ten on Monday morning, December 13, 1971. Arguing for the appellants, Sarah Weddington carefully acknowledged that "it appears the members of the Court in [*Griswold*] were obviously divided as to the specific constitutional framework of the right which they held to exist." Nevertheless, "the Ninth Amendment is an appropriate place for that freedom to rest. . . . I think in as far as liberty is meaningful, that liberty to these women would mean liberty from being forced to continue the unwanted pregnancy."[111] Weddington's case was grounded heavily in the right to decisional privacy implied by the broad and ambiguous wording of the Ninth and Fourteenth Amendments, arguing that "I think in as far as the Court has said that there is a penumbra that exists to encompass the entire purpose of the Constitution, that I think one of the purposes of the Constitution was to guarantee to the individual the right to determine the course of their own lives."[112]

But when oral arguments were finished, Chief Justice Burger urged postponing the case until October, since the Court was not at full strength. Black and Harlan had left the Court, and Powell and Rehnquist were not yet confirmed. In her second appearance, Weddington again stressed the *Griswold* privacy precedent repeatedly, along with the "definitive statement of ethics of the medical profession." The Court, particularly Justice Stewart, pressed her often on the issue of whether "it was established that an unborn fetus is a person . . . because if it was you would have an almost impossible case here, would you not?" To which Weddington replied, "it is up to the Court to make that determination."[113]

Robert Flowers, arguing for Texas, anchored his remarks in that question of whether a fetus is entitled to the rights of "personhood," holding that it was "upon conception we have a human being, a person within the concept of the Constitution." Justice Blackmun frequently interjected on this point, sarcastically remarking once that Flowers should just "sit down" as he had already "won his case" if Texas indeed spoke for the entire nation.[114]

By a vote of 7-2, with Justices White and Rehnquist in dissent, the Court upheld Roe's right to terminate a pregnancy in the first trimester (ninety days). Justice Blackmun, writing for the majority, observed that the Fourteenth Amendment contained three references to "persons" but that for nearly all such references in the Constitution, "use of the word is such that it has application only postnatally" and that "none indicates, with any assurance, that it has any possible prenatal application."[115]

Blackmun's opinion carefully steered between the right to privacy and a state's compelling interest to protect all human life. On the first point, he wrote that the majority of the justices "do not agree" with Texas that the state "may override the rights of the pregnant woman that are at stake." The "right of privacy," outlined in *Griswold* and *Eisenstadt*, "whether it be founded in the Fourteenth Amendment . . . or in the Ninth Amendment's reservation of rights to the people, is broad enough to encompass a woman's decision whether or not to terminate her pregnancy." He concluded that "the right of personal privacy includes the abortion decision, but that this right is not unqualified, and must be considered against important state interests in regulation." But Blackmun also recognized that the state does have an "important and legitimate interest in protecting the potentiality of human life" and in protecting the mother's health.

Blackmun's decision held that during the first trimester a woman, in consultation with her physician, had an unrestricted right to an abortion. During the second trimester, states could regulate abortion to protect a woman's health. Finally, during the third trimester, the state's interest in protecting the potential life of the fetus was sufficient to justify severe restrictions because the fetus was capable of living on its own at that point. It had, as it is popularly called, "fetal viability."[116]

The Court essentially had had four options in *Roe*. It could have ducked the case. It could have affirmed solely on privacy grounds. It could have upheld the Texas ban. Or it could do what it did—steer a middle course between privacy and the prevailing medical standards of the 1970s. The point Blackmun made on behalf of the Court was that the right to decisional privacy in childbirth should not be taken as absolute, even if the demarcations of viability he drew struck everyone as rather arbitrary and vague.[117]

As for privacy, there was always the chance that the right to contraception could have been distinguished from the right to have an abortion. But then the overlaps are a bit too glaring to ignore. *Roe* essentially brought *marital* privacy into the realm of *decisional* privacy. *Roe* shows us that the Court evidently thought that a refusal to extend the right to privacy established in *Griswold* to an issue so clearly related might be interpreted as a repudiation of that right. In a legal sense, both cases did offer a clear line of precedent.[118]

From a constitutional standpoint the decision is a mess. *Roe* did not establish a right to *sexual* privacy, but it was a landmark ruling nevertheless and a crucial victory for a women's movement that had come to embrace *decisional* privacy in reproductive choices as a prerequisite for equality.

IX

Elated, women's rights groups drew comparisons to *Brown v. Board of Education* almost immediately. Lawrence Lader, a figurehead of the abortion rights movement since the mid-1960s, claimed the decision "climaxed a social revolution whose magnitude and speed were probably unequaled in United States history." Alas, there were no more living abolitionists left to challenge his opinion on the matter.[119]

Ten years after *Roe* legal scholars, very much influenced by the theorist judge Richard Posner, constructed four larger "tiers of privacy" that were implied by the ruling: privacy of the home, bodily integrity, informational privacy, and decisional privacy. Privacy of the home was not explicitly addressed by the Court, but to the extent abortion is tied to the contraception issue it "helps women create seclusion, solitude, and conditions of limited attention-paying at home." The second, bodily integrity, speak to the universally recognized desire for individuals to manage the functions of their corporeal selves. The third, informational privacy, lives in the protection of doctor-patient confidentiality so that women can elect to have abortions without fear of reprisals or embarrassment. And finally, decisional privacy, the most pronounced of the four tiers, held that through the passage of laws that restricted access to abortion, the government was deemed to have entered a sphere of free decision making that should be the exclusive domain of women and beyond the reach of the state.[120]

Roe solidified the place of decisional privacy as a cornerstone of the women's rights movement—not just because of its rejection of older understandings of the private sphere, but also because decisional privacy has distinct implications for the ability of women to secure other forms of meaningful privacy. The freedom of choice implied by decisional privacy can serve the ends of those seeking anonymity, seclusion, solitude, and the protection of personal information. It allows women to reject traditional roles of caretaker and nurturer and assert instead roles rooted in gender equality and economic mobility.[121]

But rather surprisingly, while privacy was central to the legal justification of abortion, it received little attention in the debates over *Roe v. Wade* that tore across the final decades of the twentieth century. The reason for this absence lay in the tactical realities of America's culture wars. Women's groups recognized almost immediately that opponents of abortion would likely respond with a series of maneuverings designed to limit access and forestall compliance. Hospitals in some cases would need to be forced to comply with the Court's rulings, and Catholic communities especially would be eager to challenge implementation.[122] The blowback was slow in coming, though; early on, most of it came, predictably, from the Catholic Church. By the end of 1973 the church had spent over $4 million toward anti-abortion activities.[123] When attacking abortion rights, the Catholic Church and its chief affiliate (the National Right to Life Committee) decided not to engage the privacy aspects of the *Roe* decision. Instead, they adopted the language of human rights: To support abortion was to support genocide.[124] Neither political party was roused by this.[125]

So then how did the abortion issue evolve into one of the paramount issues in American politics? The power behind the elevation of the abortion issue was a concerted effort by the GOP to increase its appeal among traditionally Democratic Catholics. Polls indicate that Republican voters in the mid-1970s were, for the most part, more pro-choice than Democrats. At the 1976 Republican National Convention fewer that 40 percent of the delegates identified as pro-life.[126]

The Republican Party's strategic shift on abortion policy, according to political theorist Daniel K. Williams, "reflected the party's struggle over issues of religion and cultural politics." For most of the 1960s Republicans had viewed the right to an abortion as a mainline Protestant cause that was very much in the best interest of middle-class white women and doctors. "But when they began to view 'abortion on demand' as a symptom of the sexual revolution, the feminist movement, and cultural liberalism, Republicans became less supportive of abortion rights, and they became more amenable to" finding ways to bring more Evangelicals and Catholics into the party.[127]

Early in his administration, and after some reluctance, Nixon agreed to the "Catholic strategy" and began incorporating phrases like "sanctity of human life" and "abortion on demand" into his speeches.[128] By 1980 a strong endorsement of the pro-life position had become a way for many Americans to communicate their opposition to second-wave feminism and the sexual revolution. The social and cultural were informing the political, as is often true. By 2009 only 26 percent of Republicans identified as pro-choice.[129]

Yet neither Republicans nor Democrats spent much energy discussing the merits of privacy either as a legitimate constitutional right or as a philosophical concept. In key speeches and tracts throughout the culture wars the right to privacy was largely ignored.[130] However, abortion advocates did begin conflating decisional privacy with larger notions of liberty when constructing their pro-choice platform. By the 1990s pro-choice supporters were speaking much more about their "freedom to choose" than about their right to decisional privacy. That privacy rights had been almost wholly eclipsed by broader language is evidenced in the Supreme Court's reaffirming of the *Roe* decision in 1992's *Planned Parenthood v. Casey*.

In *Casey* the plaintiffs challenged five imaginative provisions of the Pennsylvania Abortion Control Act of 1982, viewed by many as that state's attempt to create an "undue burden" restricting abortion.

The provisions were informed consent rules, spousal notice, parental consent for minors, medical necessity, and various recordkeeping requirements.

Casey was the first major case to provide an opportunity for the justices—a very different set of justices—to overturn *Roe*. The Rehnquist Court of the early 1990s had a firm conservative majority made up of eight Republican-appointed justices—six of whom had been appointed by President Ronald Reagan or George H. W. Bush. Pro-lifers braced for a reversal. Yet Justice Souter defied expectations and joined Justices O'Connor, Stevens, and Blackmun to create a precarious five-justice majority after Justice Kennedy changed his mind as well. Kennedy joined O'Connor and Souter in writing a plurality opinion that would reaffirm *Roe*.[131]

The right to privacy was mentioned, of course, but only sparsely and only as a secondary concern to broader understandings of "liberty." Certainly not as a distinct entity as it had in *Griswold*. It was almost an afterthought. O'Connor, Kennedy, and Souter noted:

> Liberty finds no refuge in a jurisprudence of doubt yet 19 years after our holding that the Constitution protects a woman's right to terminate her pregnancy in its early stages, *Roe v. Wade* (1973), that definition of liberty is still questioned. Joining the respondents as *amicus curiae*, the United States, as it has done in five other cases in the last decade, again asks us to overrule *Roe*.[132]

Conscious of the fragility of judicial authority, the plurality acknowledged that it was important for the Court to stand by prior decisions lest it damage its prestige. There had been no change in the fundamental reasoning underpinning the previous decision:

> An entire generation has come of age free to assume *Roe*'s concept of liberty in defining the capacity of women to act in society, and to make reproductive decisions; no erosion of principle going to liberty or personal autonomy has left *Roe*'s central holding a doctrinal remnant. . . . The Court must take

care to speak and act in ways that allow people to accept its decisions on the terms the Court claims for them, as grounded truly in principle, not as compromises with social and political pressures having, as such, no bearing on the principled choices that the Court is obliged to make.[133]

Although the plurality did uphold *Roe*'s "essential holding" that women have a constitutional right to privacy (they used the term "liberty") to terminate their pregnancies, they also overturned the *Roe* trimester framework in favor of a "viability analysis." In doing so, the plurality also replaced the strict scrutiny analysis of *Roe* with a new "undue burden" standard to protect women facing a substantial obstacle when seeking an abortion.[134]

"The *Casey* decision did indeed say that the government has an interest in unborn life from the beginning of pregnancy and that it can adopt policies that allow it to express that interest," according to Pulitzer Prize winner Linda Greenhouse, "including seeking to persuade a woman to change her mind and carry the pregnancy to term. But crucially, the *Casey* decision held that while the government can endeavor to *persuade* a woman to choose childbirth over abortion, at the end of the day it may not *prevent* her from choosing otherwise."[135]

When all was said and done, *Casey* demonstrated that while the right to privacy was still part of the legal grounding surrounding the abortion issue, it had largely been subsumed in broader notions of "liberty" to choose reproductive options. Counting all opinions, the justices used the word "privacy" forty-eight times in *Griswold*, whereas "liberty" appeared thirty-six times. Likewise in *Roe*, the "privacy" to "liberty" ratio is 27 to 17. In all of the *Casey* opinions, the ratio is 21 to 114. Privacy was no longer a distinct concept in the reproductive debates; instead it took a place under the umbrella of liberty. Under the umbrella of "choice."[136]

In the decades after *Roe*, many political commentators argued that the case not only started the conflict over abortion but the common assumption, both outside and within the legal academy, became that *Roe* had driven the realignment of Republican and Democratic voters around abortion. David Brooks, for example, argued in 2005 that "Justice Harry Blackmun did more inadvertent damage to our democracy than any other 20th-century American. When he and his Supreme Court colleagues issued the *Roe v. Wade* decision, they set off a cycle of political viciousness and counter-viciousness that has poisoned public life ever since."[137]

X

By wholly embracing arguments rooted in privacy, the champions of reproductive rights achieved much. Then, on the heels of their greatest victory, they set those arguments aside. Figuring out the *when* here is considerably easier than figuring out the *why*.

The practical and transactional nature of political rhetoric is likely a good place to start. When dealing with an emotionally charged issue like abortion in an emotionally charged political landscape, broadsides aimed at "the sanctity of life" and punchier notions of "liberty" are much more effective than the philosophy lectures that usually accompany conversations about privacy. We've seen this same reluctance in debates over national security and data collection. Also, because the Court was by no means rigid when it proclaimed a right to privacy in *Griswold* and *Roe*, opponents and advocates chose instead to focus on the more immediate "fetal viability" aspect of the decision, along with the enduring legal questions around the appropriate definition of "personhood" and the scope of the state's compelling interest to protect life.

Regardless, the right to privacy was, for a time, a cornerstone of the women's movement and its quest for reproductive rights. There, privacy found a context for its eventual constitutional recognition. That context proved a considerably more effective vehicle than the perils of surveillance, or national security concerns, or tabloid journalism, or large-scale data collection.

While the Warren Court stopped short of recognizing a right to *sexual privacy*, the judiciary was instrumental in galvanizing the sexual revolution and facilitating drastic changes in sexual norms—even if that wasn't its intention. One ACLU survey conducted in

1994 is particularly telling. Six in ten Americans polled believed that homosexuality was "against God's law," yet 80 percent of those who held that view believed that all sex between consenting adults, even homosexuals, remained a private matter. As for abortion, 80 percent of respondents agreed that abortion was a personal decision for all women, even though 61 percent held that it was morally wrong. Illustrating America's persistent ambivalence in matters of privacy, nearly half of the respondents agreed with *both* statements: they felt that abortion was a private matter *and* morally reprehensible.[138]

7

TAKING STOCK

I

Capitol Hill, early afternoon, Thursday, October 25, 2001. The senators sat in the north wing of the US Capitol and awaited their turn to vote. The nation had been attacked six weeks earlier. Thousands were killed, another terrorist strike might be imminent, and the president of the United States was asking for broad new powers so that he might better take the fight to the enemy and keep his country safe. Federal surveillance, he argued, needed to be expanded. Probable cause standards needed to be reduced. Methods formerly reserved only for foreign intelligence gathering would need to be used on some American citizens. The senators, for the most part, were eager to oblige.

"We simply cannot prevail in the battle against terrorism if the right hand of our government has no idea what the left hand is doing," argued John Edwards (D-MA). "When we are facing a war where it is more likely that more civilians will die than military personnel, the home front *is* a warfront," announced Chuck Schumer (D-NY). "The FBI could get a wiretap to investigate the Mafia, but they could not get one to investigate terrorists. To put it bluntly, that was crazy!" said Joe Biden (D-DE). The American public seemed to agree. The proposed bill, the USA PATRIOT Act, had passed overwhelmingly in the House of Representatives the day before to the cheers of many. The Senate would not disappoint. The final vote was 98-1.[1]

The lone dissenter, Wisconsin's Russ Feingold, a former Rhodes scholar and graduate of Harvard Law School, stood in the pit of the Senate chamber and explained his reluctance:

> There have been periods in our nation's history when civil liberties have taken a back seat to what appeared at the time to be the legitimate exigencies of war. Our national consciousness still bears the stain and the scars of those events: the Alien and Sedition Acts, the suspension of habeas corpus during the Civil War, the internment of Japanese-Americans, German-Americans, and Italian-Americans during World War II, the blacklisting of supposed communist sympathizers during the McCarthy era, and the surveillance and harassment of antiwar protesters, including Dr. Martin Luther King Jr., during the Vietnam War. We must not allow these pieces of our past to become prologue. . . . [I]f we lived in a country where police were allowed to search your home at any time for any reason; if we lived in a country where the government was allowed to open your mail, eavesdrop on your phone conversations, or intercept your email communications . . . the government would probably discover and arrest more terrorists, or would-be terrorists . . . but that would not be a country in which we would want to live.[2]

The years to come would bring considerable technological change. Very quickly Americans developed much more intimate and highly dependent relationships with the internet. Very quickly the phones they carried would become integral and highly visible aspects of their daily lives. Very quickly constituent letter-writing campaigns would give way to online petitions and blogs, and politicians would no longer rely on mere microphones to communicate with the public but on the far-reaching platforms of social media. That wondrous period of scientific innovation, whose impact reached into almost every corner of the world in ways no less significant than the Renaissance, or the Enlightenment, or the Industrial Revolution, was a period in which American standards of privacy shifted more rapidly and became more complicated than ever before.

II

It is the privilege of historians to keep a certain distance from current events. Distance lends perspective. It reminds us that our understanding of the present is often short-sighted and incomplete, and that our predictions about the future are often wrong. Which is not to say there isn't first-rate work being done on contemporary privacy issues. Quite the opposite. Today's privacy advocates are operating at the vanguard of one of the most important issues of their age. But in the end, this is a book about what happened, not what's happening. That said, history can help shape the way we view the present and offer perspective on how we got here. Since our recent turn toward the digital, what about the privacy problems outlined in this book has changed and what has stayed the same?

As should be clear by now, the coming of the internet age did not invent the modern American conversation about privacy; neither is it likely to bring about privacy's complete and utter demise. That conversation began in the late nineteenth century and was constantly repackaged as it branched off into a variety of different directions across an array of contexts as it squared off against different countervailing interests, many of which served the public good. This is still very much the case today. The way Americans think and talk about privacy continues to evolve in the face of new legitimate pressures, only more rapidly than before and in many regards with a greater sense of urgency.

What seems especially conspicuous about the internet age is how it has made the themes that traditionally comprised the modern American conversation about privacy considerably more muddled — particularly as modern technology continues to amplify the capacity of individuals and organizations to circumscribe both their own privacy and the privacy of others in powerful new ways.

With regard to newspapers — it's no secret that American print journalism found itself in dire straits with the expansion of the internet, as more and more readers abandoned their hardcopy subscriptions for the convenience of consuming current events on their computers and smartphones. But despite years of layoffs, salary buy-outs, and bankruptcies, papers that embraced the human interest genre, with a few painful adjustments, successfully adapted to the online format and embraced the new advantages it afforded them. In many ways the privacy problems of human interest journalism born in the days of Brandeis and Warren carried over into the twenty-first century — they've just been enhanced and grown more complicated.[3]

As it has for more than a century human interest journalism, now mostly web-based, still trades largely in the disclosure of private information beyond expected boundaries, can damage reputations, and inhibits people from authoring their own self-narratives. When a paper's sights are trained on a subject, there is still little distinction to be found between its treatment of public and private figures. Any citizen enveloped in a story deemed entertaining is considered by these outlets as deserving of media attention, and modern-day media moguls still lean heavily on the argument (also born in the days of Warren and Brandeis) that at the end of the day, as the CEO of Reuters Group put it, "people get the media they deserve." All the while, the many virtues of the human interest genre have also remained the same: gossip is not always harmful, is still incredibly entertaining, can be a welcome respite from the burdens of the day and the exhaustion of the twenty-four-hour political news cycle, and is both something many people are still willing to pay for and a platform many companies are still eager to advertise on.[4]

But the internet age complicated these well-established trends in a number of ways. First, thanks to the rapid proliferation of smartphone technology, almost every American now has a camera in his or her pocket at all times — a development Brandeis would likely have found detestable. When combined with the meteoric expansion of social media and the cultural embrace of popularized "confessional" narratives in which individuals publicly share highly personal information about themselves, the result has been an endless supply of publishable material (complete with photos and video footage) pouring in from every corner of the nation. And thanks to greatly enhanced levels of public and private data collection coupled with advances in search engine technology, the personal histories of the actors involved in those stories are better known to the journalists investigating them than they ever were in the past. This additional context can yield either positive or negative results depending on the larger goals of a particular journalist. It also demonstrates the extent to which the privacy problems traditionally associated with big data and surveillance have become embedded in those associated with human interest journalism.[5]

Second, and perhaps even more consequential, is how the switch to online publishing has brought a troubling new level of permanence to the human interest genre. Before the internet, those who had stories published about their private affairs could take a measure of comfort in the fact that after an initial wave of attention the details of that ordeal would be forgotten by the majority of the public as time went on.

In the twentieth century, to discover whether an individual was ever the subject of a news report required pouring over stacks of old editions in an archive or sifting through roles of microfilm. In the twenty-first century, all one need do to acquire that information is type a name into a search engine. This increased accessibility makes the perils of one becoming a prisoner of his or her recorded past that much more pronounced and has been the motivation behind a series of legal actions (particularly in Europe) designed to regulate search engine content in the name of establishing a "right to be forgotten." The legal and cultural nuances of this movement are anything but clear-cut—particularly at a time where people go to great lengths to willingly share personal information on the internet in ways that suggest some are more afraid of *not* being seen—but the "right to be forgotten" is no doubt a fascinating new battlefront in the fight for privacy and worthy of our attention.[6]

On the subject of national security—the passage of the Patriot Act in 2001, the expansion of the Foreign Intelligence Surveillance Act (FISA) in 2008, and numerous other post-9/11 developments appear on the surface to be very much in line with America's well-established history of curtailing privacy rights to protect the nation from the very real threats posed by dangerous enemy combatants operating within our borders. Senator Feingold certainly recognized as much. But again, this trend has taken on strikingly new proportions in the internet age precisely because technological advances have vastly increased the capacity of the government to monitor its citizens while attempting to root out that threat. The impulse isn't new—it's just the potential harms that accompany these trends are so much more pronounced.[7]

The wiretaps, miniature microphones, snail mail, membership lists, and other tools that proved so valuable to the investigators of the twentieth century have expanded to include GPS and RFID technology, mobile phones, drones, satellite imaging, email, social media activity, internet browsing histories, and, most important, vast stores of consumer data held by private companies. When taken in aggregate, the modern American living in the digital age can be investigated, tracked, and monitored by the state in a way that entails almost total awareness. This reality was aptly (and foolishly) articulated in the chosen moniker of the 2003 federal surveillance program Total Information Awareness, which after an initial surge of unpopularity quickly changed its name to Terrorism Information Awareness. The growing practice of the state turning to privately held consumer data for surveillance purposes has given rise to a reality in which, according to privacy expert David Lyon, the government and the private sector "cooperate extensively, the one taking methods from the other . . . with potentially pernicious results as the 'successful' methods in one area are applied in ways deleterious of human rights in another."[8]

And much like it did in the twentieth century, the federal government still demonstrates a willingness to use its surveillance prerogatives in dangerously broad ways that are tantamount to dragnet searches—at times illegally. Among the more famous revelations to come from former National Security Agency contractor Edward Snowden in 2013 (who, it should be noted, committed an illegal invasion of privacy *against* the federal government when he turned over thousands of classified documents to the press) was that America's national security apparatus had collaborated with major telecommunications carriers to collect and store metadata on every American citizen who had either made or received a call from certain nations of interest. The US Second Circuit Court of Appeals deemed the program unlawful two years later, citing "that to allow the government to collect phone records only because they may become relevant to a possible authorized investigation in the future fails even the permissive 'relevance' test." The actual national security benefits and dangers of bulk metadata collection are still being hotly contested.[9]

The Patriot Act did not give rise to Big Brother. At least not in the aggressively totalitarian sense that George Orwell predicted. The public response, as usual, remains largely torn between the undoubtedly positive security benefits of modern surveillance technology and the pressures that technology places on privacy and civil liberties. The many positive aspects that accompany our government's increased surveillance capacity should not be ignored. CCTV technology, for example, was instrumental in capturing the perpetrators responsible for the 2013 bombing of the Boston Marathon. But we must also be aware that those positives aspects are still, as they have been throughout our history, sometimes overstated, as evidenced in a 2015 White House review panel report that concluded the NSA metadata program "was not essential in preventing attacks."[10]

And so our ambivalence about the relationship between privacy and national security endures. And it can be seen both in the persistent reluctance of the Senate to roll back many troubling provisions of the Patriot Act as they come up for renewal and in the concerted efforts by groups such as the ACLU, the Electronic Privacy Information Center, and the Obama administration's Review Group on Intelligence and Technology to raise enough public awareness and political capital to pass the Protecting Rights of Individuals Act of 2015, which, among other things, increased judicial review standards for broad monitoring programs, limited "secret searches" of American homes, and eliminated FBI usage of nameless (or "John

Doe") roving wiretaps. These developments suggest that the privacy versus security debate is far from lost, and that in the face of new technologies and an unprecedented level of data sharing between the state and modern corporate conglomerates it is more important than ever for Americans to keep a watchful eye on the institutions responsible for protecting national security. But then we do still tend to talk about this issue in all-or-nothing terms.[11]

On the subject of big data—without a doubt the most significant historical break from the privacy problems of the twentieth century has been the complete obliteration of any hope to stem the tide of data collection. To put it another way, information generally flows across three stages. It is first *collected*, which presents one set of privacy problems. It is then *processed* and sorted, which presents different kinds of privacy problems. And finally, it is *disseminated* to others, which presents still other kinds of privacy problems. By the early twenty-first century, collection of huge volumes of personal and demographic information had become unavoidable—indeed, it was the basis of a large sector of the economy. Perhaps we can make some tweaks here and there, maybe even important ones. But in its entirety the issue is a dead letter. We were trending in this direction for decades, and somewhere, probably around the passage of the 1974 Privacy Act, a line was crossed. There's no going back.[12]

We've continued our tendency, more of a knee-jerk reaction really, when presented with news about some hacking scandal or a blatant misuse of private information, to shrug and remark knowingly that "privacy is dead." Americans have been making such claims since the Gilded Age, but in the modern context this lament is perhaps best understood as a recognition that in the struggle to find an appropriate privacy balance for information, the battle over *collection* has been lost.

This isn't necessarily a bad thing. It was largely our own doing, and in many ways we've benefited from it. The immense popularity of online shopping, the proliferation of social media, the smartphone, the marked preference of credit and debit transactions over cash, voice-activated in-home digital assistants who make life more convenient and whose microphones are always listening—these consumer choices, and they were most certainly choices, made our lives easier while we left more and more snippets of ourselves behind for others to pick up. As the saying goes, nobody forced the tracking and listening devices on us: we bought them ourselves and we bought them eagerly. When coupled with a post-9/11 security mindset, which many Americans embrace wholeheartedly, any effort to reverse the flow of large-scale data collection in a broad and meaningful way seems a waste of energy.

What this means is that the greatest privacy question facing Americans in the twenty-first century is how best to ensure that those who have our data do not misuse it—especially at a time in which big data has, in the internet age, enmeshed itself in the other themes discussed in this book. Certainly not the easiest question for a civilization to face down, especially when considering the wide range of people and entities that have our information to one degree or another. Nevertheless, information *processing* is the new key battleground.

To even begin addressing this question, it has become increasingly necessary for Americans to ask ourselves what we believe an appropriate flow of information really looks like—ask ourselves, as Helen Nissenbaum puts it, where the lines should be drawn so that we can establish firm "informational norms" based on "substantive moral and political principles" that reflect who we are as a civilization.[13] Two paths forward seem the most obvious ones. The first involves the law—a top-down approach. If our leaders enact comprehensive policies regulating what information holders can and cannot do with the information they hold and outline strict penalties for violators, penalties with teeth, then a balance may well be struck. The second is the marketplace—a bottom-up solution. Consumers who are rightly concerned about how their information is being used and stored can let it be known, with their wallets, that they will enrich companies that protect their privacy and boycott those that do not. This would mean that to achieve an appropriate privacy balance, Americans must force businesses to think of privacy as a commodity.

III

First to the law. The United States entered the digital age without uniform federal laws regulating privacy—what the legal community calls "omnibus" protections. A few decades in, while almost every other advanced democracy in the world embraced an omnibus approach, we did not. Instead most privacy law stayed at the state level, where it had lived for most of the twentieth century. Some states, like California, have a rich tradition of passing aggressive and innovative privacy protections. Others not so much. We have a patchwork system because keeping privacy regulation a state matter wasn't a conscious choice. It is a product mostly of the glaring inability of Congress to keep pace with changing technologies, along with a large measure of popular and political apathy.[14]

Our patchwork system does have some advantages. It gives us flexibility. It creates space to experiment with different kinds of privacy solutions. It allows decisions about privacy to be made at different levels of government, which is more pluralistic, and it insulates privacy law from any gridlock or dysfunction in Washington. It also means that privacy advocates can launch campaigns on numerous fronts with a large degree of specialization and nuance. Supporters of the patchwork system sometimes call it "privacy federalism," and it's important not to ignore its upsides.[15]

But an omnibus approach, when enforced properly, can be a real game changer. There is power in centralization. Also clarity. And as the world grows increasingly more connected, many legal experts believe that the models embraced by our allies are America's best chance at protecting privacy from the dangers to it in a global information economy. Such was the rationale behind the passage of Europe's omnibus privacy law, the General Data Protection Regulation, which was implemented in 2018.

As an example, for decades many lawmakers and experts were comfortable giving corporations and the government a wide berth on what they did with people's information as long as they promised to follow certain rules about anonymity. Basically, keep people's names separate from their data and the entities could do what they liked. But by the early twenty-first century digital algorithms had grown so advanced that tech experts started realizing that even without names all of the snippets of data lying around the internet would be enough to identify an individual regardless. At least with 90+ percent accuracy. Such is the true reality of modern metadata. So anonymity became a myth. People may not be identifiable from the outset, but they can eventually be found.[16]

Also, while private companies have been forced since the 1970s to get consent from consumers before they gather and share their information, numerous studies have shown that people in the early digital age were dangerously uninformed about what they were consenting to. It also turned out, after much digging, that many companies simply ignored their own privacy policies whenever it suited their needs, with little in the way of repercussions. Almost all privacy scholars agree that we need a better process to inform Americans about what is happening with their information. And it wasn't just scholars. By the early 2000s the confusing nature of privacy policies became the subject of hundreds of jokes for comedians, actors, and television personalities. A patchwork approach seems ill suited to solve the problems of anonymity and consent, and many believe that only uniform standards that apply to all states can address these kinds of concerns.[17]

The question ahead of us is whether the United States will maintain the legal tradition it embraced over the twentieth century and keep most privacy law at the state level, or do what everyone else did and adopt a more centralized omnibus approach to privacy. But the prospect of an omnibus approach instantly begets more questions. How will that approach be structured? Will the Federal Trade Commission take the reins, as it did partially in the Obama years?[18] Will companies be forced to hire privacy officers, like investment bankers have to, to ensure compliance with these laws? How will advocates of such a system push against the predictable cries about the burdens of regulation? Would omnibus laws just end up being paper tigers and thus hurt more than they help?

As American privacy law transitioned from the analog to the digital, it moved into the mainstream of legal studies. As privacy problems grew, and continue to grow, more severe, the number of legal scholars offering solutions has grown exponentially. In the 1960s Allen Westin was a pioneer. By the early twenty-first century privacy law had evolved into a vast arena of jurisprudence covering governmental policy, consumer protection, medicine, international law, and much more. Small seminars have become gigantic international conferences. Papers and poster sessions have become books and edited volumes. Cramped single-room offices that housed two or three privacy advocates have become sprawling think tanks, watch dogs, and policy centers. And privacy doesn't seem to be a topic lawyers and policymakers will be talking *less* about as the century rolls on. From a professional standpoint, privacy is not dead at all.

IV

The second avenue of our salvation may lie in the marketplace. Those with little faith in the ability of lawmakers to provide effective privacy solutions should find some comfort in the knowledge that a number of developments suggest another way. Privacy, a thing traditionally discarded in favor of earnings, is increasingly becoming a marketable commodity. Privacy advocates now have a powerful and somewhat unfamiliar new weapon at their disposal: the profit motive.

The history of American data collection is that information privacy has been shaped largely by economics. Since the 1970s profits and privacy have mostly been at odds, and attempts to properly regulate big data were repeatedly thwarted by claims that increased regulations would be too burdensome for private businesses. That more privacy meant less efficiency. Which meant less profits. Which meant crippling job creators and the economy and so on.

But something changed in the early decades of the digital age. For the first time threats to personal privacy grew so powerful in the national consciousness that the market made room for the protection of personal information as a profitable enterprise. To be sure, companies still make billions trading in private data, but privacy finally has something of a counterweight. The market has opened to this new trend in a variety of ways. Cybersecurity is a multibillion dollar industry, with a range of services catering to multinational corporations, governments, small businesses, and individuals working alone out of studio apartments. There has also been a sharp increase in the use and marketing of what are called privacy enhancing technologies, or PETs. Cellphones that are advertised as "uncrackable"— even to law enforcement. Search engines that vow never to share user info regardless of circumstance. Email and messaging services that boast the most advanced encryption. Virtual private networks. Crypto-currency. Signal-blocking cellphone pouches. Stylish little stickers to place over laptop webcams. Mock life-alert bracelets that read "delete my browser history." Not to mention a slew of new "privacy upgrades" offered on a range of services from banking to credit to web design.[19]

What makes the economic approach to privacy so attractive is that it doesn't rely on our better angels or popular will. It relies on self-interest and greed. If companies in a capitalist society see that they can get rich protecting privacy, or that they can go broke if they don't, change is that much more likely. What hope there is for privacy at this crucial moment rests in its potential as a profitable venture for those with the clout and means to effect substantive change. We can, in effect, buy our way to a more private society.

But there are some red flags here as well. Obviously, there is potential for this trend to usher in a large degree of privacy inequality. If privacy is something one can increasingly purchase, it stands to reason that those with limited means will have fewer options for ensuring their privacy. There is also the chance that Americans will be fooled—businesses that sense privacy is growing fashionable may rope in customers by claiming to protect one kind of privacy, like communications, while simultaneously attacking privacy in another way, like selling purchase histories without consent. Like all movements that push against established interests, a demand for privacy can be coopted. So Americans will still need to care enough to see the whole picture and ensure they're not being taken for a ride by companies claiming to be their protectors.

Still, as long as there are vast sums of money to be made selling services to those who wish to keep their communications and data free from prying eyes or vast sums of money to be lost by not protecting that information, privacy will always have a heartbeat in the digital age. The rather recent commodification of privacy is privacy's best hope of surviving the twenty-first century. It is very much in America's interest to keep privacy profitable. And make no mistake, if the law continues to fail us then privacy-enhancing technologies may well be the greatest investment opportunity of the coming generation.

V

Which brings us back to Mr. Zuckerberg. The CEO, by most immediate accounts, performed exceedingly well during his visit to the Hill. He projected both concern and contrition in his exchanges with American lawmakers and promised that he and his company were in the process of "a broad philosophical shift" that would no doubt yield meaningful action to protect the privacy of their constituents. By the time his testimony concluded Facebook's stock had risen approximately 5 percent over those two days, and a few weeks later Zuckerberg surpassed Warren Buffett to become the third richest person on Earth.

But then, in late July of that year, following slower than projected second quarter earnings, Facebook stock plunged nearly 20 percent (or approximately $120 billion)—the greatest single-day loss of market capital ever experienced in the history of corporate capitalism (up to that point). The plunge was due to a confluence of multiple factors, not the least of which was the company's promise to "put privacy first" for its American users in the wake of the Cambridge Analytica scandal and diminished ad revenue in the wake of Europe's new omnibus data protection laws that had gone into effect that May.[20]

The crisis faced by Zuckerberg is still unfolding as this book goes to press, and much about the future of that company remains unclear. But in these early stages we can already see the potential impact of pro-privacy pressures when they are thrust simultaneously from the legal and consumer realms.

The threat of a not-too-distant future in which Congress could pass stronger data privacy legislation is increasingly becoming more real, though exactly what that legislation would look like is hard to gauge. The frequency of hearings on data privacy have reached record highs in the twenty-first century, and the larger political dangers inherent to targeted misinformation campaigns by foreign powers engaged in information warfare certainly have the potential to help reframe America's privacy debate on *societal* terms. And while many pundits have claimed that the decline of Facebook's stock price is evidence that "privacy and profits are mutually exclusive," all the plunge has really demonstrated is that privacy and *unlimited* profits are mutually exclusive. After all, Facebook employed these new protections not out of altruism but as a way to insulate itself from total annihilation. The real question is the extent to which these changes are legitimate or mere window dressing. Only time will tell.[21]

Moving forward, we mustn't forget that there will always be some Americans who simply don't care much about their own privacy. Particularly with the advent of social media, again, the bigger fear for many individuals is that they're *not* being watched. Those who find such behavior troubling should remember that the larger value of privacy is located on the *societal* level—it's about more than individual rights. Should you find yourself speaking to such a person, try reminding them of that fact. And don't be too judgy if they remain unconvinced. Some groups of people have been oblivious about their privacy for more than a century.

Among the more important lessons to be learned from a study of American privacy is the need to abandon our stubborn and persistent line of thinking that imagines privacy and those interests that push against it as mutually exclusive. This paves the way for a false perception that people tend to care about privacy somewhat, but they care about other things more, and so privacy must suffer. Only by transcending this zero-sum mindset will we come to enjoy the benefits of both privacy and curiosity. Of privacy and freedom from fear. Of privacy and technological innovation. Of privacy and convenience. Of privacy and all the wondrous things our digital golden age has to offer.

ACKNOWLEDGMENTS

This is my first book. Writing it would have been considerably harder were it not for the help of numerous advisors, colleagues, pupils, friends, and frenemies. Any valuable insights found within are largely because of their efforts. Any errors are mine alone.

Andrew Wylie and Kristina Moore somehow transformed a simple proposal into a book contract with a publisher I've admired all of my adult life. There is no better home for a writer than the Wylie Agency.

Timothy Mennel is an incomparable editor with an impeccable sense of style and taste in all things. He is master of both stick and carrot. I am very grateful for his guidance.

Three historians are most responsible for shepherding this project to completion. The always collegial Robert "KC" Johnson set aside hours of time he certainly didn't have to patiently explore with me what privacy even is, why it matters, and what the law has to say about it. David Nasaw offered crucial guidance and frequently reminded me, as he does all of his students, that authors hailing from the City University of New York (CUNY) have an obligation to write for two audiences. James Oakes, whose office door I darkened far too often, ended up being, through our many discussions, the best advisor a guy never had.

My sincere thanks to Joel Allen, Laird Bergad, Joshua Brown, Martin Burke, Peter Connolly-Smith (a teacher of teachers), Michael

Crowder, Tanya Domi, Gregory Downs, Joshua Freeman, Dagmar Herzog, Micki Kaufman, the indomitable Teresita Levy, Kathleen McCarthy, Helena Rosenblatt, Frank Warren, and Barbara Welter—all of whom shaped this work in one important way or another.

Two students from my time teaching at CUNY Queens College require mentioning. The ever incisive Emily Abrams showed me that Americans can be hilarious when it comes to the subject of privacy. Kaitlin McDermott's intimidatingly brilliant observations helped me to articulate the value and dangers of privacy in much clearer terms and pressed me to think about a future with privacy solutions. They are both smarter than me. Thankfully, I am older.

The New York City–based public lecture organization ThinkOlio, brainchild of David Kurfirst and Chris Zumtobel, allowed me, while writing, to bring my ideas to a general audience and get a better sense of why people care, and don't care, about their privacy.

I am grateful to Kelly Unger Rachel and Lisa Wehrle at the University of Chicago Press for their meticulous work, attention, and professionalism.

A condensed version of my chapter on data collection was first published as "Big Iron and the Small Government: A History of Privacy and Data Collection in the United States," in the *Journal of Policy History*, and sections are reprinted here with the journal's permission.

Generous financial support from the Intercollegiate Studies Institute, the John Anson Kittredge Fund, and the Graduate Center of the City University of New York, for which I am most appreciative, also helped make this book a reality.

Carol Tambasco stands above all others (it's not even close). Katherine Brown is my rock. Phil Tambasco is the toughest and classiest guy I know. Yumi Aschkar—thunder buddy for life. And I would be remiss if I didn't also thank Salvatore, Denise, and Lauren Cappello.

My wife Victoria, whom I love madly, often finds herself in the acknowledgment sections of better books than this, and so I'm not entirely sure how to compete. My best shot: Party Buns. *Double-Slap-High-Five*. All of the feelings.

NOTES

INTRODUCTION

1 See "Transcript of Mark Zuckerberg's Senate Hearing," *Washington Post*, 10 April 2018, https://www.washingtonpost.com/news/the-switch/wp/2018/04/10/transcript-of-mark-zuckerbergs-senate-hearing/?noredirect=on&utm_term=.1dc6598d2a71.

2 Ibid.

3 The "all-or-nothing" character of post-9/11 American privacy debates has been well illustrated by privacy scholar Daniel Solove, who refers to this conceptualization as the "all-or-nothing fallacy" in his work *Nothing to Hide: The False Tradeoff Between Privacy and Security* (New Haven, CT: Yale University Press, 2011), esp. 21–38.

4 Ibid.

5 Barbara Welter, "The Cult of True Womanhood," *American Quarterly* 18, no. 2 (Summer 1966): 151–74.

6 The terms *dissemination* and *aggregation* as used here refer to Daniel Solove's "Taxonomy of Privacy," *University of Pennsylvania Law Review* 154, no. 3 (January 2006): 477–560.

7 Ibid.

8 See Anita Allen, *Uneasy Access: Privacy for Women in a Free Society* (Totowa, NJ: Rowman and Littlefield, 1988), 50–62.

9 See Daniel Solove, *Understanding Privacy* (Cambridge, MA: Harvard University Press, 2010); Helen Nissenbaum, *Privacy in Context: Technology, Policy, and the Integrity of Social Life* (Stanford, CA: Stanford Law Books, 2010).

10 Sarah Elizabeth Igo, *The Known Citizen: A History of Privacy in Modern America* (Cambridge, MA: Harvard University Press, 2018), 1.

PART ONE

1 While a total of fifty-five delegates were present at the Constitutional Convention, only twenty-nine had arrived in Philadelphia by May 29, which was enough for a quorum; the definitive primary source collection of the Convention is spread over

four volumes in United States and Max Farrand, *The Records of the Federal Convention of 1787* (New Haven, CT: Yale University Press, 1934).

2   The sheer number of articles and monographs regarding Madison's role in the Convention are legion. Among the finest are Carol Berkin, *A Brilliant Solution: Inventing the American Constitution* (Orlando: Harcourt, 2003); and Robert Middlekauff's *The Glorious Cause: The American Revolution, 1763-1789* (New York: Oxford University Press, 2007).

3   See Farrand, *Records*, vol. 1; Berkin, *Brilliant Solution*, 30-67.

4   Or more precisely, one most influential *American* privacy scholars. Alan F. Westin, *Privacy and Freedom* (New York: Atheneum, 1970), 7; Samuel Warren and Louis Brandeis, "The Right to Privacy," *Harvard Law Review* 4 (1890): 193.

5   This idea of privacy as an "umbrella term" is articulated in Daniel Solove's seminal article, "A Taxonomy of Privacy," *University of Pennsylvania Law Review* 154, no. 3 (January 2006): 477-560, and again in his *Understanding Privacy* (Cambridge, MA: Harvard University Press, 2010). Raymond Wacks also takes considerable pains to identify the difficulties in pinning down privacy's definition (he calls it "large and unwieldy") in *Privacy: A Very Short Introduction* (Oxford: Oxford University Press, 2010); and *Privacy*, vol. 1, *The Concept of Privacy* (Aldershot: Dartmouth, 1993).

6   Melvin Urofsky and Paul Finkelman, *A March of Liberty: A Constitutional History of the United States* (New York: Oxford University Press, 2002), 91-105.

7   Letter from Henry Lee to George Washington, 8 September 1876, in *The Papers of George Washington*, digital ed., ed. Theodore J. Crackel (Charlottesville: University of Virginia Press, Rotunda, 2008); Letter from George Washington to David Humphreys, 22 October 1876, in "Founders Online," US National Archives, https://founders.archives.gov/documents/Washington/04-04-02-0272.

8   Berkin, *Brilliant Solution*, 65; Westin, *Privacy and Freedom*, 46-47.

9   It should be noted that at its inception the machines and anti-immigrant groups had some success using the Australian ballot to disenfranchise large groups of voters. Despite this rocky start, the overall contributions of private voting are considered by most scholars to be immensely positive in the larger history of American democracy. The first comprehensive work on the introduction of the secret (or "Australian") ballot in the United States was Eldon Cobb Evan's University of Chicago dissertation, *A History of the Australian Ballot System in the United States* (Ann Arbor: University of Michigan Library, 1917).

10   Of course, we now know thanks to declassified documents that the FBI under Director J. Edgar Hoover and later under the instructions of the Nixon administration launched surveillance operations targeting both the SCLC and NAACP, but these operations were far from successful, they were widely condemned when brought to light, and both groups still preserved large amounts of privacy in their planning sessions. See part IV.

11   Pricilla Regan is among the first legal scholars to recognize the importance of privacy's *societal value*; see *Legislating Privacy: Technology, Social Values, and Public Policy* (Chapel Hill: University of North Carolina Press, 1995).

12   See Richard Estes and Daniel Otte, *The Behavior Guide to African Mammals: Including Hoofed Mammals, Carnivores, Primates* (Berkeley: University of California Press, 2012); D. Lukas and H. Clutton Brock, "The Evolution of Social Monogamy in Mammals," *Science*, 29 July 2013, http://science.sciencemag.org/content/sci/early/2013/07/29/science.1238677.full.pdf; Robert Ardrey, *The*

Territorial Imperative: A Personal Inquiry into the Animal Origins of Property and Nations (New York: Atheneum, 1966); Vero Copner Wynne-Edwards, *Animal Dispersion in Relation to Social Behaviour* (New York: Hafner, 1972); W. C. Allee, *The Social Life of Animals* (New York: AMS Press, 1976); "social distance" argument also noted in Westin, *Privacy and Freedom*, 8-9.

13   Margaret Mead, *Coming of Age in Samoa: A Psychological Study of Primitive Youth for Western Civilization* (New York: Morrow, 1961), 82-87; also Dorothy Lee, *Freedom and Culture* (Prospect Heights, IL: Waveland Press, 1987); Cotton Mather, *The Religion of the Closet* (Boston, 1705), 6; see also Westin, *Privacy and Freedom*, 8-9; also in David H. Flaherty, *Privacy in Colonial New England* (Charlottesville: University Press of Virginia, 1972), 1. Flaherty, a Westin protégée, was among the first (and few) historians to apply an advanced understanding of privacy to the US historical narrative, starting first with the Colonial period.

14   Jeffery Rosen, *The Unwanted Gaze: The Destruction of Privacy in America* (New York: Vintage Books, 2001), 8.

15   The term *privacy problem*, coined by Solove, is among the more preferred terms used by privacy scholars. It recognizes the reality that many individuals and organizations that push against privacy do so for legitimate reasons, whereas terms like *intrusion* or *invasion* tend to be more value laden and imply that all attempts against privacy are inherently wrong; see William Miller, *The Anatomy of Disgust* (Cambridge, MA: Harvard University Press, 1998). This observation is also present in numerous works, including Regan, *Legislating Privacy*; Solove, *Understanding Privacy*; Westin, *Privacy and Freedom*; and Nissenbaum, *Privacy in Context*.

16   Walt Whitman, "Song of Myself," in *Leaves of Grass* (Brooklyn, 1855; London: Penguin Classics, 2017).

17   See Deborah Hurley, "Taking the Long Way Home: The Human Right of Privacy," in *Privacy in the Modern Age: The Search for Solutions*, ed. Marc Rotenberg, Julia Horwitz, and Jeramie Scott, 70-77 (New York: The New Press, 2015); Alan Wolfe, "Public and Private in Theory and Practice: Some Implications of an Uncertain Boundary," in *Public and Private in Thought and Practice: Perspectives on a Grand Dichotomy*, ed. Jeff Weintraub, Alan and Krishan Kumar (Chicago: University of Chicago Press, 1997), 186-87; this quote also in Solove, *Understanding Privacy*, 99.

18   Ancient Jewish law, in particular, took great pains to protect individuals from the prying eyes of their neighbors.

19   This is a central claim by Westin in *Privacy and Freedom*, 20-21.

PART TWO

1   Samuel Warren and Louis Brandeis, "The Right to Privacy," *Harvard Law Review* 4 (1890): 193.

2   See Melvin Urofsky, *Louis D. Brandeis: A Life* (New York: Pantheon Books, 2009); *Olmstead v. United States*, 277 U.S. 438 (1928).

3   Warren and Brandeis, "Right to Privacy," 196.

4   *Life*, January-June, 1891 (emphasis added); *Cox Broadcasting Corp. v. Cohn*, 420 U.S. 469 (1975). For representative scholarship, see William L. Prosser, "Privacy," *California Law Review* 48 (1960): 383; Wilbur Larremore, "The Law of Privacy," *Columbia Law Review* 12, no. 8 (1912): 693; Daniel J. Solove, *Understanding Pri-*

vacy (Cambridge, MA: Harvard University Press, 2010); Ken I. Kersch, "The Reconstruction of Constitutional Privacy Rights and the New American State," *Studies in American Political Development* 16, no. 1 (2002): 61–87; also by Kersch, *Constructing Civil Liberties: Discontinuities in the Development of American Constitutional Law* (Cambridge: Cambridge University Press, 2004); David J. Bodenhamer and James W. Ely, *The Bill of Rights in Modern America* (Bloomington: Indiana University Press, 2008); Colin J. Bennett and Charles D. Raab, The Governance of Privacy: Policy Instruments in Global Perspective (Cambridge, MA: MIT Press, 2006).

5   See Solove, *Understanding Privacy*, 15–17.

6   "Patrician lawyer-merchant" being Westin's categorization in *Privacy and Freedom*, 348.

7   *Olmstead v. United States*, 277 U.S. 438, 473 (1928).

8   "Mr. Tilton's Sworn Statement," as reprinted in the New *York Times*, 22 July 1874.

9   Ibid.

10   *Woodhull & Claflin's Weekly*, 2 November 1872; Woodhull took pains to make it clear that she was not admonishing Beecher's sexual acts but his rhetorical hypocrisy; Richard Wightman Fox, *Trials of Intimacy: Love and Loss in the Beecher-Tilton Scandal* (Chicago: University of Chicago Press, 1999); Helen Lefkowitz Horowitz, *Rereading Sex: Battles Over Sexual Knowledge and Suppression in Nineteenth-Century America* (New York: Knopf, 2002), 346–57. For more on Woodhall, see also Amanda Frisken, *Victoria Woodhull's Sexual Revolution: Political Theater and the Popular Press in Nineteenth-Century America* (Philadelphia: University of Pennsylvania Press, 2004).

11   See Helen Lefkowitz Horowitz, "Victoria Woodhull, Anthony Comstock, and Conflict Over Sex in the United States in the 1870s," *Journal of American History* 87, no. 2 (September 2000): 403–34.

12   See especially Patricia Cline Cohen, Timothy J. Gilfoyle, and Helen Lefkowitz Horowitz, *The Flash Press: Sporting Male Weeklies in 1840s New York* (Chicago: University of Chicago Press, 2008). The "flash press" of the 1840s had been largely ignored by scholars until the American Antiquarian Society established a substantive collection of sources in 1985, which was used by Cohen, Gilfoyle, and Horowitz.

13   Joshua Brown, *Beyond the Lines: Pictorial Reporting, Everyday Life, and the Crisis of Gilded-Age America* (Berkeley: University of California Press, 2002), 4–15.

14   See Glenn Wallach "'A Depraved Taste for Publicity': The Press and Private Life in the Gilded Age," *American Studies* 39, no. 1 (Spring 1998): 31–57; also in Fox, *Trials of Intimacy*; Frisken, *Victoria Woodhull's Sexual Revolution*.

15   Wallach, "'A Depraved Taste for Publicity,'" 36, 42–50.

16   Ibid.

17   "The Abolition of Privacy," *New York Times*, 4 August 1874; also noted in Wallach, "'A Depraved Taste for Publicity.'"

18   "We Have Received the Following Letter from a Correspondent," *New York Times*, 12 February 1875; also noted in Wallach, "'A Depraved Taste for Publicity.'"

19   "We Have Received the Following Letter"; also noted in Wallach, "'A Depraved Taste for Publicity.'"

20   "Reporters Endeavoring to Obtain Admission to a Meeting of the Investigation Committee at Mr. Storrs's House," *Frank Leslie's Illustrated Newspaper*, 8 August 1874; "The Parlor of Mr. Rossiter Raymond, 123 Henry Street, Brooklyn—

Reporters and Stenographers Making Copies of Mr. Beecher's Statement for the Daily Papers," *Frank Leslie's Illustrated Newspaper*, 29 August 1874; "Mrs. Tilton," *Chicago Daily Tribune*, 3 October 1874; also in Wallach, "'A Depraved Taste for Publicity,'" 39, 41, 43, 50–53.

21 For examples of press coverage surrounding the Warrens and the Bayards, see Amy Gajda, "What If Samuel Warren Hadn't Married a Senator's Daughter? Uncovering the Press Coverage That Led to *The Right to Privacy*," Illinois Public Law and Legal Theory Research Papers Series, no. 07-06, 1 November 2007.

22 E. L. Godkin, "Chromo-Civilization," *Nation*, 24 September 1874, 201–2.

23 E. L. Godkin, "The Rights of the Citizen: To His Reputation," *Scribner's Magazine*, July 1890, 58–68.

24 Rochelle Gurstein, *The Repeal of Reticence: America's Cultural and Legal Struggles over Free Speech, Obscenity, Sexual Liberation, and Modern Art* (New York: Hill and Wang, 1996), 50.

25 Ibid., 59–60. Gurstein puts it particularly well: "it was the party of exposure's attempt to turn what was distinctive, unique, or individual into common coin that mortified the party of reticence."

26 "Fire Wrecks the Home of the Police Gazette," *New York Times*, 18 December 1906; for more on the *Gazette*, see Guy Reel, *The National Police Gazette and the Making of the Modern American Man, 1879–1906* (New York: Palgrave Macmillan, 2006); also Dan Schiller, *Objectivity and the News: The Public and the Rise of Commercial Journalism* (Philadelphia: University of Pennsylvania Press, 1981).

27 "Tragedy on a Train—Congressman Thompson Encounters the Seducer of His Wife and Kills Him in His Tracks," *National Police Gazette*, 12 May 1883; "A Jilted Woman's Revenge," "Killed by Her Husband," and "Her Young Life Ruined, Romance of Christie Jackson, of Sharon Springs, N.Y., "Eloped with a Rascal," all in *National Police Gazette*, 28 May 1892.

28 "Tragedy on a Train"; "Jilted Woman's Revenge," "Killed by Her Husband"; "Her Young Life Ruined"; "Eloped with a Rascal."

29 "Caught in the Shafting," *National Police Gazette*, 28 May 1892; "A Girl's Fight for Life," *National Police Gazette*, 28 May 1892.

30 Solove, *Understanding Privacy*, 10, 140–46.

31 Ibid.; a key difference is that the harm in a breach of confidentiality is usually the violation of trust in the relationship not necessarily embarrassment or damage to one's reputation.

32 Kathleen A. Hansen and Nora Paul, *Future Proofing the News: Preserving the First Draft of History* (Lanham, MD: Rowman and Littlefield, 2017), 2–10; Shannon E. Martin and Kathleen Hansen, *Newspapers of Record in a Digital Age: From Hot Type to Hot Link* (Westport, CT: Greenwood, 1998),79–90.

33 "Rush Buck Knocked Out," *National Police Gazette*, 28 May 1892; "Free Fight in a Cotton Mill," *National Police Gazette*, 28 May 1892.

34 "Caught in the Shafting," wood engraving, *National Police Gazette*, 28 May 1892; "Rush Buck Knocked Out," wood engraving, *National Police Gazette*, 28 May 1892.

35 "A Girl's Fight for Life," wood engraving, *National Police Gazette*, 28 May 1892; "Free Fight in a Cotton Mill."

36 *National Police Gazette*, 10 February 1891.

37 Louis Brandeis, "Other People's Money," *Harper's Weekly*, 13 December 1913.

38 See "Religious Notes" of *National Police Gazette*, 11 March 1882; 6 December 1890; 21 January 1888; 31 March 1883.

39   "Snap Shots on the Beach," *National Police Gazette*, 29 August 1891.

40   Neil Harris, "Iconography and Intellectual History: The Half-Tone Effect," in *New Directions in American Intellectual History*, ed. J. Higham and P. K. Conklin, 196-211 (Baltimore: Johns Hopkins University Press, 1979).

41   Ibid.

42   Ibid.; see also Michael L. Carlebach, *The Origins of Photojournalism in America* (Washington, DC: Smithsonian Institution Press, 1992), 5; also in Frederick S. Lane, *American Privacy: The 400 Year History of Our Most Sacred Right* (Boston: Beacon Press, 2009), 65-70.

43   *Roberson v. Rochester Folding Box Co.*, 64 N.E. 442 (N.Y. 1902); see also Robert Mensel, "Kodakers Lying in Wait: Amateur Photography and the Right of Privacy in New York, 1885-1915," *American Quarterly* 43, no. 1 (1991): 24-45; Victoria Prussen Spears, "The Case That Started It All: *Robertson v Rochester Folding Box Company*," *Privacy & Data Security Law Journal*, November 2008.

44   See Mensel, "Kodakers," 39; Spears, "Case That Started It All," 44.

45   Mensel, "Kodakers," 37-39.

46   *Henry v. Cherry & Webb*, 73 A. 97 (R.I. 1909); see also Lane, *American Privacy*, 69-70.

47   Solove, *Understanding Privacy*, 129-33, 154-58.

48   Ibid.

49   *Pavesich v. New England Life Ins. Co.*, 50 S.E. 68 (Ga. 1905); John Henry Wigmore, *Select Cases on the Law of Torts* (Boston: Little, Brown, 1912).

50   *Pavesich*, 50 S.E. 68.

51   *Henry v. Cherry & Webb*, 73 A. 97 (R.I. 1909); *Pavesich*, 50 S.E. 68; Wigmore, *Select Cases*; Lane, *American Privacy*, 55, 70-72.

52   See Gurstein, *Repeal of Reticence*, 163; Mensel, "Kodakers," 37.

53   Robert Allen Rutland, *The Newsmongers; Journalism in the Life of the Nation, 1690-1972* (New York: Dial Press, 1973), 319; John D. Stevens, *Sensationalism and the New York Press* (New York: Columbia University Press, 1991), 115.

54   Stevens, *Sensationalism*, 123.

55   Stephen Vaughn, *Encyclopedia of American Journalism* (New York: Routledge, 2009), 332; Stevens, *Sensationalism*, 119.

56   Arthur Sarell Rudd, "The Development of Illustrated Tabloid Journalism in the United States" (PhD thesis, Columbia University, 1925); Stevens, *Sensationalism*, 119.

57   See Miles Orvell, *The Real Thing: Imitation and Authenticity in American Culture, 1880-1940* (Chapel Hill: University of North Carolina Press, 1989), 73; Orvell holds that the tension between imitation and authenticity is a primary category in American civilization, and that "a major shift occurred within the arts and material culture from the late nineteenth century to the twentieth century, a shift from a culture in which the arts of imitation and illusion were valorized to a culture in which the notion of authenticity became of primary value." Ibid., xv. He also notes that by 1900 "vicarious experience had become a major commodity in the American marketplace and the habit of surrogates had grown strong and indelible in American life, preparing the grounds for mass-market visual narrative that were to come in the twentieth century in the form of movies and television." Ibid., 73.

58   Carlebach, *Origins of Photojournalism*, 1-22, 34-60; Frank Mallen, *Sauce for the Gander* (White Plains, NY: Baldwin Books, 1954); also in Orvell, *Real Thing*.

59   The debates over visual objectivity in photography are voluminous. See Henry P. Robinson, *The Elements of a Pictorial Photography* (1896; repr., New York: Arno, 1973); also Orvell, *Real Thing*, 197–240; see also nn.46 & 47.

60   Orvell, *Real Thing*, quote on 94, see also 198–241; Susan Sontag, *On Photography* (New York: Farrar, Straus and Giroux, 1977); John Berger and Geoff Dyer, *Understanding a Photograph* (New York: Aperture, 2013); see also Abigail Solomon-Godeau, *Photography at the Dock: Essays on Photographic History, Institutions, and Practices* (Minneapolis: University of Minnesota Press, 1991).

61   Mensel notes in his study of the Roberson case and "inviolate personality" that cultural trends in this period were such that many people understood that they "were responsible for the visible evidence of their feelings at every moment. If they were caught betraying an inappropriate or indelicate feeling, there was no escape from embarrassment, and at that moment were captured in a photograph, embarrassment could be perpetual." Mensel, "Kodakers," 31–32.

62   "73, Righting Wrong, He'll Wed the Girl, 15," *New York Daily News*, 19 June 1926.

63   David J. Krajicek, "Ruthless Ruth," *New York Daily News*, 25 March 2018.

64   Ibid.

65   Ibid.

66   Ibid.

67   Ibid.

68   See also Troy Taylor, "Dead Men Do Tell Tales," https://www.prairieghosts.com /ruth_judd.html (last accessed 18 December 2018).

69   "Dead!," *Daily News*, 13 January 1928, extra edition; see also "Ruthless Ruth," *Daily News*, 25 March 2008; "Snyder Murdered," *Chicago Sunday Tribune*, 29 December 1935; Ann Jones, "She Had to Die!" *American Heritage* 31 no. 6 (1980).

70   "Dead!," *Daily News*, 14 January 1928.

71   Solove, *Understanding Privacy*, 147; "Bar Press at Executions: Bill Filed at Albany is Seen as Sequel to Snyder Incident," *New York Times*, 8 February 1928; see also Jessie Ramey, "The Bloody Blonde and the Marble Woman: Gender and Power in the Case of Ruth Snyder," *Journal of Social History* 37 no. 3 (Spring 2004): 625–50.

72   Michel Foucault, *Discipline and Punish: The Birth of the Prison* (New York: Pantheon Books, 1977).

73   Austin Sarat, *Gruesome Spectacles: Botched Executions and America's Death Penalty* (Stanford, CA: Stanford University Press, 2014); Annulla Linders, "The Execution Spectacle and State Legitimacy: The Changing Nature of the American Execution Audience, 1833-1937," *Law and Society Review* (2002): 607–56. Linders provides an excellent survey of the debates over humanitarian versus state concerns; Sarat notes that the growing aversion to the gallows might be explained in four interrelated ways: a newly sensitized and class conscious middle class recoiled from it as crass and offensive; that the middle class developed an aversion to death in general; that the structural parallels between judicial hanging and the intensified violence of lynching troubled both state and citizen; and last, that the scientific revolution of the Gilded Age created painless and palatable execution methods.

74   The cover of the January 12 issue of the *Daily News* features two photographs, one of the "death row walk" toward the open door of the execution chamber. The electric chair can be seen at a distance. Below the photos is a hand-drawn map of the journey Snyder would take from her cell to the chair.

75   Solove, *Understanding Privacy*, 146-49.

76   Ibid, 147. Gurstein also calls attention to a similar notion concerning the corporeal and privacy, arguing "privacy, and it's most fundamental function, shelters bodily experience from the kinds of exposure that invoke shame, the feeling of degradation or dehumanization that comes from having too much attention drawn to what we all share by virtue of existing and biological time, the feeling of dread or mortification that overwhelms us whenever we experience ourself reduced to the one dimensionality of the body."

77   See *Nat'l Archives & Records Admin. v. Favish*, 541 U.S. 157 (2004). One of the earliest cases of exposure protections on record is the 1858 French case *l'affaire Rachel*, which prohibited dissemination of sketches of a famous actress on her deathbed. A larger collection of similar case histories can be found in Solove, *Understanding Privacy*.

78   "Big Crowds Vie for View of Funerals," *Daily News*, 14 January 1928.

79   Urofsky, *Brandeis*, 201.

80   Reprinted in William L. Prosser, *Handbook of the Law of Torts* (St. Paul: West, 1971).

81   Robert Wiebe, *The Search for Order, 1877-1920* (New York: Hill and Wang, 1967), 42-43; T. Jackson Leers, Richard Hofstadter, and Mensel have also made similar observations.

82   Charles L. Ponce de Leon, *Self-Exposure: Human-Interest Journalism and the Emergence of Celebrity in America, 1890-1940* (Chapel Hill: University of North Carolina Press, 2002), 12; Daniel J. Boorstin, *The Image, or What Happened to the American Dream* (New York: Atheneum, 1961).

83   See Solove, *Understanding Privacy*, 5-9; Sarah Elizabeth Igo, *The Known Citizen: A History of Privacy in Modern America* (Cambridge, MA: Harvard University Press, 2018), 3.

PART THREE

1   The literature is vast, among the more prominent examples include Sun Tzu's famous claim that "warfare is the way of deception," Bin Sun, Samuel B. Griffith, and Basil Henry Liddell Hart, *Sun Tzu The Art of War* (New York: Oxford University Press, 1963); both the Union and Confederacy employed spies during the Civil War and practiced various methods of counterintelligence, "The Union's Spy Game," *New York Times*, 15 August 2011; repeated examples of American intelligence and counterintelligence methods prior to the creation of CIA can be found in G. J. O'Toole, *Honorable Treachery: A History of U.S. Intelligence, Espionage, and Covert Action from the American Revolution to the CIA* (New York: Atlantic Monthly Press, 1991); Carl J. Jensen, David McElreath, and Melissa Graves, *Introduction to Intelligence Studies* (Boca Raton: CRC Press, 2013).

2   For a thorough treatment of this rhetoric and ideology, see Daniel J. Solove, *Nothing to Hide: The False Tradeoff between Privacy and Security* (New Haven, CT: Yale University Press, 2011).

3   This tradition will be made clear in numerous works cited throughout this chapter. For WWI era examples, see the rise of the American Protective League in Ann Hagedorn, *Savage Peace: Hope and Fear in America, 1919* (New York: Simon and Schuster, 2007); for the First Red Scare, see Nathan Miller, *New World*

Coming: The 1920s and the Making of Modern America (New York: Scribner, 2003); the Cold War examples are numerous: see Thomas C. Reeves, *McCarthyism* (Hinsdale, IL: Dryden Press, 1973).

4   *Final Report of the Select Committee to Study Governmental Operations with Respect to Intelligence Activities, United States Senate: Together with Additional, Supplemental, and Separate Views* (Washington, DC: Government Printing Office, 1976); also *Supplementary Reports on Intelligence Activities*, bk. 6, *Final Report* (Washington, DC: Government Printing Office, 1976).

5   See among others Lynn Dumenil, *The Modern Temper: American Culture and Society in the 1920s* (New York: Hill and Wang, 1995); Edwin P. Hoyt, *The Palmer Raids, 1919-1920; An Attempt to Suppress Dissent* (New York: Seabury Press, 1969); Robert K. Murray, *Red Scare; A Study in National Hysteria, 1919-1920* (Minneapolis: University of Minnesota Press, 1955).

6   Walter Goodman, *The Committee: The Extraordinary Career of the House Committee on Un-American Activities* (New York: Farrar, Straus, and Giroux, 1968).

7   Solove's *Nothing to Hide: The False Tradeoff Between Privacy and Security* (New Haven, CT: Yale University Press, 2011), offers a thorough treatment of the "all-or-nothing fallacy" (he coined the term).

8   Ibid., esp. 1-2, 29-37, 59-61.

9   Ibid.

10   George F. Kennan, *Memoirs* (Boston: Little, Brown, 1967).

11   J1.14 Sundry Civil Appropriations Act of May 27, 1908, as listed in *Checklist of United States Public Documents 1789-1909*, vol. 1 (Washington, DC: Government Printing Office, 1911); also in Max Lowenthal, *The Federal Bureau of Investigation* (New York: Sloane, 1950), 3-10; Don Whitehead, *The FBI Story; A Report to the People* (New York: Random House, 1956), 13-16; Charles H. McCormick, *Seeing Reds: Federal Surveillance of Radicals in the Pittsburgh Mill District, 1917-1921* (Pittsburgh: University of Pittsburgh Press, 2003), 9-10.

12   Mann Act, 18 U.S.C. § 2421; see also Jessica Pliley, *Policing Sexuality: The Mann Act and the Making of the FBI* (Cambridge, MA: Harvard University Press, 2014).

13   McCormick, *Seeing Reds*, 9-15.

14   Ibid.

15   Miller, *New World Coming*, 35-39; see also Alan Brinkley, *The Unfinished Nation: A Concise History of the American People* (Boston: McGraw-Hill, 2004).

16   The APL was but one of many such volunteer civilian organizations, including the Boy Spies of America, the American Defense Society, the Sedition Slammers, the Knights of Liberty, and the Terrible Threateners. Quote from Hagedorn, *Savage Peace*, 27; see also the authoritative text on the subject by Joan M. Jensen, *The Price of Vigilance* (Chicago: Rand McNally, 1969); Harold Relyea, *Evolution and Organization of Intelligence Activities in the United States* (Laguna Hills, CA: Aegean Park Press, 1980); and most recently, Bill Mills, *The League: The True Story of Average Americans on the Hunt for WWI Spies* (New York: Skyhorse, 2013).

17   Hagedorn, *Savage Peace*, 24-37.

18   Peter Conolly-Smith, "Reading Between the Lines: The Bureau of Investigation, the United States Post Office, and Domestic Surveillance During World War I," *Social Justice* 36, no. 1 (2009): 7-8.

19   Ibid.; Espionage Act of June 15, 1917, 18 U.S.C. §§ 793-798; Trading with the Enemy Act of October 6, 1917, 40 Stat. 411, §§ 1-44.

20   Case File #47748, *Records of the Post Office Department* 40, Records Relating to the Espionage Act; Conolly-Smith, 11–12.

21   As Conolly-Smith notes, this loophole has gone largely unnoticed by many scholars; see also Jensen, *Price of Vigilance*, 147–50.

22   See Lane, *American Privacy*, 6–7, 20, 30.

23   Julie Cohen, "Examined Lives: Informational Privacy and the Subject as Object," in *Georgetown University Law Center Scholarship* (Washington, DC: Georgetown University Law Center, 2000), 14–26.

24   Zechariah Chafee Jr., *Free Speech in the United States* (Cambridge, MA: Harvard University Press, 1941), xiii; Yiddish *Daily Forward* announcement reprinted in the *New York Times*, 7 October 1917; Stephen M. Feldman, *Free Expression and Democracy in America: A History* (Chicago: University of Chicago Press, 2015), 456–59; Harry N. Scheiber, *The Wilson Administration and Civil Liberties, 1917–1921* (Ithaca, NY: Cornell University Press, 1960).

25   Dumenil, *Modern Temper*, 60–63.

26   See Jacob Spolansky, *The Communist Trail in America* (New York: Macmillan, 1951); also in McCormick, *Seeing Reds*, 18–23.

27   McCormick, *Seeing Reds*, 19–24.

28   Ibid.

29   Regin Schmidt, *Red Scare: FBI and the Origins of Anticommunism in the United States, 1919–1943* (Copenhagen: Museum Tusculanum Press, University of Copenhagen, 2000).

30   McCormick, *Seeing Reds*, 42–70.

31   For more on the nonviolent character of the IWW, see Lawrence Cappello, "In Harm's Way: The Lawrence Textile Strike Children's Affair," in *The Great Lawrence Textile Strike of 1912: New Scholarship on the Bread and Roses Strike*, ed. R. Forrant and J. Siegenthaler (Amityville, NY: Baywood, 2014).

32   See among others, Kenneth D. Ackerman, *Young J. Edgar: Hoover, the Red Scare, and the Assault on Civil Liberties* (New York: Carroll and Graf, 2007); R.G. Brown et al., *To the American People: Report Upon the Illegal Practices of the United States Department of Justice* (Washington, DC: National Popular Government League, 1920); Stanley Coben, *A. Mitchell Palmer: Politician* (New York: Columbia University Press, 1963); John Milton Cooper Jr., *Pivotal Decades: The United States, 1900–1920* (New York: W.W. Norton, 1990); Melvyn Dubofsky and Foster Dulles, *Labor in America: A History*, 6th ed. (Wheeling, IL: Harlan Davidson, 1999); Philip S. Foner, *History of the Labor Movement in the United States*, vol. 8, *Postwar Struggles, 1918–1920* (New York: International, 1988); David M. Kennedy, *Over Here: The First World War and American Society* (New York: Oxford University Press, 2004); William E. Leuchtenburg, *The Perils of Prosperity, 1914–32* (Chicago: University of Chicago Press, 1958); Todd J. Pfannestiel, *Rethinking the Red Scare: The Lusk Committee and New York's Crusade against Radicalism, 1919–1923* (New York: Routledge, 2003).

33   Dumenil, *Modern Temper*, 218–19; Miller, *New World Coming*, 39–42.

34   Miller, *New World Coming*, 40–42

35   Ibid., 50–55; Kennedy, *Over Here*, 19–27.

36   Hoyt, *Palmer Raids*, 12–19; Murray, *Red Scare*, 40–49, Miller, *New World Coming*, 32–34.

37   Schmidt, *Red Scare*, 55.

38   Solove, *Understanding Privacy*, 67–69.

39   United States Federal Office of Technology Assessment, "Update on Computerized Criminal History Record Systems" (Washington, DC: Government Printing
Office, 1986), app. A.

40   Ibid.

41   Ibid.

42   Dumenil, *Modern Temper*, 220-21.

43   Stanley Coben, *A. Mitchell Palmer: Politician* (New York: Columbia University
Press, 1963), 2-6.

44   Richard G. Powers, *Not Without Honor: The History of American Anticommunism*
(New York: Free Press, 1995); also in McCormick, *Seeing Reds*, 187; and Igo,
Known Citizen, 49.

45   Interview of Marge Frantz, 22 August 1981, Oral History Transcripts, interviews
by James Klein and Julia Reichart for *Seeing Red*, Oral History of the American
Left, Tamiment Institute Library, New York University; *Hearings on H.R. 1884
and H.R. 2122, Before the House Committee on Un-American Activities*, 80th Cong.,
1st Sess. (1947) (testimony of J. Edgar Hoover, Director, FBI).

46   Interview of Howard Johnson, 16 November 1979, and David Friedman, 23 October 1979, Oral History Transcripts, interviews by James Klein and Julia Reichart
for *Seeing Red*, Oral History of the American Left, Tamiment Institute Library,
New York University; the quip about witchcraft is from Ellen Schrecker, *The
Age of McCarthyism: A Brief History with Documents* (Boston: Bedford Books,
1994), 15.

47   See Frank A. Warren, *Liberals and Communism: The "Red Decade" Revisited*
(Bloomington: Indiana University Press, 1966).

48   *Hearings Before Special House Committee to Investigate Communism in the US*,
71st Cong., 2nd Sess. (1930).

49   Goodman, *Committee*, 9-11.

50   Ibid., 14.

51   Goodman, *Committee*, 6-7.

52   *Congressional Digest*, November 1939, 282; Soviet archival evidence uncovered
decades later revealed that Dickstein, in fact, had been on the payroll of the Russian Security Service from 1937 to 1940 under the codename "crook"; see Sam
Roberts, "A Soviet Spy in Congress Still Has His Street," *New York Times*, 22 May
2013.

53   Schrecker, *Age of McCarthyism*, 15; see also Thomas Patrick Doherty, *Cold War,
Cool Medium: Television, McCarthyism, and American Culture* (New York: Colum-
bia University Press, 2003); Carol Sicherman, *Rude Awakenings: An American
Historian's Encounter with Nazism, Communism and McCarthyism* (Washington,
DC: New Academia, 2012).

54   Earl Latham, *The Communist Controversy in Washington: From the New Deal to
McCarthy* (Cambridge, MA: Harvard University Press, 1966); also in Warren,
Liberals and Communism, 89-93; also in Schrecker, *Age of McCarthyism*, 15-19.

55   James F. O'Neil, "How You Can Fight Communism," *American Legion Magazine*,
August 1948, 16-17, 42-44; also in Schrecker, *Age of McCarthyism*, 109-12.

56   *Hearings on H.R. 1884 and H.R. 2122* (Hoover testimony).

57   Congress made the issue of registration moot in 1954 with the passage of the
Communist Control Act, which outlawed the existence of the party. These laws
were repealed in the 1960s and 1990s, except for the Communist Control Act,
which has never been enforced by the Justice Department.

58   Internal Security Act, 1950, Veto Message from the President of the United States, 22 September 1950, in H.R. Doc. No. 708, 81st Cong., 2nd Sess., at 6 (1950).

59   Solove, *Nothing to Hide*, 57.

60   Expression noted in Goodman, *Committee*, introduction.

61   See ibid., 3–23.

62   Ibid.; Felix Frankfurter, "Hands Off the Investigations," *New Republic*, 21 May 1924.

63   Ibid.

64   Solove, *Understanding Privacy*, 112–16.

65   *Brown v. Walker*, 161 U.S. 591, 637 (1896); *Ullman v. United States*, 350 U.S. 422, 455 (1956); Charles Fried, "Privacy," *Yale Law Journal* 77 (1968): 475, 488; see also Solove, *Understanding Privacy*, 112–13.

66   The *Congressional Record* is littered with such routine instances. For an excellent treatment of this ritual, see Schrecker, *Age of McCarthyism*, 64–67.

67   See Ralph S. Brown, *Loyalty and Security: Employment Tests in the United States* (New Haven, CT: Yale University Press, 1958).

68   Brown also notes that this figure does not include rejected applications and other persons who were dismissed for ostensibly different reasons. See Brown, *Loyalty and Security*.

69   83 Cong. Rec. 2 (1938).

70   Goodman, *Committee*, 43–46.

71   "Communist 'Front' Attacked by Dies; Will List Members; At Dies Session," *New York Times*, 25 October 1939; 85 Cong. Rec. 6213 (1939) (testimony of Dr. Ward before HUAC); see also Matthew A McNiece, "Un-Americans and Anti-Communists: The Rhetorical Battle to Define Twentieth-Century America" (PhD diss., Texas Christian University, 2008), 92–96; Goodman, *Committee*, 65–75.

72   Goodman, *Committee*, 65–75.

73   Ibid.; for the debate in Congress on the publication of the ALPD lists, see 85 Cong. Rec. 485 (1939); "Sordid Procedure," *New York Times*, 28 October 1939.

74   Oral history interview with M. Wesley Swearingen in Griffin Fariello, *Red Scare: Memories of the American Inquisition: An Oral History* (New York: W. W. Norton, 1995), 84–99.

75   Solove, *Understanding Privacy*, 117–21, 149–53.

76   *Anti-Fascist Refugee Committee: Hearings Before the House Committee on Un-American Activities*, 79th Cong., 1st Sess. (1946); 92 Cong. Rec. 2744 (1946); Goodman, *Committee*, 176–81

77   *NAACP v. Alabama*, 357 U.S. 449 (1958).

78   Ibid.

79   *Barenblatt v. United States*, 360 U.S. 109 (1959).

80   Goodman, *Committee*, 390.

81   Schrecker, *Age of McCarthyism*, 28–33.

82   Goodman, *Committee*, 226–71.

83   Ibid., 251; Thomas quote in *Hearings Before the House Committee on Un-American Activities*, 80th Cong., 2nd Sess. (1948), 1310.

84   *Hearings Before the House Committee on Un-American Activities*, 80th Cong., 1st Sess. (1947); Lawson in ibid.

85   *Investigation of Communist Activities, New York Area (Entertainment): Hearings Before the House Committee on Un-American Activities*, 84th Cong., 1st Sess. (1955).

86   *Hearings Before the House Committee on Un-American Activities*, 80th Cong., 2nd Sess. (1948).

87   See Goodman, *Committee*, 351-56.

88   See Schrecker, *Age of McCarthyism*, 244-45.

89   Testimony, *John Henry Faulk v. AWARE Inc.*, in John Henry Faulk, *Fear on Trial*, 2nd ed. (Austin: University of Texas Press, 1983), 157-62.

90   Reprinted in Goodman, *Committee*, 358-59.

91   *Watkins v. United States*, 354 U.S. 178 (1957); "Treason Has Won Its Biggest Victory," *U.S. News*, 28 June 1957.

92   "Thomas Jailed," *New York Times*, 9 November 1948; also Goodman, *Committee*, 269-73.

93   See Schrecker, *Age of McCarthyism*, 24-25; John Lewis Gaddis, *The Cold War: A New History* (New York: Penguin Press, 2005); James T. Patterson, *Grand Expectations: The United States, 1945-1974* (New York: Oxford University Press, 1996); Samuel Walker, *In Defense of American Liberties: A History of the ACLU* (New York: Oxford University Press, 1990); Allan M. Winkler, *The Cold War: A History in Documents* (Oxford: Oxford University Press, 2000).

94   Schrecker, *Age of McCarthyism*, 24-25.

95   Exec. Order No. 9835, 3 C.F.R. 627 (1943-1948) ("Prescribing for the Administration of an Employees' Loyalty Program in the Executive Branch of the Government"); Schrecker, *Age of McCarthyism*, 151-54.

96   Ibid.

97   Schrecker, *Age of McCarthyism*, 44-45.

98   Adam Yarmolinsky, ed., *Case Studies in Personnel Security* (Washington, DC: Bureau of National Affairs, 1955), 142-47.

99   Ibid., 152.

100 Ibid., 153-54.

101 Ibid., 158-59.

102 Swearingen interview, in Fariello, *Red Scare*, 90-91.

103 Herbert Brownell interview, in Fariello, *Red Scare*, 110-12.

104 See Solove, *Understanding Privacy*, 135.

105 Joseph Rauh interview, in Fariello, *Red Scare*, 138-41.

106 Al Bernstein interview, in Fariello, *Red Scare*, 142-45

107 Interview reprinted in Fariello, *Red Scare*, 37.

108 For more on the history of executive privacy protections, see Lawrence Cappello, "Can Government Function Without Privacy?" *Atlantic*, 1 November 2015.

109 The length of time Dies was forced to wait changed in his second speech from thirty minutes to forty-five; noted in Goodman, *Committee*, 111-12.

110 The Senate, however, did not pass a concurring resolution, and so the vote did not carry the force of law; see Goodman, *Committee*, 231-41.

111 Westin, *Privacy and Freedom*, 165-68.

112 Arthur M. Schlesinger Jr., *The Imperial Presidency* (Boston: Houghton Mifflin, 1973), 156; for more on Ike resistance, see Goodman, *Committee*, 354-66.

113 Stephen E. Ambrose, *Eisenhower* (New York: Simon and Schuster, 1983), 147-50; Thomas C. Reeves, *The Life and Times of Joe McCarthy: A Biography* (New York: Stein and Day, 1982), 627-31.

114 Patterson, *Grand Expectations*, 269.

115 Similar observation about McCargtyism's legacy made in Schrecker, *Age of McCarthyism*, 92-94.

116   Ibid.
117   See Goodman, *Committee*, 491–93; Patterson, *Grand Expectations*, 260–89; Schrecker, *Age of McCarthyism*, 92–94; and Westin, *Privacy and Freedom*, 23–28.
118   In Solove, *Nothing to Hide*, 55–57.
119   Ibid.
120   William O. Douglas, "The Black Silence of Fear," *New York Times Magazine*, 13 January 1952, 37–39.

PART FOUR

1   Lyndon B. Johnson, "State of the Union Address," 10 January 1967.
2   The bill was cosponsored by Senators Howard Cannon (D-N) and Jennings Randolph (D-WV); *Right of Privacy Act of 1967: Hearings Before the Subcommittee on Administrative Practice and Procedure of the Senate Committee on the Judiciary*, 90th Cong., 1st Sess. (1967) (statement of Ramsey Clark, US Attorney General); *Right of Privacy Act of 1967: Hearings Before the Subcommittee on Administrative Practice and Procedure of the Senate Committee on the Judiciary Pursuant to S. Res. 25, on S. 928, to Protect the Right of Privacy by Prohibiting Wire Interception and Eavesdropping, and for Other Purposes*, 90th Cong., 1st Sess. (1967).
3   For more on the etymology of surveillance, see David Lyon, *Surveillance Society: Monitoring Everyday Life* (Buckingham: Open University Press, 2002), 2–4.
4   See Raymond Wacks, *Privacy: A Very Short Introduction* (Oxford: Oxford University Press, 2010), 6–19; Alan F. Westin makes the same point in *Privacy and Freedom* (New York: Atheneum, 1970), 21, 57–63.
5   This dialectic is noted in most privacy literature; see, among others, Daniel J. Solove, *Understanding Privacy* (Cambridge, MA: Harvard University Press, 2010); David Lyon, *The Electronic Eye: The Rise of Surveillance Society* (Minneapolis: University of Minnesota Press, 1994); Wacks, *Privacy*.
6   See Julie Cohen, "Examined Lives: Informational Privacy and the Subject as Object," in *Georgetown University Law Center Scholarship* (Washington, DC: Georgetown University Law Center, 2000), 1426; Cohen also quoted in Solove, *Understanding Privacy*, 108; study in Henry A. Landsberger, *Hawthorne Revisited* (Ithaca, NY: Cornell University Press, 1958).
7   Westin, *Privacy and Freedom*, 368
8   Milan Kundera. *The Unbearable Lightness of Being* (New York: Harper and Row, 1984); the point about Kundera is also found in Jeffery Rosen, *The Unwanted Gaze: The Destruction of Privacy in America* (New York: Vintage Books, 2001).
9   Solove, *Understanding Privacy*, 109.
10   See, among others, Hannah Arendt, *The Origins of Totalitarianism* (New York: Harcourt, Brace and World, 1966); Roger Griffin, *Fascism* (Oxford: Oxford University Press, 1995); Juan J. Linz, *Totalitarian and Authoritarian Regimes* (Boulder, CO: Lynne Rienner, 2000); Leonard Schapiro, T. H. Rigby, Archie Brown, and Peter Reddaway *Authority, Power, and Policy in the USSR: Essays Dedicated to Leonard Schapiro* (New York: St. Martin's Press, 1980).
11   The libertarian impulse of the anti-Federalist movement (and, ironically, the Federalist James Madison) deserves most of the credit in its pushing for the creation of a Bill of Rights to the US Constitution. See particularly the First, Third, Fourth, and Fifth Amendments.

12   Sarah Elizabeth Igo, *The Known Citizen: A History of Privacy in Modern America* (Cambridge, MA: Harvard University Press, 2018), 142.

13   Westin served as chair of the New York Bar Association's Committee on Science and Law, which provided reports and expert testimony to numerous congressional committees; see Westin, *Privacy and Freedom*, 320; Communications Act of 1934, Omnibus Crime Control and Safe Streets Act of 1968, and Electronic Communications Privacy Act of 1986, respectively.

14   This observation is also noted in the excellent book by Robert Ellis Smith, *Ben Franklin's Web Site: Privacy and Curiosity from Plymouth Rock to the Internet* (Providence, RI: Privacy Journal, 2004), 153–54; see also Nathan G. Theoharis, *Spying on Americans: Political Surveillance from Hoover to the Huston Plan* (Philadelphia: Temple University Press, 1978), 2–18, regarding impeachment — the incriminating role played by Nixon's secret White House recordings and the secret telephone recordings performed by Linda Tripp during the Clinton-Lewinsky scandal.

15   George Orwell, *Nineteen Eighty-Four: A Novel* (New York: Harcourt, Brace, 1949); Michel Foucault, *Discipline and Punish: The Birth of the Prison* (New York: Vintage Books, 1995).

16   This chronology can be found in Smith, *Ben Franklin's Web Site*; also Samuel Dash, Richard F. Schwartz, and Robert E. Knowlton, *The Eavesdroppers* (New Brunswick, NJ: Rutgers University Press, 1959), 14–18.

17   See Smith, *Ben Franklin's Web Site*, 151–91; the microphone and dictograph were developed through a series of smaller inventions over the course of the 1870s and 1880s; Grover Cleveland, *Report of the Postmaster-General of the United States; Being Part of the Message and Documents Communicated to the Two Houses of Congress at the Beginning of the First Session of the Fifty-Fourth Congress* (Washington, DC: Government Printing Office, 1895).

18   The "Strowger Switch" was invented in 1891, but switchboards did not become widely used until the early 1900s and 1910s. See Herbert Newton Casson, *The History of the Telephone* (Miami: HardPress, 2014), 13–22.

19   Smith, *Ben Franklin's Web Site*, 151–91.

20   Ibid.; also in Casson, *History of the Telephone*, 25–28; Louise Spilsbury and Richard Spilsbury, *The Telephone* (Oxford: Raintree, 2011), 33–59.

21   *Olmstead v. United States*, 277 U.S. 438 (1928).

22   US Constitution amend. IV.

23   Ibid.

24   See Richard Hamm, *Olmstead v. United States: The Constitutional Challenges of Prohibition Enforcement*, Federal Trials and Great Debates in United States History Project (Washington, DC: Federal Judicial Center, 2010), https://www.fjc.gov/history/famous-federal-trials/olmstead-v-us-prohibition-trial-seattle-bootlegger.

25   Ibid.

26   *Olmstead v. United States*, 277 U.S. 438, 464 (1928).

27   Ibid., 438.

28   Ibid., 474.

29   Ibid., 478.

30   See Melvin I. Urofsky, *Louis D. Brandeis: A Life* (New York: Pantheon Books, 2009); Brandeis legacy mentioned in Ken I. Kersch, "The Reconstruction of Constitutional Privacy Rights and the New American State," *Studies in Ameri-*

can Political Development 16, no. 1 (2002): 61–87; David J. Bodenhamer, *The Bill of Rights in Modern America: After 200 Years* (Bloomington: Indiana University Press, 1993); Anita L. Allen, Marc Rotenberg, and Rok Lampe, *Privacy Law and Society* (St. Paul: Thompson/West Academic, 2007), 5–7; *Katz v. United States* 389 U.S. 347 (1967); *Griswold v. Connecticut*, 381 U.S. 479 (1965);

31   Noted in Smith, *Ben Franklin's Web Site*, 158; also in Hamm, *Olmstead v. United States*, 57.

32   The culprits in the first three cases remain a mystery for the most part. See Dash, *Eavesdroppers*, p. 30; Smith, p. 153.

33   The Communications Act of 1934, 47 U.S.C. § 151

34   Argued in Dash, Schwartz, and Knowlton, *Eavesdroppers*, 11; Westin, *Privacy and Freedom*, 175; Smith, *Ben Franklin's Web Site*, 158.

35   See Westin, *Privacy and Freedom*, 68–72, 90–101.

36   Smith, *Ben Franklin's Web Site*, 159–60; see also J. K Petersen, *Handbook of Surveillance Technologies* (Boca Raton: CRC Press, 2012), 14–18.

37   Patterson, *Grand Expectations*, 61–82.

38   The proliferation of the private detective industry and the existence and training methods of surveillance schools are detailed in *Invasions of Privacy: Hearings before the Subcommittee on Administrative Practice and Procedure of the Committee on the Judiciary*, 89th Cong., 1st Sess. (1965), 205–6, 869–74, 953; also in Westin, *Privacy and Freedom*, 90.

39   Reprinted in Westin, *Privacy and Freedom*, 91–110.

40   Ibid., 98.

41   "Everything's Bugged as Gumshoes Meet," *Long Island City Star Journal*, 7 September 1965; see also Westin, *Privacy and Freedom*, 98–104.

42   Assortment of advertisements were collected in Westin, *Privacy and Freedom*, 91–105; "Memocord" ad in *New York Times*, 27 July 1965; "The Bird" and Gelso Electronics in *Dinners Club Magazine*, February 1963; see also "Build the Shotgun Sound Snooper" *Popular Electronics*, June 1964; John Meshna Jr., Surplus Electronic Material Catalogue, Spring 1964, offers "sniper scopes," "infrared viewers," "phone patches," "gold-plated concealed microphone buttons," and various other items; Paul Bunker, "Twenty-Four Hour Monitoring," *Law and Order*, January 1958; William Shaw, "Applied Electronics . . . Radio Beacon Trails," *Law and Order*, November 1962; "Camera Surveillance of Sex Deviates," *Law and Order*, November 1963.

43   "You Too Can Bug People . . . and Their Phones," *Miami Herald*, 23 September 1965.

44   Q, for example, in the James Bond series is a recurring character who introduces Bond and the viewers to new technology. Audiences would have been astonished if Q was missing from a Bond film, just as they would have if the Mission Impossible team or Maxwell Smart went an entire episode without using some kind of futuristic device.

45   A similar point was made in James Chapman, *License to Thrill: A Cultural History of the James Bond Films* (New York: Columbia University Press, 2000), 12–14, and in Smith, *Ben Franklin's Web Site*.

46   *Wiretapping, Eavesdropping, and the Bill of Rights: Hearings Before the Subcommittee on Constitutional Rights of the Senate on the Judiciary*, 86th Cong., 1st Sess. at (1959),1467–69 (testimony of Harold Lipset); Lipset's many exploits are chronicled in Patricia Holt, *The Bug in the Martini Olive: And Other True Cases*

from the Files of Hal Lipset, Private Eye (Boston: Little, Brown, 1991); also in Smith, *Ben Franklin's Web Site*, 164–65, 186.

47 Ibid.

48 Survey on business espionage in "Section VII," *New York Times*, 6 February 1966; also in Westin, *Privacy and Freedom*.

49 Westin, *Privacy and Freedom*, 108–12; *UAW Solidarity*, March 1965, 4; *CWA News*, October 1963, 5.

50 Westin, *Privacy and Freedom*, 108–12; "Exterminating the Electronic Bugs," *New York Herald Tribune*, 29 March 1964; *Los Angeles Herald Examiner*, 21 October 1965; see also California State Senate, *Report on the Interception of Messages by the Use of Electronic and Other Devices and the Use of Such in the Suppression of Crime and the Use of Such by Private Parties for Their Own Use* (1957).

51 See *New York Journal American*, 20 June 1965; also in Westin, *Privacy and Freedom*, 110–12.

52 *New York Journal American*, 20 June 1965; Marie Smith, "Mrs. Knutson Sidesteps Mate's Plea to Quit Congress and Return Home," *Washington Post*, 9 May 1958.

53 Dash, Schwartz, and Knowlton, *Eavesdroppers*, 67–72; Westin, *Privacy and Freedom*, 112–18.

54 Westin, *Privacy and Freedom*, 119.

55 The Long committee hearings of the mid-1960s featured many shocking revelations concerning the proliferation of government surveillance and are most responsible for "pulling the lid off" of what was by then a troubling development. See also Miriam Ottenberg, *The Federal Investigators* (Englewood Cliffs, NJ: Prentice-Hall, 1962).

56 *Wiretapping for National Security: Hearings Before Subcommittee No. 3, House Committee on the Judiciary, on H.R. 408, to Regulate the Interception of Communications in the Interest of National Security and the Safety of Human Life; H.R. 477, to Authorize Acquisition and Interception of Communications in Interest of National Security and Defense; H.R. 3552, Authorizing Acquisition and Interception of Communications in Interest of National Security; H.R. 5149, to Authorize the Use in Criminal Proceedings in Any Court Established by Act of Congress of Information Intercepted in National Security Investigations, May 4, 20, and July 8, 1953*, 83rd Cong., 1st Sess. (1953).

57 See Westin, *Privacy and Freedom*, 127–31.

58 Act of the State of Pennsylvania no. 411, July 1956; Dash, Schwartz, and Knowlton, *Eavesdroppers*, 118–19.

59 Quote and Coplon episode in Lane, *American Privacy*, 132–133; see also Herbert Brownell Jr., "Public Security and Wire Tapping," *Cornell Law Review* 39, no. 2 (1954): 195–212.

60 *Benanti v. United States*, 355 U.S. 96 (1957); Lane, *American Privacy*, 134–36; Thaddeus Russell, *Out of the Jungle: Jimmy Hoffa and the Remaking of the American Working Class* (New York: Knopf, 2001); also in Westin, *Privacy and Freedom*, 192–94.

61 Lane, *American Privacy*, 135–36.

62 See Fred J. Cook, *The FBI Nobody Knows* (New York: Macmillan, 1964); also in Westin, *Privacy and Freedom*, 160–61.

63 Theoharis, *Spying on Americans*, 105–12.

64 See Justin Peters, "On This Day in 1957, the FBI Finally Had to Admit That the Mafia Existed," *Slate*, 14 November 2013, https://slate.com/news-and-politics

/2013/11/apalachin-meeting-on-this-day-in-1957-the-fbi-finally-had-to-admit
-that-the-mafia-existed.html.

65   Smith, *Ben Franklin's Web Site*, 160–65; also in Edith J. Lapidus, *Eavesdropping on Trial* (Rochelle Park, NJ: Hayden, 1973).

66   As mentioned, media coverage of the "surveillance craze" did not peak until the mid-1960s despite the late 1940s beginnings of the expansion of the surveillance state; Westin is among the first writers to note this ambivalence.

67   "Big Brother is Listening," *Saturday Evening Post*, 6 June 1964. Westin notes that media coverage had expanded considerably in this period; see *Privacy and Freedom*, 195–98; also appears in Smith, *Ben Franklin's Web Site*, 166–67.

68   ABC program featured in *Time*, TV section, 22 May 1964; NBC Universal Archives, http://www.nbcuniversalarchives.com/nbcuni/clip/5112768928_s01.do (last accessed 2 May 2016).

69   Vance Packard, *The Naked Society* (New York: D. McKay, 1964), 40; Myron Brenton, *The Privacy Invaders* (New York: Coward-McCann, 1964).

70   Smith, *Ben Franklin's Web Site*, 164–68; "The Bug in the Martini," *Life*, 20 May 1966; see also *Invasions of Privacy: Hearings Before the Subcommittee on Administrative Practice and Procedure of the Senate Committee on the Judiciary, on February 18, 23, 24, March 2, 3, 1965*, pt. 1, 88th Cong., 1st Sess. (1965) (hereafter cited as *Invasions of Privacy Hearings*); also in Westin, *Privacy and Freedom*, 112–23, 125–26, 196–98, 207.

71   *Invasions of Privacy Hearings*, pt. 3; ibid., pt. 2; also in Westin, *Privacy and Freedom*, 121–23, 125–26, 196-98, 207

72   *Invasions of Privacy Hearings*, pt. 3; ibid., pt. 4; also referenced in US Government Accountability Office, GAO/IMTEC-87-4S, *FBI Voice Privacy: Cost, Status, and Future Direction: Report to the Chairman, Subcommittee on Civil and Constitutional Rights, House Committee on the Judiciary* (1987), 155–77.

73   Long helped keep the issue alive by frequently reading into the *Congressional Record* a "Big Brother Item for the Day," see 111 Cong. Rec. 17591 (1965), and 112 Cong. Rec. 2131 (1966); Alan Westin provides a survey of the media response to the Long committee in *Privacy and Freedom*, 198–99; a particularly scathing editorial was Alan Barth, "Lawless Lawmen," *New Republic*, 30 July 1966; William F. Buckley, "What We Need is a Law," *National Review*, 1 June 1965.

74   As listed in Westin, *Privacy and Freedom*, 108–32; the Hamburgers actually lost their suit when their landlord claimed the microphone was installed to monitor a broken heating pump. See *Hamburger v. Eastman*, 206 A.2d 239 (N.H. 1964); also in Lane, *American Privacy*, 143–44.

75   See L. A. Scot Powe, *The Warren Court and American Politics* (Cambridge, MA: Belknap Press of Harvard University Press, 2000), xiii–xvii.

76   *Elkins v. United States*, 364 U.S. 206 (1960); *Silverman v. United States*, 365 U.S. 505 (1961).

77   Powe, *Warren Court and American Politics*, 193–99.

78   Ibid.

79   *Mapp v. Ohio*, 367 U.S. 643 (1961).

80   Walter P. Signorelli, *The Constable Has Blundered: The Exclusionary Rule, Crime, and Corruption* (Durham, NC: Carolina Academic Press, 2010), 12–16.

81   *Katz v. United States*, 389 U.S. 347 (1967).

82   Ibid., 349.

83   Ibid.

84 Ibid., 351.

85 Ibid., 359.

86 Ibid., 364.

87 See Powe, *Warren Court and American Politics,* for more on the Warren Court's contribution toward making the judiciary a "coequal" branch.

88 "Paint-it-Blue" syndrome noted in Smith, *Ben Franklin's Web Site,* 173; see Electronics and Communication," *Law and Order,* July 1965; Jack Rytten, "How to Tap a Telephone" and "Recording and the Police Profession," *Law and Order,* January and May 1965.

89 New York University's Brennan Center is an excellent resource for the measurement of local and national crime statistics (http://www.brennancenter.org); the rise of rights consciousness in this period is regarded by most historians as one of its defining characteristics. See also Thomas J. Sugrue, *The Origins of the Urban Crisis: Race and Inequality in Postwar Detroit* (Princeton, NJ: Princeton University Press, 1996).

90 See Institute for Defense Analyses, *Task Force Report: Science and Technology; A Report to the President's Commission on Law Enforcement and Administration of Justice* (Washington, DC: Government Printing Office, 1967); and Robert Wallace Winslow, *Crime in a Free Society; Selections from the President's Commission on Law Enforcement and Administration of Justice, the National Advisory Commission on Civil Disorder, the National Commission on the Causes and Prevention of Violence, and the Commission on Obscenity and Pornography* (Encino, CA: Dickenson, 1972).

91 Johnson himself was later accused of engaging in illegal wiretapping for political purposes; Lyndon B. Johnson, "State of the Union Address," 10 January 1967; and "Special Message to Congress," 6 February 1967.

92 *Right of Privacy Act of 1967: Hearings Before the Subcommittee on Administrative Practice and Procedure of the Senate Committee on the Judiciary Pursuant to S. Res. 25, on S. 928, to Protect the Right of Privacy by Prohibiting Wire Interception and Eavesdropping, and for Other Purposes,* 90th Cong., 1st Sess. (1967) (hereafter cited as *Right of Privacy Act Hearings*).

93 "The Case Against Wiretapping: Some of LBJ's Own Doubt It," *Harvard Crimson,* 8 May 1967.

94 Ibid.

95 Ibid.

96 Institute for Defense Analyses, *Task Force Report.*

97 112 Cong. Rec. A4417-A4418 (1966); Westin, *Privacy and Freedom,* 207.

98 Smith, *Ben Franklin's Web Site,* 153-54

99 *Right of Privacy Act Hearings,* pt. 2.

100 Westin repeatedly (and correctly) cites the lack of comprehensive surveillance data as a key detriment to the surveillance debate in *Privacy and Freedom,* 200-215.

101 See David Garrow, "The FBI and Martin Luther King," *Atlantic,* July 2002.

102 Ibid.; also in Stanford University's *King Encyclopedia,* http://kingencyclopedia .stanford.edu/encyclopedia/federal-bureau-investigation-fbi (last accessed 18 December 2018).

103 "What an Uncensored Letter to M.L.K Reveals," *New York Times Magazine,* 11 November 2014.

104 Select Committee on Intelligence Activities Within the United States (Church

Committee), *Intelligence Activities and the Rights of Americans: 1976 U.S. Senate Report on Illegal Wiretaps and Domestic Spying by the FBI, CIA and NSA*, bk. 3, *Supplementary Detailed Staff Reports on Intelligence Activities and the Rights of Americans* (1976); also in Garrow, "FBI and Martin Luther King"; and *King Encyclopedia*.

105   See *Legislative History of the Omnibus Crime Control and Safe Streets Act of 1968* (Washington, DC: Office of General Counsel, Law Enforcement Assistance Administration, 1973).

106   See Richard M. Nixon, *Toward Freedom from Fear: A Statement* (New York: Nixon for President Committee, 1968); Richard Nixon, *The Memoirs of Richard Nixon* (New York: Grosset and Dunlap, 1978); also Stephen E. Ambrose, *Nixon* (New York: Simon and Schuster, 1987) and Lane, *American Privacy*, 159–61.

107   Michael W. Flamm, *Law and Order: Street Crime, Civil Disorder, and the Crisis of Liberalism* (New York: Columbia University Press, 2005), 2–4.

108   Ibid., 12–14.

109   Lyndon Baines Johnson, *The Vantage Point: Perspectives of the Presidency, 1963–1969* (New York: Holt, Rinehart and Winston, 1971), 549.

110   Flamm, *Law and Order*, 16–25.

111   William G. Mayer, *The Changing American Mind: How and Why American Public Opinion Changed between 1960 and 1988* (Ann Arbor: University of Michigan Press, 1992), 19–21; Robert Mason, *Richard Nixon and the Quest for a New Majority* (Chapel Hill: University of North Carolina, 2004), 20–22.

112   Center for National Security Studies and Sarah C. Carey, *Law and Disorder IV: A Review of the Federal Anti-Crime Program Created by Title I of the Omnibus Crime Control and Safe Streets Act of 1968* (Washington, DC: Center for National Security Studies, 1976); see Lane, *American Privacy*, 159–63.

113   S. Rep. No. 1097, 90th Cong., 2nd Sess., at 182 (1968); Fong quote also in Arthur R. Miller, *The Assault on Privacy: Computers, Data Banks, and Dossiers* (Ann Arbor: University of Michigan Press, 1971), 161; also appears in Smith's *Ben Franklin's Web Site*, 178.

114   Language in Omnibus Crime Control and Safe Streets Act of 1968, tit. 3, Pub. L. No. 90-351, 82 Stat. 19 (codified at 34 U.S.C. § 10101).

115   "Statement by the President Upon Signing the Omnibus Crime Control and Safe Streets Act of 1968," 19 June 1968; also in Lane, *American Privacy*, 163.

116   Department of Justice data from David Burnham at Trac Inc, Washington DC, reprinted in Smith, *Ben Franklin's Web Site*, 172.

117   Quote from Miller in *Assault on Privacy*, 162; observations about dataveillance ibid., 160–65.

118   "Statement by the President Upon Signing the Omnibus Crime Control and Safe Streets Act of 1968," 19 June 1968. Recently, scholars have also begun making connections between Johnson's War on Crime and the contemporary reality of mass incarceration in America, distinguished by a rate of imprisonment far above all other industrialized nations and involving the systematic confinement of entire groups of citizens. Jonathan Simon positions the Safe Streets Act as ushering in "a new way of imagining the needs of the citizenry as framed by the problem of crime, the purposes and means of intervention, and the means of achieving a higher level of success against crime"—what he calls the beginning of "governing through crime" in America. LBJ understood how dangerous violent crime was to the post–New Deal coalition he was seeking to reestablish even while leading

liberal criminologists of the day continued to doubt the seriousness of the surge in armed robberies in the very largest cities; see Elizabeth Kai Hinton, *From the War on Poverty to the War on Crime: The Making of Mass Incarceration in America* (Cambridge, MA: Harvard University Press, 2016); Marie Gottschalk, *The Prison and the Gallows: The Politics of Mass Incarceration in America* (New York: Cambridge University Press, 2006); Bruce Western, *Punishment and Inequality in America* (New York: R. Sage Foundation, 2006); David Garland, *The Culture of Control: Crime and Social Order in Contemporary Society* (Chicago: University of Chicago Press, 2001); National Research Council, Committee of Law and Justice, Jeremy Travis, and Bruce Western *The Growth of Incarceration in the United States: Exploring Causes and Consequences* (Washington, DC: National Academies Press, 2014); Barry Mahoney, "The Politics of the Safe Streets Act, 1965–1973: A Case Study in Evolving Federalism and the National Legislative Process" (Ph.D. diss., Columbia University, 1976); Christian Parenti, *Lockdown America: Police and Prisons in the Age of Crisis* (London: Verso, 2001); Jonathan Simon, *Governing Through Crime: How the War on Crime Transformed American Democracy and Created a Culture of Fear* (Oxford: Oxford University Press, 2009), 73–81.

119   Lane, *American Privacy*, 173–81; William Doyle, *Inside the Oval Office: The White House Tapes from FDR to Clinton* (New York: Kodansha International, 1999).

120   Lapidus, *Eavesdropping on Trial*, 7–8.

121   *United States v. United States District Court*, 407 U.S. 297 (1972); in Lane, *American Privacy*, 167–83.

122   The literature on the Watergate affair is extensive; see, among others, Kevin Hillstrom, Archibald Cox, John W. Dean, John Ehrlichman, Sam J. Ervin, H. R. Haldeman, Leon Jaworski, John N. Mitchell, Richard M. Nixon, and John J. Sirica, *Watergate* (Detroit: Omnigraphics, 2004); Alex Cruden, *Watergate* (Detroit: Greenhaven Press, 2012); Leon Jaworski, *The Right and the Power: The Prosecution of Watergate* (New York: Reader's Digest Press, 1976); Tim Weiner, *One Man Against the World: The Tragedy of Richard Nixon* (New York: Macmillan, 2015); Jonathan Aitken, *Nixon: A Life* (Washington, D.C.: Regnery, 2015); Rick Perlstein, *Nixonland: The Rise of a President and the Fracturing of America* (New York, Simon and Schuster, 2010); John A. Farrell, *Richard Nixon: The Life* (New York: Doubleday, 2017).

123   Recorded conversations transcribed in Richard M. Nixon, *The White House Transcripts: Submission of Recorded Presidential Conversations to the Committee on the Judiciary of the House of Representatives* (Toronto: Bantam Books, 1974); also in Theoharis, *Spying on Americans*.

124   Sam Dash, *Chief Counsel: Inside the Ervin Committee—The Untold Story of Watergate* (New York: Random House, 1976), 120–34; a collection of previously unpublished Watergate source material compiled by Butterfield can be found in Bob Woodward, *The Last of the President's Men* (London: Simon and Schuster, 2015); Fred Thompson, *At That Point in Time: The Inside Story of the Senate Watergate Committee* (New York: Quadrangle, 1975).

125   *United States v. Nixon*, 418 U.S. 683 (1974).

126   Ibid., 711.

127   Arthur M. Schlesinger, *The Imperial Presidency* (Boston: Houghton Mifflin, 1973), 331–37; see also Jaworski, *Right and the Power*; Jeb Stuart Magruder, *An American Life; One Man's Road to Watergate* (New York: Atheneum, 1974); Mary McCarthy, *The Mask of State: Watergate Portraits* (New York: Harcourt Brace Jovanovich,

1974); Theodore H. White, *Breach of Faith: The Fall of Richard Nixon* (New York: Atheneum Publishers, 1975); and, of course, Carl Bernstein and Bob Woodward, *All the President's Men* (New York: Simon and Schuster, 1974).

128   Theoharis, *Spying on Americans*, 109.

129   "Huge CIA Operation Reported in U.S.," *New York Times*, 22 December 1974. The literature on Congress and the intelligence community in this period is extensive. See, among others, Roger H. Davidson and Walter J. Oleszek, *Congress and Its Members* (Washington, DC: Congressional Quarterly Press, 1981); Roger Davidson, "The Political Dimensions of Congressional Investigations," *Capitol Studies* 5 (Fall 1997): 41–63; *The Tethered Presidency: Congressional Restraints on Executive Power*, ed. Thomas Franck (New York: New York University Press, 1981); James Hamilton, *The Power to Probe: A Study of Congressional Investigations* (New York: Random House, 1976).

130   Theoharis, *Spying on Americans*, 7–12.

131   For the debate on the creation of these committees, see 112 Cong. Rec. S542–S529 (1966) & 121 Cong. Rec. S967–S984 (1975); *Final Report of the Select Committee to Study Governmental Operations with Respect to Intelligence Activities, United States Senate: Together with Additional, Supplemental, and Separate Views* (Washington, DC: Government Printing Office, 1976); see also Senate Select Committee on Intelligence, *Annual Report to the Senate*, 18 May 1977, 95–217.

132   The Church committee's chief counsel, F. A. O. Schwartz Jr., offered an analysis of the findings in a 1976 address to the New York Bar Association, reprinted in 123 Cong. Rec. 52602–52605 (1977); see also Senate Select Committee on Intelligence, *Report to the Senate*, 14 May 1979, 96–141; see also House Permanent Select Committee on Intelligence, *Compilation of Intelligence Laws and Related Laws and Executive Orders of Interest to the National Intelligence Community*, April 1983, 343–51.

133   Frank J. Donner, *The Age of Surveillance: The Aims and Methods of America's Political Intelligence System* (New York: Knopf, 1980).

134   Frank Church on NBC's "Meet the Press," 17 August 1975, https://youtu.be/YAG1 N4a84Dk.

135   Loch K. Johnson, *A Season of Inquiry: The Senate Intelligence Investigation* (Lexington: University Press of Kentucky, 1985), 266–75. The Church committee's *Final Reports* comprise *Foreign and Military Intelligence* (bk. 1); *Intelligence Activities and the Rights of Americans* (bk. 2); *Supplementary Detailed Staff Reports on Intelligence Activities and the Rights of Americans* (bk. 3, which includes studies of the MLK wiretaps and COINTELPRO); *Supplementary Detailed Staff Reports on Foreign and Military Intelligence* (bk. 4, a history of the CIA); *The Investigation of the Assassination of John F. Kennedy: Performance of the Intelligence Agencies* (bk. 5); and *Supplementary Reports on Intelligence Activities* (bk. 6, relationship between the CIA and the executive).

136   Donner, *Age of Surveillance*, 231–32.

137   Ibid.

138   James Angleton and Charles J. V. Murphy, "On the Separation of Church and State," *American Cause, Special Report* (June 1976); David Atlee Phillips, "Of Rogue Mice and Men," *Periscope* (the official organ of the Association of Retired Intelligence Officers), May 1976.

139   "The Trial of the CIA," *New York Times Magazine*, 12 September 1976; Nixon quote in *Supplemental Detailed Staff Reports on Foreign and Military Intelligence*

(bk. 4 of the Church committee's *Final Reports*), 171; James Angleton and Charles J. V. Murphy, "On the Separation of Church and State," *American Cause*, June 1967; argued in Ernest W. Lefever and Roy Godson. *The CIA and the American Ethic: An Unfinished Debate* (Washington, DC: Ethics and Public Policy Center, Georgetown University, 1979).

140   Johnson, *Season of Inquiry*, 265; see also "The Spying Inquiry," *Washington Post*, 4 February 1975; "The Names in the CIA Files: Some Belong Some Don't," *Washington Post*, 2 February 1975; "CIA: Power and Arrogence," *Washington Post*, 27 April 1975; David Wise, *The American Police State* (New York: Random House, 1976), 213–19.

141   Henry Steele Commager, "Intelligence: The Constitution Betrayed," *New York Review of Books*, 30 September 1976, 32.

142   Reprints of original documents such as floor debates, hearings, and testimony can be found in Tyrus G. Fain, Katharine C. Plant, and Ross Milloy, eds., *The Intelligence Community: History, Organization, and Issues* (New York: R. R. Bowker, 1977); and House Permanent Select Committee on Intelligence, *Compilation of Intelligence Laws and Related Laws and Executive Orders of Interest to the National Intelligence Community* (Washington, DC: Government Printing Office, 1983).

143   Donner, *Age of Surveillance*, 471.

144   See Vlado Damjanovski, *CCTV: From Light to Pixels* (Waltham, MA: Butterworth-Heinemann, 2014); Clive Norris and Gary Armstrong, *The Maximum Surveillance Society: The Rise of CCTV* (Oxford: Berg, 1999).

145   Herman Kruegle, *CCTV Surveillance: Analog and Digital Video Practices and Technology* (Amsterdam: Elsevier Butterworth Heinemann, 2007).

146   "First Surveillance Cameras in Olean," *Olean Times Herald*, 5 October 2008.

147   Ibid.

148   Report cited in "DC's Virtual Panopticon," *Nation*, 16 May 2002.

149   For more on this debate, see Kate Painter and Nick Tilley, *Surveillance of Public Space: CCTV, Street Lighting and Crime Prevention* (Monsey, NY: Criminal Justice Press, 1999); Nick Tilley, *Understanding Car Parks, Crime, and CCTV: Evaluation Lessons from Safer Cities* (London: Home Office Police Department, 1993); Brandon Welsh and David P. Farrington, *Making Public Places Safer: Surveillance and Crime Prevention*, (Oxford: Oxford University Press, 2009).

150   Parenti, *Lockdown America*, 110–12.

151   Ibid., 193–94.

152   Smith, *Ben Franklin's Web Site*, 188–89; also in Solove, *Nothing to Hide*; the case in question, *United States. v. Torres*, 751 F.2d 875 (7th Cir. 1984), concerned the use of over 100 hours of FBI videotaping of alleged bomb making by a secret Puerto Rican terrorist group.

153   Smith, *Ben Franklin's Web Site*, 185–91.

154   Ibid.; Electronic Communications Privacy Act of 1986, 18 U.S.C. § 2510 et seq.

155   Smith, *Ben Franklin's Web Site*, 185–91.

156   Ibid.

157   Ibid.

158   Tripp exploited one of the many loopholes in the Omnibus Crime Control Act that allows for the surreptitious recording of private phone conversation as long as *one* party consents. See Helen Nissenbaum, *Privacy in Context: Technology, Policy, and the Integrity of Social Life* (Stanford, CA: Stanford Law Books, 2010),

151–55; also the subject of Jeffery Rosen's *The Unwanted Gaze: The Destruction of Privacy in America* (New York: Vintage Books, 2001).

PART FIVE

1   Robert Gannon, "Big Brother 7074 Is Watching You," *Popular Science*, March 1963, 86–88, 206–8.

2   Ibid.; *Bergen Evening Record*, March 21, 1963; *Time*, "1410 is Watching," 23 August 1963, 53, which concerned the computerization of driver records by the Department of Commerce; David Bergamini, "Government by Computers?," *Reporter*, 17 August 1961, 21.

3   *Computer Privacy: Hearings Before the United States Senate Committee on the Judiciary, Subcommittee on Administrative Practice and Procedure, on Mar. 14–15, 1967, Feb. 6, 1968*, 90th Cong., 2nd Sess. (1967) (hereafter cited as *1967 Senate Hearings on Computer Privacy*); J. W. Ramey, "Computer Information Sharing—Threat to Individual Freedom," in *Proceedings of the American Documentation Institute* (Washington, DC: American Documentation Institute, 1967), 273–77.

4   *The Computer and Invasion of Privacy: Hearings Before the Special Subcommittee on the Invasion of Privacy of the House Committee on Government Operations, July 26–28*, 89th Cong., 2nd sess. (1966) (hereafter cited as *1966 House Hearings on the Computer and Invasion of Privacy*); Carl Kaysen, "Data Banks and Dossiers," *Public Interest* 7 (1967): 52–60; *1967 Senate Hearings on Computer Privacy*; Priscilla M. Regan, *Legislating Privacy: Technology, Social Values, and Public Policy* (Chapel Hill: University of North Carolina Press, 1995), 72–73.

5   United States and Willis H. Ware, *Records, Computers, and the Rights of Citizens: Report of the Secretary's Advisory Committee on Automated Personal Data Systems, U.S. Department of Health, Education & Welfare* (Washington, DC: US Department of Health, Education and Welfare, 1973); Alan F. Westin and Michael A. Baker, *Databanks in a Free Society; Computers, Record-Keeping, and Privacy; Report* (New York: Quadrangle Books, 1972); *Federal Data Banks, Computers, and the Bill of Rights: Hearings Before the Subcommittee on Constitutional Rights of the Senate Committee on the Judiciary, February 23, 24 and 25, and March 2, 3, 4, 9, 10, 11, 15, and 17, 1971*, 92nd Cong., 1st Sess. (1971); Regan, *Legislating Privacy*, 72–87; Frederick S. Lane, *American Privacy: The 400 Year History of Our Most Sacred Right* (Boston: Beacon Press, 2009), 193–96, 217, 257.

6   Patricia Russell Evans, *Privacy Act of 1974: Legislative History of Public Law 93–579* (Washington, DC: US Supreme Court Library, 1975); *Legislative History of the Privacy Act of 1974, S. 3418, Public Law 93–579: Source Book on Privacy* (Washington, DC: Government Printing Office, 1976).

7   *Oversight of Computer Matching to Detect Fraud and Mismanagement in Government Programs: Hearings Before the Subcommittee on Oversight of Government Management of the Senate Committee on Governmental Affairs, December 15 and 16, 1982*, 97th Cong., 2nd Sess. (1983) (hereafter cited as *Oversight Hearings*).

8   John Shattuck, "Computer Matching Is a Serious Threat to Individual Rights," *Communications of the ACM* 27, no. 6 (1984): 538–41.

9   This line of thought was debated in *Oversight Hearings*.

10   Regan's *Legislating Privacy* is among the first books to chronical this legislative history, see 95–108; Daniel Solove, *Understanding Privacy* (Cambridge, MA: Har-

vard University Press, 2010), 172–90; Raymond Wacks, *Privacy: A Very Short Introduction* (Oxford: Oxford University Press, 2010), 32–38.

11 *Return of the Whole Number of Persons Within the Several Districts of the United States* (Philadelphia: Childs and Swaine, 1791); Nevyle Shackleford, "First Census Takers Had Their Problems," *Kentucky Farmer*, January 1, 2006; also cited in Lane, *American Privacy*, 39.

12 US Census Bureau, "Through the Decades: 1790 Overview," http://www.census .gov/history/www/through_the_decades/overview/1790.html (last accessed 3 May 2016); Regan, *Legislating Privacy*, 68.

13 US Constitution art. 1, § 2; *An Act Providing for the Actual Enumeration of the Inhabitants of the United States* (New York: Printed by Thomas Greenleaf, 1790); United States and Carroll Davidson Wright, *The History and Growth of the United States Census* (Washington, DC: Government Printing Office, 1900).

14 Responsibility for the census ultimately fell on Jefferson as secretary of state, who was informed about the progress and obstacles faced by census takers; US Census Bureau, "Through the Decades"; *The Papers of James Madison*, vols. 1–10, ed. William T. Hutchinson et al. (Chicago: University of Chicago Press, 1962–77); George Tucker, *Progress of the United States in Population and Wealth in Fifty Years As Exhibited by the Decennial Census* (New York: Hunt's Merchants' Magazine, 1843), 15–16.

15 Shaves, Goosehorn, and Rainwater may or may not have been false, but the Census Bureau certainly thought they were; in US Census Bureau, *A Century of Population Growth 1790–1900* (Washington, DC: Government Printing Office, 1907), 113–14.

16 Reprinted in Steven Kelman, "The Political Foundations of American Statistical Policy," in *The Politics of Numbers*, ed. William Alonso and Paul Starr (New York: Russell Sage Foundation, 1989).

17 United States and Wright, *History and Growth of the United States*, 18–20; "1800 Memorial of the American Philosophical Society," reprinted in "Garfield's Report on the Ninth Census," *House Reports*, 41st Cong., 2nd sess., vol. 1, no. 3, 36–37.

18 United States and Wright, *History and Growth of the United States*, 39–52; Thomas McKennan, "Circular to Marshals, Etc. — Census of 1850," reprinted in IPUMS, https://usa.ipums.org/usa/voliii/inst1850.shtml (last accessed 20 October 2017).

19 McKennan, "Circular to Marshals"; also in Lane, *American Privacy*, 42–46.

20 United States and Wright, *History and Growth of the United States*, 56–79; Lane, *American Privacy*, 42–46.

21 Lane, *American Privacy*, 43–44.

22 T. C. Martin, "The Hollerith Electric Census System," *Technology Quarterly and Proceedings from the Society for the Arts* 5 (1982): 49–55; also in Lane, *American Privacy*, 42–46.

23 Lane, *American Privacy*, 42–46.

24 Martin, "Hollerith Electric Census System," 49–55; Martin Campbell-Kelly and William Aspray, *Computer: A History of the Information Machine* (New York: Basic Books, 1996), 52; also in Daniel J. Solove, *The Digital Person: Technology and Privacy in the Information Age* (New York: New York University Press, 2004), 13–26.

25 John W. Macy Jr., *How Computers Are Being Used in Washington to Streamline Personnel Administration — To the Individual's Benefit*, in *1966 House Hearings on the Computer and Invasion of Privacy*, 35–38.

26   Vance Packard, *The Naked Society* (New York: D. McKay, 1964); Myron Brenton, *The Privacy Invaders* (New York: Coward-McCann, 1964).

27   Westin and Baker, *Databanks in a Free Society*, 1-4, 27-29.

28   Carl Kaysen, *Report of the Task Force on the Storage of and Access to Government Statistics* (Washington, DC: Executive Office of the President, Bureau of the Budget, 1965).

29   See Regan, *Legislating Privacy*, 69-108.

30   *1966 House Hearings on the Computer and Invasion of Privacy*, 4-5, 7-20.

31   Carl Kaysen, "Databanks and Dossiers," *Public Interest*, Spring 1967, 52-60; Stanford Linear Accelerator Center and L. J. Hoffman, *Computers and Privacy: A Survey* (1968), 85-90.

32   Kaysen, *Report*, 2; *1966 House Hearings on the Computer and Invasion of Privacy*, 36.

33   *1966 House Hearings on the Computer and Invasion of Privacy*, 2.

34   Ibid., 5-9, 13-18.

35   Solove, among others, argues that the more appropriate literary abstraction for privacy is Kafka's *The Trial*.

36   *1966 House Hearings on the Computer and Invasion of Privacy*, 26, 119-31.

37   Ibid., 5, 11-19.

38   Ibid., 12-22.

39   Ibid.

40   Ibid., 183.

41   Ibid.

42   Ibid., 3-12.

43   Solove, *Understanding Privacy*, 117-23.

44   Ibid., 129-33.

45   S. J. Ervin, "The Computer—Individual Privacy" *Vital Speeches of the Day* 33, no. 14 (1967): 421-16.

46   See Westin and Baker, *Databanks in a Free Society*.

47   "The Credit Card Was Invented by a Guy Who Forgot His Wallet at Dinner," *Business Insider*, 2 March 2015; Lewis Mandell, *The Credit Card Industry: A History* (Boston: Twayne, 1990); Lane, *American Privacy*, 124-26.

48   Lane, *American Privacy*, 124-26.

49   James B. Rule, *Privacy in Peril* (Oxford: Oxford University Press), 15-17.

50   *Privacy: The Collection, Use, and Computerization of Personal Data: Joint Hearings Before the Ad Hoc Subcommittee on Privacy and Information Systems of the Committee on Government Operations and the Subcommittee on Constitutional Rights of the Committee on the Judiciary, United States Senate, Ninety-Third Congress, Second Session . . . June 18, 19, and 20, 1974* (1974) (hereafter cited as *1974 Senate Hearings*) 1342, 1344-46, 1355-57, 2003, 2028.

51   See Regan, *Legislating Privacy*, 69-108; The verbal transcript of the dialogue in this film is set forth in *Hearings on H.R. 16340 Before the Subcommittee on Consumer Affairs of the House Committee on Banking and Currency*, 91st Cong., 2nd Sess. (1970); also in "The Fair Credit Reporting Act: Are Business Credit Reports Regulated?" *Duke Law Journal*, 1971, 1229-30, http://scholarship.law.duke.edu /cgi/viewcontent.cgi?article=2367&context=dlj.

52   "The Fair Credit Reporting Act: Are Business Credit Reports Regulated?" *Duke Law Journal* 1971, 1229-30.

53   "The Information Seekers: Your Privacy Is Their Concern," *Washington Star News*, 23 May 1974.

54   Ibid.

55   "The Rape of Privacy," *New York Daily News*, 25-27 May 1974.

56   Ibid.

57   Charles Fried, *An Anatomy of Values; Problems of Personal and Social Choice* (Cambridge, MA: Harvard University Press, 1970); Arthur R. Miller, *The Assault on Privacy: Computers, Data Banks, and Dossiers* (Ann Arbor: University of Michigan Press, 1971); US Department of Health, Education & Welfare, *Records, Computers, and the Rights of Citizens* (Cambridge, MA: MIT Press, 1973) (hereafter cited as 1974 HEW Report).

58   1974 HEW Report.

59   Ibid.

60   Ibid., 70-95; Sarah Elizabeth Igo, *The Known Citizen: A History of Privacy in Modern America* (Cambridge, MA: Harvard University Press, 2018), 89.

61   1974 HEW Report.

62   See Regan, *Legislating Privacy*, 69-108.

63   "The First Amendment: A Living Thought in the Computer Age," *Columbia Human Rights Law Review* 4, no. 1 (1972): 31-30.

64   *1974 Senate Hearings*, 517.

65   Ibid., 519-24.

66   Ibid., 440-81.

67   *Legislative History of the Privacy Act of 1974, S. 3418, Public Law 93-579: Source Book on Privacy* (Washington, DC: Government Printing Office, 1976); *Overview of the Privacy Act of 1974* (Washington, DC: US Department of Justice, Office of Privacy and Civil Liberties, 2010).

68   *Overview of the Privacy Act of 1974*; Regan, *Legislating Privacy*, 79-85; Igo, *Known Citizen*, 257.

69   Regan, *Legislating Privacy*, xiii-xv.

70   *Electronic Record Systems and Individual Privacy* (Washington, DC: US Congress Office of Technology Assessment, 1986) (hereafter cited as 1986 OTA Report); *Oversight Hearings*.

71   *Electronic Record Systems and Individual Privacy*, 7-9; *Oversight Hearings*, 7-8, 114.

72   1986 OTA Report, 9-22; Gary L. Galemore, *The Grace Commission* (Washington, DC: Congressional Research Service, Library of Congress, 1993); Guy B. Peters and Charles H. Levine, *The Unfinished Agenda for Civil Service Reform: Implications of the Grace Commission Report* (Washington, DC: Brookings Institution, 1985).

73   For more on the conservative ascendency of the late 1970s, see Donald T. Critchlow, *The Conservative Ascendancy: How the GOP Right Made Political History* (Cambridge, MA: Harvard University Press, 2007); James T. Patterson, *Restless Giant: The United States from Watergate to Bush v. Gore* (New York: Oxford University Press, 2005); William A. Link, *Righteous Warrior: Jesse Helms and the Rise of Modern Conservatism* (New York: St. Martin's Press, 2008).

74   1986 OTA Report, 4-5, 7.

75   Ibid.; see also Kenneth C. Laudon, *Dossier Society: Value Choices in the Design of National Information Systems* (New York: Columbia University Press, 1986).

76   SPECTRE was also the name of a fictional organization comprised of super-

villains and terrorists that appeared in a number of Ian Fleming's popular James Bond films and novels. One can only speculate that this reference was lost on the parties responsible for naming the program.

77 *Oversight Hearings*, 7–9, 17.

78 Ibid., 20–22.

79 Ibid., 20; 1986 OTA Report, 3; Regan, *Legislating Privacy*, 90.

80 *Oversight Hearings*, 79.

81 Ibid.; see also John Shattuck, "In The Shadow of 1984—National Identification Systems, Computer Matching and Privacy in the United States," *Hastings Law Journal* 35, no. 6 (1984): 991–1005.

82 *Oversight Hearings*, 82–83.

83 Ibid., 85.

84 *Computer Matching and Privacy Protection Act of 1988: Report (to Accompany H.R. 4699—Including Cost Estimate of the Congressional Budget Office)* (Washington, DC: Government Printing Office, 1988); Regan, *Legislating Privacy*, 95–99; see also Priscilla M. Regan, "Data Integrity Boards: Institutional Innovation and Congressional Oversight," *Government Information Quarterly* 10, no. 4 (1993): 433–59; US Government Accountability Office, GAO/PEMD-94-2, *Computer Matching: Quality of Decisions and Supporting Analyses Little Affected by 1988 Act* (1993).

85 Solove pushes hard for the Kafkaesque metaphor in *Nothing to Hide: The False Tradeoff between Privacy and Security* (New Haven, CT: Yale University Press, 2011), 49–50.

86 Ibid., 50; also a central argument in Regan, *Legislating Privacy*.

87 Rule, *Privacy in Peril*, x–xiii, 25–48.

88 Helen Nissenbaum, *Privacy in Context: Technology, Policy, and the Integrity of Social Life* (Stanford, CA: Stanford Law Books, 2010), 38–45.

PART SIX

1 *Griswold v. Connecticut* 381 U.S. 479 (1965).

2 *Griswold* continues to be explored by the legal community. The most comprehensive single volume history of the *Griswold* battle is David J. Garrow's *Liberty and Sexuality: The Right to Privacy and the Making of Roe v. Wade* (New York: Macmillan, 1994). In 2001 Anita Allen cited the case as a forerunner that "inspired later efforts to establish sexual privacy rights for gays and lesbians in *Bowers v. Hardwick* (1986); see "Is Privacy Now Possible? A Brief History of the Obsession," *Social Research* 68, no. 1 (2001): 301–6; Jack Harrison positions Douglas's remarks on marriage in *Griswold* as central to the gay marriage victory in *Obergefell v Hodges* (2015); see "At Long Last Marriage," *American University Journal of Gender, Social Policy & the Law* 24, no. 1 (2015): 1–56. Rachel Bisi and Patrick Horan called for an expanded reading of *Griswold* to combat persistent barriers to birth control in contemporary American society such as the disagreement over "abortifacients" and opposition by healthcare providers to pay for contraceptives; see "Access to Contraception," *Georgetown Journal of Gender and the Law* 14, no. 1 (2013): 245–79. Dana Hirschenbaum argues that *Griswold*'s privacy protections are not being properly extended to drug-addicted pregnant women; see "When CRACK is the Only Choice: The Negative Right of Privacy on Drug-

Addicted Women," *Berkeley Journal of Gender, Law, and Justice* 15, no. 1 (September 2013): 327-37. Cary Franklin sees *Griswold* as a tool through which scholars can better understand the class/poverty focused nature of the Warren Court and championing of privacy rights for the poor over reproductive rights; see "*Griswold* and the Public Dimension of the Right to Privacy," *Yale Law Journal Forum*, March 2015, 332-38. Melissa Murray explored *Griswold* as a "part of a criminal law reform effort that sought to reimagine the state's authority in the intimate lives of citizens"; see "*Griswold*'s Criminal Law," *Connecticut Law Review* 47, no. 4 (May 2015): 1045-76. Neil and Reva Siegel view *Griswold* as a path to dismantling challenges to contraception under the recent Religious Freedom Restoration Act (RFRA); see "Compelling Interests in Contraception," *Connecticut Law Review* 47, no. 4 (May 2015): 1025-1044. Priscilla Smith calls for the application of privacy ideas affirmed in *Griswold* to combat litigation challenging the Obamacare contraception coverage requirement; see "Contraceptive Comstockery: Reasoning from Immorality to Illness in the Twenty-First Century," *Connecticut Law Review* 47, no. 4 (May 2015): 971-1023. Ryan Williams argues that *Griswold* was "hardly typical of the Warren Court" and in fact shared "a greater affinity with the decisions of the later Burger Court"; see "The Paths to *Griswold*," *Notre Dame Law Review* 89 (2014): 2155-90. Debbie V. S. Kasper believes the right to privacy established in *Griswold* should be extended to surveillance rights under the doctrine of "privacy as a larger social good"; see "Privacy as a Social Good," *Social Thought and Research* 28 (2007): 165-89. Dawn Johnson traces how the right to privacy affirmed in *Griswold* has "routinely" come up in legislative vetting of federal and state judges; see "State Court Protections of Reproductive Rights: The Past, The Perils, and the Promise," *Columbia Journal of Gender and Law* 29, no. 1 (Spring 2015): 41-88; see also Malcolm Potts, Peter Diggory, and John Peel, *Abortion* (Cambridge: Cambridge University Press, 1977); N. E. H. Hill and Peter Charles Hoffer, *Roe v. Wade: The Abortion Rights Controversy in American History* (Lawrence: University Press of Kansas, 2001); and Eva R. Rubin, *Abortion, Politics, and the Courts: Roe v. Wade and Its Aftermath* (Westport, CT: Greenwood Press, 1982).

3   This separation of public and private spheres has been noted by many scholars. See particularly Barbara Welter, "The Cult of True Womanhood: 1820-1860," *American Quarterly* 18, no. 2 (1966): 151-74; Eleanor Flexner, *Century of Struggle: The Woman's Rights Movement in the United States* (Cambridge, MA: Belknap Press of Harvard University Press, 1975), ix-xvi.

4   Anita L. Allen, *Uneasy Access: Privacy for Women in a Free Society* (Totowa, NJ: Rowman and Littlefield, 1988), 72.

5   Flexner, *Century of Struggle*, 56-60; also in Jennifer Joline Anderson and Arzoo Osanloo, *The Women's Rights Movement* (Minneapolis: ABDO, 2013); and Garrow, *Liberty and Sexuality*.

6   See Marc Robert Stein, *Sexual Injustice: Supreme Court Decisions from Griswold to Roe* (Chapel Hill: University of North Carolina Press, 2013), 2-9.

7   This transition is noted by Cornell University's Legal Information Institute (LII), https://www.law.cornell.edu/wex/planned_parenthood_of_southeastern_penn sylvania_v_casey_%281992%29; also noted in Rickie Solinger, *Reproductive Politics: What Everyone Needs to Know* (New York: Oxford University Press, 2013), 2-6; Minky Worden's, *The Unfinished Revolution: Voices from the Global Fight for*

Women's Rights (New York: Seven Stories Press, 2012), also frames the issue as one of "liberty" and not "decisional privacy"; *Planned Parenthood of Southeastern Pa. v. Casey*, 505 U.S. 833 (1992).

8   *De May v. Roberts*, 9 N.W. 146 (Mich. 1881); also in Allen, *Uneasy Access*, 113–14.

9   Allen, *Uneasy Access*, 113–17.

10 Rubin, *Abortion, Politics, and the Courts*, 9–11; James George Jr., "The Evolving Law of Abortion," in *Abortion, Society, and the Law*, ed. David F. Walbert and J. Douglas Butler, 3–32 (Cleveland: Press of Case Western Reserve University, 1973).

11 Historian James C. Mohr's *Abortion in America: The Origins and Evolution of National Policy, 1800–1900* (New York: Oxford University Press, 1978), is the seminal text on nineteenth-century abortion law; see 20–45.

12 George, "Evolving Law of Abortion," 31–33.

13 Rubin, *Abortion, Politics, and the Courts*, 12–14; see also Barbara Laslett and Johanna Brenner, "Gender and Social Reproduction: Historical Perspectives," *Annual Review of Sociology* 15 (1989): 381–404.

14 Rubin, *Abortion, Politics, and the Courts*, 12–14; C. R. King, *Abortion in Nineteenth Century America* (New York: Arno Press, 1974), 49–60.

15 Zad Levy and Jerome Kummer, "Criminal Abortion: Human Hardship and Unyielding Laws," *Southern California Law Review* 35 (Winter 1962): 126–27; Harold Rosen, "A Case Study in Social Hypocrisy," in *Abortion in America*, ed. Harold Rosen (Boston: Beacon Press, 1967), 298–300; see also Daniel Callahan, *Abortion: Law, Choice, and Morality* (New York: Macmillan, 1970), 132–36; also in Rubin, *Abortion, Politics, and the Courts*, 14–21.

16 Rubin, *Abortion, Politics, and the Courts*, 18–21.

17 S. Boyer, *Purity in Print: The Vice Society Movement and Book Censorship in America* (New York: Scribner's, 1968), 2–14.

18 Anthony Comstock, *Traps for the Young* (1883; repr., Cambridge, MA: Belknap Press of Harvard University Press, 1967), 56–71.

19 Nicola Beisel, *Imperiled Innocents: Anthony Comstock and Family Reproduction in Victorian America* (Princeton, NJ: Princeton University Press, 1998), 2–5.

20 Ibid.; "Obscene Literature," *New York Times*, 15 March 1873.

21 Boyer, *Purity in Print*, 14–18.

22 Ibid., 51.

23 Beisel, *Imperiled Innocents*, 38–42.

24 Ibid.; Leta Hollingsworth, "Social Devices for Impelling Women to Bear and Rear Children," *American Journal of Sociology* 22 (1916): 19–29.

25 Noted extensively in Garrow, *Liberty and Sexuality*; see also Margaret Sanger, Esther Katz, Cathy Moran Hajo, and Peter Engelman, *The Selected Papers of Margaret Sanger* (Urbana: University of Illinois Press, 2002), 14–51; David M. Kennedy, *Birth Control in America: The Career of Margaret Sanger* (New Haven, CT: Yale University Press, 1970), 108–26. The literature on women in the Progressive Era is vast, covering a generation of women who gathered in settlement houses, formed national and international networks of women reformers, and ultimately concentrated their power in Washington and circumvented gender restrictions on political action in ways that were broadly and powerfully public. See Kathryn Kish Skylar, *Florence Kelley and the Nation's Work: The Rise of Women's Political Culture, 1830–1920* (New Haven, CT: Yale University Press, 1997); Robyn Muncy, *Creating a Female Dominion in American Reform, 1890–1935* (New York: Oxford

University Press, 1991); Leila J. Rupp, *Worlds of Women: The Making of an International Women's Movement* (Princeton, NJ: Princeton University Press, 1997); Paula Baker, *The Moral Frameworks of Public Life: Gender, Politics, and the State in Rural New York, 1870–1930* (New York: Oxford University Press, 1991); Molly Ladd-Taylor, *Mother-Work: Women, Child Welfare, and the State, 1890–1930* (Urbana: University of Illinois Press, 1994); and Patricia Schechter, *Ida B. Wells-Barnett and American Reform, 1880–1930* (Chapel Hill: University of North Carolina Press, 2001).

26   Margaret Sanger, *Family Limitations* (New York, 1917), 3-5.

27   Margaret Sanger, *Margaret Sanger: An Autobiography* (New York: Dover, 1971), 22-42; Sanger et al., *Selected Papers*, 43-52; Ellen Chesler, *Woman of Valor: Margaret Sanger and the Birth Control Movement in America* (New York: Simon and Schuster, 1992), 3-9.

28   Margaret Sanger and Havelock Ellis, *Woman and the New Race* (1920), sec. XVIII.

29   "The Raid," *Birth Control Review* 13 (June 1929): 150-56; also in Garrow, *Liberty and Sexuality*, 20-24.

30   Sanger, "Breaking into the South, A Contrast," in *Selected Papers*, 265-67.

31   "Connecticut," *Birth Control Review*, June 1938, 104.

32   Reprinted in the *Waterbury Republican*, 12 June 1939, 2-3; and Garrow, *Liberty and Sexuality*, 1-2, 62.

33   Garrow, *Liberty and Sexuality*, 1.

34   Ibid., 7.

35   Ibid., 69-70.

36   *State v. Nelson*, 126 Conn. 412, 418, 422-26 (1940); also in *Human Fertility* 5 (April 1940); "Pease to Clarence Gamble," *New Haven Journal-Courier*, 26 October 1935; reprinted in Garrow, *Liberty and Sexuality*.

37   Garrow, *Liberty and Sexuality*, 77-78.

38   Ibid. 78, 122-27.

39   In addition to those already listed, see generally Lois W. Banner, *Women in Modern America: A Brief History* (Belmont, CA: Thomson/Wadsworth, 2005); Ethel Klein, *Gender Politics: From Consciousness to Mass Politics* (Cambridge, MA: Harvard University Press, 1984); Susan Estabrook Kennedy, *If All We Did Was to Weep at Home: A History of White Working-Class Women in America* (Bloomington: Indiana University Press, 1979).

40   Alan F. Westin, *Privacy and Freedom* (New York: Atheneum, 1970), 21; Allen notes this error in *Uneasy Access*, 66-67.

41   Welter, "Cult of True Womanhood," 1-2, 5.

42   Mary Louise Roberts argues that Welter's collection of essays *Dimity Convictions: The American Woman in the Nineteenth Century* (Athens: Ohio University Press, 1976), in which "The Cult of True Womanhood" also appeared, "set the agenda for a whole generation of women's historians." See "True Womanhood Revisited," *Journal of Women's History* 14, no. 1 (2002): 150-55.

43   See Allen, *Uneasy Access*, 54-55, also Kennedy, *If All We Did*, 41-44.

44   Nancy Hewitt, "Taking the True Woman Hostage," *Journal of Women's History* 14, no. 1 (2002): 156-52. Scholarship supportive of this public/private distinction can be found in Joan Scott, "Gender: A Useful Category of Historical Analysis," in *Gender and the Politics of History* (New York: Columbia University Press, 1988), 28-50; Carroll Smith-Rosenberg, "Discourses of Sexuality and Subjectivity: The

New Woman, 1870-1936," in *Hidden from History: Reclaiming the Gay and Lesbian Past*, ed. Martin Duberman, Martha Vicinus, and George Chauncey Jr., 267-78 (New York: New American Library, 1989); Carroll Smith-Rosenberg, "The New Woman as Androgyne: Social Disorder and Gender Crisis, 1870-1936," in *Disorderly Conduct: Visions of Gender in Victorian America* (New York: Alfred Knopf, 1985), 245-96; Elsa Barkley Brown, "Womanist Consciousness: Maggie Lena Walker and the Independent Order of St. Luke," *Signs* 14 (Spring 1989): 610-33; a classic statement of the female culture model is found in Nancy Cott, *The Bonds of Womanhood: "Woman's Spheres" in New England, 1780-1835* (New Haven, CT: Yale University Press, 1977); these authors linked Welter's public/private construction to different economic and political changes, but the dominant image remains that of a middle-class housewife sacrificing a place in the labor force alongside men for the "joys" of urban domesticity and childrearing.

45 Charlotte Perkins Gilman, *Women and Economics: A Study of the Economic Relation between Men and Women in Social Evolution* (London: Putnam, 1900), 256; Smith also notes the contributions of Gilman, Welter, and Virginia Wolfe in *Ben Franklin's Web Site*, 90-101.

46 We should be wary not to plot males and females onto the public and private too rigidly. "Man is not entirely to public and woman not entirely to private," notes Mary Ryan. "It is the gender bias lodged at the border between public and private," not the terms themselves, "that is objectionable to feminists and troublesome to historians"; Mary Ryan, "The Public and the Private Good: Across the Great Divide in Woman's History," *Journal of Women's History* 15, no. 2 (Summer 2003): 10-27; see Elizabeth Cady Stanton, "The Solitude of Self," *Woman's Column*, January 1882, 2-3, reprinted in Ellen Carol DuBois, ed., *Elizabeth Cady Stanton and Susan B. Anthony: Correspondence, Writings, and Speeches* (New York: Schocken Books, 1981).

47 This is a book about privacy, not a book about gender. Gender studies is a field presently bursting with excellent scholarship on the causes and contours of gender inequality. See, as a beginning, "Further Thoughts on the Public and Private Distinction," *Journal of Women's History* 15, no. 2 (Summer 2003): 28-39. Scholarship on public/private gender distinctions provided a point of departure for later critiques in the 1980s and 1990s. Many of these critiques positioned "true womanhood" and its practitioners as inhibiting discussion about more diverse and competing histories of American women, and cast these new histories against a static image of northern, white, middle-class womanhood. This shift was noted at the time by Linda K. Kerber, "Separate Spheres, Female Worlds, Woman's Place: The Rhetoric of Women's History," *Journal of American History* 75 (June 1988): 9-39. On "respectability" among African American women in the nineteenth century, see James Oliver Horton, "Freedom's Yoke: Gender Conventions among Antebellum Free Blacks" *Feminist Studies* 12, no. 1 (Spring, 1986): 51-76; and Evelyn Brooks Higginbotham, *Righteous Discontent: The Women's Movement in the Black Baptist Church, 1880-1920* (Cambridge, MA: Harvard University Press, 1993). On working-class and immigrant women, see Christine Stansell, *City of Women: Sex and Class in New York, 1789-1860* (New York: Alfred A. Knopf, 1986). On southern and western women, see Suzanne Lebsock, *The Free Women of Petersburg: Status and Culture in a Southern Town, 1784-1860* (New York: W. W. Norton, 1984); and John Mack Faragher, *Women and Men on the Overland Trail* (New Haven, CT: Yale University Press, 1979).

48 This argument can be found in numerous studies on women in the labor movement, such as Alice Henry, *Women and the Labor Movement* (New York: Macmillan, 1927); see also Philip Foner's *Women and the American Labor Movement* (New York: Free Press, 1979); Ruth Milkman, *Women, Work, and Protest: A Century of US Women's Labor History* (London: Routledge and Kegan Paul, 1987), and Allen, *Uneasy Access*, 63, 66-67.

49 Betty Friedan, *The Feminine Mystique* (New York: W. W. Norton, 1963), 337-72.

50 Catharine A. MacKinnon, *Toward a Feminist Theory of the State* (Cambridge, MA: Harvard University Press, 1989), 191. For more on the origins of the women's movement, see, among others, William H. Chafe, *The Paradox of Change: American Women in the 20th Century* (New York: Oxford University Press, 1991); Karen Anderson, *Wartime Women: Sex Roles, Family Relations, and the Status of Women During World War II* (Westport, CT: Greenwood Press, 1981); Cynthia Ellen Harrison, *On Account of Sex: The Politics of Women's Issues, 1945-1968* (Berkeley: University of California Press, 1988); John D'Emilio and Estelle B. Freedman. *Intimate Matters: A History of Sexuality in America* (New York: Harper and Row, 1988); also noted in Jeffery Rosen, *The Unwanted Gaze: The Destruction of Privacy in America* (New York: Vintage Books, 2001), 13.

51 An excellent summary of the liberal feminist viewpoint on decisional privacy is found in Allen, *Uneasy Access*, 69-81.

52 Rubin, *Abortion, Politics, and the Courts*, 15-16; Harold Rosen, *Abortion in America; Medical, Psychiatric, Legal, Anthropological, and Religious Considerations* (Boston: Beacon Press, 1967), 319-21.

53 Alfred C. Kinsey, Wardell Baxter Pomeroy, and Clyde E. Martin, *Sexual Behavior in the Human Male* (Philadelphia: W. B. Saunders, 1948); Paul A. Robinson, *The Modernization of Sex: Havelock Ellis, Alfred Kinsey, William Masters, and Virginia Johnson* (New York: Harper and Row, 1976), 54-55; also in James T. Patterson, *Grand Expectations: The United States, 1945-1974* (New York: Oxford University Press, 1996), 343-56.

54 Glanville Llewellyn Williams, *The Sanctity of Life and the Criminal Law* (New York: Knopf, 1957); American Law Institute, Herbert Wechsler, and Mary Steichen Calderone, *Model Penal Code*, Council Draft no. 22, March 3, 1959; Rubin, *Abortion, Politics, and the Courts*, 15-18.

55 "How a German Measles Epidemic Stoked the Abortion Debate in 1965," *Time*, 2 February 2015; Rubin, *Abortion, Politics, and the Courts*, 21-28.

56 Garrow, *Liberty and Sexuality*, 170-74.

57 Fowler Harper, "Jurisdictional Statement," *Poe v. Ullman*, 367 U.S. 497 (1961); also in Garrow, *Liberty and Sexuality*, 170-74.

58 Garrow, *Liberty and Sexuality*, 171.

59 Ibid., 181-85.

60 Dissenting opinion in *Poe v. Ullman*, 367 U.S. 497 (1961); also in Garrow, *Liberty and Sexuality*, 194-95.

61 Dissenting opinion in *Poe v. Ullman*, 367 U.S. 497, 550 (1961); also in Garrow, *Liberty and Sexuality*, 195.

62 Planned Parenthood League of Connecticut, "Planned Parenthood League of Connecticut to Offer Contraceptive Services," press release, 20 June 1961; also in Garrow, *Liberty and Sexuality*, 196.

63 "Planned Parenthood League of Connecticut to Offer Contraception Services," *New Haven Journal Courier*, 21 June 1961; also in the *New Republic*, 3 July 1961.

64 *Hartford Currant,* 4 November 1961, 2; reprinted in Garrow, *Liberty and Sexuality,* 175.

65 L. A. Scot Powe, *The Warren Court and American Politics* (Cambridge, MA: Belknap Press of Harvard University Press, 2000), 372-74.

66 Thomas Emerson, "Brief for Appellants," *Griswold v. Connecticut,* U.S.S.C., O.T. 1964, #496, 11 February 1965; Garrow, *Liberty and Sexuality,* 237-38.

67 Garrow, *Liberty and Sexuality,* 237-38.

68 The four briefs are "Ernst, Pilpel, and Wechsler, "Motion for Leave to File a Brief with Brief Appendices as Amicus Curiae for Planned Parenthood Federation of America," *Griswold v. Connecticut,* U.S.S.C., O.T. 1964, #496, 15 February 1965; Seymour and Eleanor Fox, "Brief as Amici Curiae for Drs. John M. Adams et al.," *Griswold v. Connecticut,* U.S.S.C., O.T. 1964, #496, 12 February 1965; Robert Flemming, "Motion for Leave to File a Brief with Brief Appendices as Amicus Curiae for the Catholic Council on Civil Liberties and Brief Amici Curiae," *Griswold v. Connecticut,* U.S.S.C., O.T. 1964, #496, 15 February 1965; Rhoda Karpatkin and Melvin Wulf, "Motion for Leave to File a Brief with Brief Appendices as Amicus Curiae for the American Civil Liberties Union and Connecticut Civil Liberties Union and Brief Amici Curiae," *Griswold v. Connecticut,* U.S.S.C., O.T. 1964, #496, 26 February 1965; see also Garrow, *Liberty and Sexuality,* 237-38.

69 Joseph Clark, "Brief for the Appellee," *Griswold v. Connecticut,* U.S.S.C., O.T. 1964, #496, 9 March 1965.

70 U.S. Supreme Court, Fowler Harper, and Additional Contributors, *Griswold v. Connecticut U.S. Supreme Court Transcript of Record with Supporting Pleadings,* Gale, U.S. Supreme Court Records, 2011; Garrow, *Liberty and Sexuality,* 238.

71 See Garrow, *Liberty and Sexuality,* 238-40 (quote on 240).

72 Ibid., 240.

73 Powe, *Warren Court and American Politics,* 373.

74 *Griswold v. Connecticut,* 381 U.S. 479 (1965).

75 Ibid.

76 Ibid.

77 Ibid.

78 Ibid.

79 Ibid.

80 See Powe, *Warren Court and American Politics,* 372-76.

81 Igo, *Known Citizen,* 158.

82 Allen, *Uneasy Access,* 86-87.

83 Ibid.

84 Ibid.; see also Reva B. Siegel, "Before (and After) Roe v. Wade: New Questions About Backlash," *Yale Law School Faculty Scholarship Series,* Paper 4135 (2011), 2028-87.

85 Powe, *Warren Court and American Politics,* 376.

86 Garrow also notes this mixture of opinions; an excellent collection of opinions on the case can be found in these conference proceedings: Robert Galloway Dixon, *The Right of Privacy; A Symposium on the Implications of Griswold v. Connecticut, 381 U.S. 497 (1965)* (New York: Da Capo Press, 1971). Informational privacy comments can be found in Robert G. Dixon, "The *Griswold* Penumbra: Constitutional Charter for an Expanded Right to Privacy?," *Michigan Law Review* 64 (December 1965): 197-218.

87 Maryann Barakso, *Governing NOW: Grassroots Activism in the National Organiza-*

tion for Women (Ithaca, NY: Cornell University Press, 2004), 11–39; Rubin, *Abortion, Politics, and the Courts*, 22–24.

88   Betty Friedan, Address Before the First National Conference on Abortion Laws: Abortion: A Woman's Civil Right (February 1969).

89   The New York incident and the testimonials given afterward found in Diane Schulder and Florynce Kennedy, *Abortion Rap* (New York: McGraw-Hill, 1971); Barbara Sinclair Deckard, *The Women's Movement* (New York: Harper and Row, 1975), 332–36; see also Linda Greenhouse and Reva B. Siegel, *Before Roe v. Wade: Voices That Shaped the Abortion Debate Before the Supreme Court's Ruling* (New York: Kaplan, 2010); Rubin, *Abortion, Politics, and the Courts*, 23–25.

90   This popular characterization is outlined and challenged in Stein, *Sexual Injustice*, 2–4; Besides *Griswold* and *Roe*, see *Memoirs v. Attorney General of Massachusetts*, 383 U.S. 413 (1966); *Loving v. Virginia*, 388 U.S. 1 (1967); and *Eisenstadt v. Baird*, 405 U.S. 438 (1972).

91   See Hariet Pilpel, "Sex vs. the Law: A Study in Hypocrisy," *Harper's*, January 1965; Hugh Hefner, "The Legal Enforcement of Morality," *University of Colorado Law Review* 40 (1968): 199–221; Richard Posner and Katherine B. Silbaugh, *A Guide to America's Sex Laws* (Chicago: University of Chicago Press, 1996).

92   This is the central thesis of Stein, *Sexual Injustice*, 1–7.

93   Ibid., 14, 30–33.

94   See particularly Justice Stuart's concurring opinion in *Memoirs*, 383 U.S. at 421.

95   As argued in a Stein, *Sexual Injustice*, 44–46.

96   Ibid.; see also Chang Moon Sohn, "Principle and Expediency in Judicial Review: Miscegenation Cases in the Supreme Court" (Ph.D diss., Columbia University, 1970).

97   See Brennan's remarks in the majority opinion, *Eisenstadt*, 405 U.S. 438.

98   Lawrence Sager and John Roberston, "Brief of the American Civil Liberties Union and the Civil Liberties Union of Massachusetts," *Eisenstadt v. Baird*, U.S.S.C., O.T. 1970 #70-17, 26 October 1971; see also Roger P. Stokely and Stephen M. Weiner, "Brief for the Amicus Curiae Planned Parenthood League of Massachusetts," *Eisenstadt v. Baird*, U.S.S.C., O.T. 1970 #70-17, 14 June 1971; Garrow, *Liberty and Sexuality*, 536–44.

99   *Eisenstadt*, 405 U.S. at 453; also in Stein, *Sexual Injustice*, 47.

100   Stein's core thesis in *Sexual Injustice*; see also Arthur J. Goldberg, "The Warren Court and its Critics: The Supreme Court History Project: The Warren Court 1962–1969," *Santa Clara Law Review* 20, no. 1 (January 1980): 831–42; Roy Lucas, "New Historical Insights on the Curious Case of *Baird v. Eisenstad*," *Roger Williams University Law Review* 9, no. 1 (Fall 2003): 9–58.

101   *Bowers v. Hardwick*, 478 U.S. 186 (1986); Stein, *Sexual Injustice*, 286–90; see also Lisa Keen and Suzanne B. Goldberg, *Strangers to the Law: Gay People on Trial* (Ann Arbor: University of Michigan Press, 1998); Dale Carpenter, *Flagrant Conduct: The Story of Lawrence v. Texas: How a Bedroom Arrest Decriminalized Gay Americans* (New York: W. W. Norton, 2012).

102   *Bowers*, 478 U.S. 186.

103   Stein, *Sexual Injustice*, 40–57; Powe, *Warren Court and American Politics*, 298; also in Howard Ball and Phillip J. Cooper, *Of Power and Right: Hugo Black, William O. Douglas, and America's Constitutional Revolution* (New York: Oxford University Press, 1992).

104   Warren, Black, Clark, Harlan, and Goldberg were no longer serving; *Roe* con-

tinues to be a mainstay of American legal discourse. Rebecca Spence points to
a number of holes in the *Roe* decision's application to female agency in birthing
rights; see "Abandoning Women to Their Rights: What Happens When Feminist Jurisprudence Ignores Birthing Rights," *Cardozo Journal of Law & Gender*
19 (2012): 75–99; a similar observation is found in Sylvia A. Law, "Childbirth: An
Opportunity for Choice that Should Be Supported," *New York University Review
of Law, Society, and Change* 32 (2008): 345–80. Caitlin E. Borgmann argues
that *Roe* had a "paradoxical effect on women's constitutional right to privacy"
because it did not recognize an absolute right to decisional autonomy in reproductive choice; see "Abortion, the Undue Burden Standard, and the Eviscera-
tion of Women's Privacy," *William and Mary Journal of Women and the Law* 16,
no. 2 (2010): 291–327. Mary Ziegler claims that *Roe* serves as "the most prominent example of the damage judicial review can do to the larger society" because
it precluded any form of productive compromise between pro-choice and pro-
life camps; see "Beyond Backlash: Legal History, Polarization, and *Roe v. Wade*,"
Washington and Lee Law Review 71, no. 2 (Spring 2014): 969–1023. Rima Kund-
nani outlined the problems of applying *Roe*'s decisional privacy to the mentally ill;
see "Protecting the Right to Procreate for Mentally Ill Women," *Southern California Review of Law and Social Justice* 59, no. 4 (Fall 2013): 59–92. Rebecca Green
explored the negative impact of *Roe*'s privacy implications toward the prevention of domestic violence; see "Privacy and Domestic Violence in Court," *William
and Mary Journal of Women and the Law* 16, no. 2 (2010): 237–90. Khiara Bridges
notes the class inequalities present for contemporary pregnant mothers seeking
government assistance and positions them as ananthema to the spirit of *Roe*'s privacy protections; see "Privacy Right and Public Families," *Harvard Journal of Law
and Gender* 34, no. 1 (2011): 113–77. Judith Baer showcases a number of arguments
against scholars who disagree with the findings of *Roe*; see "Privacy at 50: The
Bedroom, the Courtroom, and the Spaces in Between," *Maryland Law Review* 75,
no. 1 (2015): 233–47. Rebecca Rausch investigates whether "the absence of positive rights and the lack of express constitutional language" inherent in the right
to privacy might be redressed by reframing *Roe* in the language of property, and
specifically a woman's property right in her uterus; see "Reframing Roe: Property over Privacy," *Berkeley Journal of Gender, Law & Justice* 27, no. 1 (2012):
28–55. Richard Meyers argues that a close reading of *Roe* with a "de-emphasis on
women's rights" will lead to its eventual reversal; see "Re-reading *Roe v. Wade*,"
Washington and Lee Law Review 71, no. 2 (Spring 2014): 1025–48. Dahlia Lithwick
examines how *Roe* has become "a starting point for any conversation about the
appropriate role of courts in modern life"; see "*Roe v. Wade* at Forty," *Ohio State
Law Journal* 74, no. 1 (2013): 5–14. Mark Osler speaks to the inherent problems
of "fetal viability" in the *Roe* decision; see *Stanford Law & Policy Review* 24, no. 1
(January 2013): 215–46. Bridget Crawford addresses the tax implications of *Roe*
and privacy for surrogates; see "Taxation, Pregnancy, and Privacy," *William and
Mary Journal of Women and the Law* 16, no. 2 (2010): 327–70. Lynn Wardle speaks
to the impact of *Roe* on the creation of "cause lawyering" and the positive and
negative impact of that trend; see "The Use and Abuse of 'Cause Lawyering': The
Bad Example of *Roe v Wade*," *University of La Verne Law Review* 35, no. 1 (July
2014): 217–44.

105   See Norma McCorvey and Andy Meisler, *I Am Roe: My Life, Roe v. Wade, and
Freedom of Choice* (New York: Harper Collins, 1994); also *The 25th Anniversary of*

Roe v. Wade: Has It Stood the Test of Time? Hearing Before the Subcommittee on the Constitution, Federalism, and Property Rights of the Senate Committee on the Judiciary, 105th Cong., 2nd Sess. (1998).

106 See Jane Roe, Henry Wade, Mary Doe, Arthur K. Bolton, and Robert E. Ratermann, *Oral Arguments in the Supreme Court Abortion Decisions: In the Cases in the Supreme Court of the United States Roe et al. v. Wade, District Attorney of Dallas County (Texas) no. 70-18 and Doe et al. v. Bolton, Attorney General of Georgia et al. no. 70-40, Oral Arguments Monday, December 13, 1971, Wednesday, October 11, 1972, Decisions and Opinions Monday, January 22, 1973, As Reported in 410 U.S. at 113, 179* (1973).

107 Garrow, *Liberty and Sexuality*, 473–599.

108 "Doctors Ask Supreme Court to Ease Curbs on Abortion," *New York Times*, 15 August 1971.

109 Roy Lucas, "Brief as Amici Curiae for the American College of Obstetricians and Gynecologists et al.," *Doe v. Bolto*, U.S.S.C., O.T. 1971, #70-40, 14 August 1971; Lucas et al., "Brief for the Appellants," *Roe v. Wade*, U.S.S.C., O.T. 1971, #70-40, 18 August 1971.

110 Hariet Pilpel, Nancy Wechsler, and Ruth Zuckerman, "Brief for Planned Parenthood Federation of America," *Roe v. Wade* and *Doe v. Bolton*, 11 August 1971; all briefs and oral arguments are outlined masterfully in Garrow's *Liberty and Sexuality*, 473–599.

111 Jane Roe, John Doe, Mary Doe, James Hubert Hallford, Henry Wade, and Sarah Ragle Weddington, *Roe v. Wade: Proceedings of Arguments Before the U.S. Supreme Court* (Washington, DC, 1975).

112 Ibid.

113 Ibid.

114 Ibid.

115 *Roe v. Wade*, 410 U.S. 113, 157 (1973).

116 Ibid. "Fetal viability" is a popular term used by both sides of the abortion debate; see Lyle Denniston, "Constitution Check: Will Changes in Fetal Medicine Diminish Abortion Rights?" National Constitution Center, 4 June 2015, https://constitutioncenter.org/blog/constitution-check-will-changes-in-fetal-medicine-diminish-abortion-rights.

117 Garrow makes this observation in *Liberty and Sexuality*, 547–52.

118 A similar point is found in United States, *The Consequences of Roe v. Wade and Doe v. Bolton: Hearing Before the Subcommittee on the Constitution, Civil Rights, and Property Rights of the Senate Committee on the Judiciary, June 23, 2005*, 109th Cong., 1st Sess. (2009); also Rubin, *Abortion Politics*, 75–79; Garrow, *Liberty and Sexuality*, 471.

119 Janice Goodman, Rhonda Copeland Schoenbrod, and Nancy Stearns, "Doe and Roe, Where Do We Go from Here?" *Women's Rights Law Reporter*, Spring 1973, 24–26; Lawrence Lader, *Abortion II: Making the Revolution* (Boston: Beacon Press, 1973), i–ii; Garrow, *Liberty and Sexuality*, 601–10.

120 As outlined in Allen, *Uneasy Access*, 90–92; the structure of these tiers are very similar to Judge Prosner's "Four Privacy Torts."

121 See Allen, *Uneasy Access*, 89–92, 97–100.

122 See Goodman, Schoenbrod, and Stearns, "Doe and Roe"; Barbara Mutnick and Susan La Mont, "The Meaning of the Supreme Court Decisions," *WONAAC Newsletter*, February 1973; Roberta Gratz, "Never Again," *Ms.*, April 1973.

123   Marion K. Sanders, "Enemies of Abortion," *Harper's*, March 1974; "Bishops Begin Anti-Abortion Drive," *Washington Post*, 21 November 1975; Paul Weber, "Bishops in Politics: The Big Plunge," *America*, May 1976.

124   James Armstrong, "The Politics of Abortion," *Christian Century*, March 10, 1976, 47–48.

125   This chronology used in Rubin, *Abortion, Politics, and the Courts*, 80–92.

126   An excellent treatment of the initial reaction to *Roe* can be found in Greenhouse and Siegel, *Before Roe v. Wade*, 33–48; also Daniel K. Williams, "The GOP's Abortion Strategy: Why Pro-Choice Republicans Became Pro-Life in the 1970s," *Journal of Policy History* 23, no. 4 (2011), 513–22.

127   Williams, "GOP's Abortion Strategy," 513–14; see also Donald T. Critchlow, *Intended Consequences: Birth Control, Abortion, and the Federal Government in Modern America* (Oxford: Oxford University Press, 2010), 85–112.

128   Williams, "GOP's Abortion Strategy," 518–19; also Kristin Luker, *Abortion and the Politics of Motherhood* (Berkeley: University of California Press, 1984), 126–58.

129   "Ford Abortion Stance Draws Criticism," *New York Times*, 5 February 1976; Michele McKeegan, *Abortion Politics: Mutiny in the Ranks of the Right* (New York: Free Press, 1992), ii–xiii; also in Williams, "GOP's Abortion Strategy."

130   See generally John Rice, "The Murder of the Helpless Unborn," *Sword of the Land*, 22 October 1971; "Reagan on God and Morality," *Christianity Today*, 2 July 1976; "Ford Abortion Stand Draws Criticism," *New York Times*, 5 February 1976; "Anti-Abortion: Not Parochial," *Christianity Today*, 8 August 1975; "Flare Up Over Abortion," *Time*, 13 September 1976; "Dole Camp Accepts Uncompromising Abortion Plank," *New York Times*, 6 August 1996; also absent in secondary studies by Critchlow, *Intended Consequences*; Garrow, *Liberty and Sexuality*; and McKeegan, *Abortion Politics*.

131   Chris Whitman, "Looking Back on *Planned Parenthood v. Casey*," *Michigan Law Review* 100, no. 7 (June 2002): 1980–96; *Parenthood of Southeastern Pa. v. Casey*, 505 U.S. 833 (1992).

132   *Casey*, 505 U.S. at 844.

133   Ibid., 860.

134   Ibid., 837.

135   "The Worrisome Future of Abortion Rights," *New York Times*, 9 November 2017.

136   Cornell University Law School's Legal Information Institute notes this conflation of privacy and liberty as well, writing in its overview of the case: "[In *Casey*] the Court characterized the issue as one of "liberty" rather than "privacy"; this opened the door for substantive due process analysis. Referring to past Supreme Court cases such as *Griswold v. Connecticut* (1965), *Eisenstadt v. Baird* (1972), and *Carey v. Population Services International* (1977), the Court put an emphasis on the liberty interests and decisional autonomy of the woman seeking an abortion [rather than privacy]." *Parenthood of Southeastern Pa. v. Casey* (1992), Legal Information Institute, https://www.law.cornell.edu/wex/planned_parenthood_of_southeastern_pennsylvania_v_casey_%281992%29 (last accessed 20 December 2018).

137   David Brooks, "Roe's Birth, and Death," *New York Times*, 21 April 2005; according to Benjamin Wittes, "One effect of *Roe* was to mobilize a permanent constituency for criminalizing abortion—a constituency that has driven much of the southern realignment toward conservatism"; "Letting Go of *Roe*," *Atlantic*, January/February 2005. Cass Sunstein writes that "the decision may well have created the

Moral Majority, helped defeat the equal rights amendment, and undermined the women's movement by spurring opposition and demobilizing potential adherents"; "Three Civil Rights Fallacies," *California Law Review* 79 (1991): 766. Sandford Levinson called *Roe* "the *gift* that keeps on giving inasmuch as it has served to send many, good, decent, committed largely (though certainly not exclusively) working-class voters into the arms of a party that works systematically against their material interests but is willing to pander to their serious value commitment to a 'right to life'"; "Should Liberals Stop Defending Roe? Sanford Levinson and Jack M. Balkin Debate," reprinted in *Legal Affairs*, 28 November 2005.

138   Albert Hadley Cantril and Susan Davis Cantril, *Live and Let Live: American Public Opinion About Privacy at Home and at Work* (New York: American Civil Liberties Union Foundation, 1994).

PART SEVEN

1   147 Cong. Rec. D1050–D1051, D1053 (2001); post-vote remarks in Howard Ball, *The USA Patriot Act of 2001: Balancing Civil Liberties and National Security* (Santa Barbara: ABC-CLIO, 2005), 46–49.

2   147 Cong. Rec. S11020 (2001).

3   See Mathew Ingram, "The Media Today: Layoffs, Shutdowns, and Salary Outrage," *Columbia Journalism Review*, 1 February 2018; also John Nichols, "These Are the Worst of Times for American Journalism," *Nation*, 25 July 2018.

4   Quote in Pothik Gosh, "People Get the Media They Deserve," *Economic Times*, 13 December 2005.

5   Confessional culture is now the subject of numerous articles and monographs. The topic comprised an entire chapter in Sarah Elizabeth Igo's *The Known Citizen*, in which she argues self-exposure is in many regards a way for individuals to reclaim control over their self-narratives in a significantly less private world; see *The Known Citizen: A History of Privacy in Modern America* (Cambridge, MA: Harvard University Press, 2018), chap. 8. See also, among others, Peter Brooks, *Troubling Confessions* (Chicago: University of Chicago Press, 2000); Bernard E. Harcourt, *Exposed: Desire and Disobedience in the Digital Age* (Cambridge, MA: Harvard University Press, 2015); and Daniel Mendelsohn, "But Enough About Me: What Does the Popularity of Memoirs Tell Us About Ourselves," *New Yorker*, 25 January 2010.

6   See, among others, Jeffery Rosen, "The Right to be Forgotten," *Stanford Law Review* Sarah Elizabeth Igo, *The Known Citizen: A History of Privacy in Modern America* (Cambridge, MA: Harvard University Press, 2018), February 2012; Juan Olano, "The Rise of the Right to be Forgotten," *University of Miami Law Review*, February 2017.

7   While the Patriot Act was certainly responsible for significant privacy intrusions, particularly with regard to the Fourth Amendment, it is a common practice in popular parlance to use Patriot Act as a symbol for the many other privacy intrusions that occurred in the name of "national security" since 2001—particularly the increased role of FISA courts thanks to the FISA Amendments Act of 2008, the warrantless wiretapping programs of the Bush and Obama administrations (PRISM, which was revealed by Edward Snowden, being the most famous), and the embracing of numerous privacy-invading technologies by law enforcement

both on the ground and in the sky. A number of excellent books and articles have emerged from these developments—a list too long to include here. An excellent breakdown of contemporary issues surrounding national security and post-9/11 surveillance use can be found at the ALCU's subdivision on privacy and surveillance: https://www.aclu.org/issues/national-security/privacy-and-surveillance and also at the Electronic Privacy Information Center (EPIC), https://www.epic .org/.

8   David Lyon, "Surveillance, Snowden, and Big Data: Capacities, Consequences, and Critique," *Big Data & Society*, July 2014.

9   *ACLU v. Clapper*, 785 F.3d 787, 818 (2d Cir. 2015); for more on Snowden see Glenn Greenwald, "NSA Collecting Phone Records on Millions of Verizon Customers Daily," *Guardian*, 6 June 2013; Kenneth Roth and Salil Shetty, "Pardon Edward Snowden," *New York Times*, 15 September 2016; Josh Barro, "Here's Why Edward Snowden Deserves a Long Prison Sentence," *Business Insider*, 6 January 2014.

10 "Boston Marathon Surveillance Raises Privacy Concerns Long After Bombing," *NPR Morning Edition*, 17 April 2017; "Obama: 'Lives Have Been Saved' by NSA Programs," Associated Press, 19 June 2013; Michael Isikoff, "NSA Program Stopped No Terror Attacks, says White House Panel Member," *NBC News*, 2 November 2015.

11 See UC Berkeley's Jim Dempsey, "Section 702 Renewal: Opportunities Lost and Gained," *Blog of the American Constitution*, 29 January 2018, https://www.acslaw .org/acsblog/section-702-renewal-opportunities-lost-and-gained/; Consumer Privacy Protection Act of 2015, S. 1158, 114th Cong. (2015).

12 The three stages of information flow are outlined by Solove in *Understanding Privacy*. This point expertly explained by Andrew Burt and Dan Geer in "The End of Privacy," *New York Times*, 5 October 2017, https://www.nytimes.com/2017/10/05 /opinion/privacy-rights-security-breaches.html.

13 A core idea of Nissenbaum's work is "the necessity to understand privacy expectations and their implications developed in the literature on law, public policy, and political philosophy"—again, what she calls "contextual integrity"; see particularly her book *Privacy in Context*; quoted in *Privacy, Dig Data, and the Public Good*, 46; see also Benjamin Wittes and Jodie Liu, "The Privacy Paradox: The Privacy Benefits of Privacy Threats," *Brookings Institute*, 21 May 2015, https://www .brookings.edu/research/the-privacy-paradox-the-privacy-benefits-of-privacy -threats/.

14 Europe had broader privacy protections than the United States for the second half of the twentieth century but was less eager to enforce them, whereas the United States had mostly state-level protections but enforced them with vigor. This changed with the advent of the digital age, when Europe started enforcing its omnibus system more aggressively. See especially the European Data Protection Directive of 1995. Also, among others, Lee Bygrave, *Data Privacy Law: An International Perspective* (Oxford: Oxford University Press, 2014); Lothar Determann, *Determann's Field Guide to Data Privacy Law: International Corporate Compliance* (Cheltenham, UK: Northampton, 2017); Gregory Voss & Katherine Woodcock, *Navigating EU Privacy and Data Protection Laws* (Chicago: American Bar Association, 2015). Regarding California privacy law, see, among others, the 2015 Electronic Communications Privacy Act, which imposes very restrictive warrant requirements for law enforcement collection of all digital metadata from private

business—what the ACLU called the best "model for the rest of the nation in protecting our digital privacy rights."

15   See Paul M. Schwartz, "The Value of Privacy Federalism," in Beate Roessler & D. Mokrosinska, *Social Dimensions of Privacy: Interdisciplinary Perspectives*, (Cambridge: Cambridge University Press, 2015).

16   See Solon Barocas and Helen Nissenbaum "Big Data's End Run Around Anonymity and Consent," in *Privacy, Big Data, and the Public Good: Frameworks for Engagement*, ed. Julia Lane et al., 44–75 (Cambridge University Press, 2014).

17   Ibid.; also in Omri Ben-Shahar, *More Than You Wanted to Know: The Failure of Mandated Disclosure* (Princeton, NJ: Princeton University Press, 2016); and Florencia Marotta-Wurgler, "Self-Regulation and Competition in Privacy Policies," *Journal of Legal Studies* 45 no. 2 (June 2016): S13–S39.

18   The relationship between privacy and the Federal Trade Commission has received excellent attention from Chris Jay Hoofnagle in *Federal Trade Commission Law and Policy* (New York: Cambridge University Press, 2016); see also Daniel Solove and Woodrow Hartzog, "The FTC and the New Common Law of Privacy," *Columbia Law Review* 114 (2014): 583; also in Marotta-Wurgler, "Self-Regulation and Competition."

19   Specific trends outlined in Lawrence Cappello, "Privacy and the Profit Motive," *Nation*, 4 May 2015, and "Privacy's Best Hope: Keep it Profitable," *Hill*, January 2016; Steve Morgan, "Cybersecurity Market Reaches $75 Billion in 2015; Expected to Reach $170 Billion by 2020," *Forbes*, 20 December 2015; Anna Lysyanskaya, "Cryptography is the Future," in *Privacy in the Modern Age: The Search for Solutions*, ed. Marc Rotenberg, Jeramie Scott, and Julia Horwitz, 112–17 (New York: New Press, 2015); Aleecia McDonald, "When Self-Help Helps: User Adoption of Privacy Technologies," in *Privacy in the Modern Age*, 127–37.

20   "Facebook Stock Drops Roughly 20%, Loses $120 Billion in Value after Warning that Revenue Growth Will Take a Hit," *MarketWatch*, 26 July 2018.

21   For the potential reframing toward *societal* privacy, see Gideon Lewis-Krauss, "Facebook and the Dead Body Problem," *New York Times Magazine*, 24 April 2018. For claims that privacy and profits are mutually exclusive, see Kalev Leetaru, "Profit Versus Privacy: Facebook's Stock Collapse and Its Empty 'Privacy First' Promise," *Forbes*, 29 July 2018. For a more positive outlook on Facebook's potential growth, see Richard Saintvilus, "Why Now is the Perfect Time to Buy Facebook Stock," *Nasdaq.com*, 28 March 2018; and Gillian Brassil, "Don't Lose Faith in Facebook Now, Because Its Valuation Remains Solid, Analysts Say," *CNBC*, 26 July 2018.

INDEX

Page references in italics refer to illustrations.